The Tavern

Recent Titles in
History of Human Spaces

The Schoolroom: A Social History of Teaching and Learning
Dale Allen Gyure

The Bathroom: A Social History of Cleanliness and the Body
Alison K. Hoagland

The Factory: A Social History of Work and Technology
Allison Marsh

THE TAVERN

A Social History of Drinking and Conviviality

Steven D. Barleen

History of Human Spaces

An Imprint of ABC-CLIO, LLC
Santa Barbara, California • Denver, Colorado

Library of Congress Cataloging-in-Publication Data

Names: Barleen, Steven (Steven D.), author.
Title: The tavern : a social history of drinking and conviviality / Steven D. Barleen.
Description: Santa Barbara, California : Greenwood, [2019] | Series: History of human spaces | Includes bibliographical references and index.
Identifiers: LCCN 2019007066 | ISBN 9781440852725 (print : alk. paper) | ISBN 9781440852732 (ebook)
Subjects: LCSH: Bars (Drinking establishments)—Social aspects—United States—History. | Taverns (Inns)—Social aspects—United States—History. | United States—Social life and customs.
Classification: LCC TX950.56 .B37 2019 | DDC 647.9573—dc23
LC record available at https://lccn.loc.gov/2019007066

ISBN: 978-1-4408-5272-5 (print)
978-1-4408-5273-2 (ebook)

23 22 21 20 19 1 2 3 4 5

This book is also available as an eBook.

Greenwood
An Imprint of ABC-CLIO, LLC

ABC-CLIO, LLC
147 Castilian Drive
Santa Barbara, California 93117
www.abc-clio.com

This book is printed on acid-free paper ∞
Manufactured in the United States of America

For my children, the ones in life who matter most.
May they never spend too much time in taverns.

CONTENTS

PREFACE

This book is a history of the tavern, and it examines this timeless institution as both a social and physical space. The American tavern is the primary focus of this effort. However, the role of the tavern as a mainstay in most societies since the beginning of civilization is also considered, demonstrating how the tavern has been one of the most important spaces throughout history, where people have gathered to interact with friends, neighbors, and others whom they may not have already known well. For the most part, the purpose of the tavern has stayed very consistent. People typically gather in taverns to socialize while consuming alcoholic beverages, and this work will discuss what has drawn people to this institution. In this effort, it will also consider the other services that taverns have provided and how these have changed, depending on time and circumstance. Finally, this work will examine the resistance that the tavern has received from those who have seen it as a disruptive and problematic presence in their communities.

The Tavern is designed for a wide variety of audiences. Taverns have always fascinated the public imagination. They have been viewed as centers of mirth, community, and chaos, and readers will enjoy the many aspects of the institution that are discussed in this book along with anecdotes and narratives about tavern life. It is also filled with detailed descriptions of the physical aspects of taverns. This work is a good resource for students of history who seek to better understand the role the tavern has played in the American experience.

At various times in American history, taverns have been called by other names, such as "public house," "ordinary," "dramshop," "bar," "speakeasy," and "saloon." When appropriate, these terms will be used, but generally "tavern" will be used most often. This is because, as with the institution itself, this term has a long life in Western culture. We get the word "tavern" from the Greek *taverna* and later the Latin *tabernae.*

This book is broken into four chapters. Chapter 1 provides a brief history of the role of drinking establishments from colonial times until the present. This chapter focuses on the functions of the institution while also considering its role as a perpetual mainstay for communities. Chapter 2 examines how drinking establishments represent themselves to their communities. It also considers the tavern's external physical structure, which is designed to draw customers in. Chapter 3 considers where tavern customers congregate—the barroom. This chapter considers how the physical spaces of drinking establishments reflect the values of their occupants. It also considers why they frequent bars and what they expect from the barroom. Chapter 4 concludes by considering life behind the bar. This chapter examines the objects behind the bar and the physical spaces in which the bartender works as well as some of the challenges faced by those behind the bar as they work hard to provide society with a service that it very much craves.

Several works have strongly influenced this effort, and I will just mention a few of them. First and foremost, I will frequently refer to George Ade's *The Old Time Saloon*, written in 1931, which is both an insightful and humorous look at the saloon period from a writer who had himself experienced saloons in the king of saloon towns, Chicago. I also very much recommend *John Barleycorn*, written by Jack London in 1913, just three years before his untimely death. London, one of the United States' greatest writers, provides a semiautobiographical account of his relationship with taverns and drinking. I also strongly recommend Madelon Power's *Faces along the Bar.* Powers provides a lively analysis of tavern culture that is unequaled. I would also recommend Perry Duis's *The Saloon*, which primarily focuses on the saloon as a business, providing a comparison of the tavern business in Boston and Chicago. For the early American tavern period, I suggest *Taverns and Drinking in Early America* by Sharon Sallinger, *Rum Punch and Revolution* by Peter Thompson, and *The Alcoholic Republic* by W. J. Rorabaugh.

INTRODUCTION

> Work is the curse of the drinking class.
>
> —Oscar Wilde

The year 1976 represented a significant milestone in the United States. That year marked the bicentennial of the founding of the republic, and the occasion evoked many sentimental thoughts about how far the improbable American experiment in democracy had come. The nation had very recently endured many tumultuous and divisive events, and Watergate, the long nightmare of Vietnam, and the intense social unrest of the previous decade were still wounds that stung the national psyche. Many were looking to the bicentennial year as an occasion to heal divisions and find the common bonds that make Americans American. In this spirit, Harry Warner, an editorial writer in Hagerstown, Maryland, wrote a lengthy column in the fall of that year in his local newspaper. Warner pointed out that in his community much had been done in recent months to reflect on local history and how Hagerstown fit into the overall American story. However, Warner lamented, a major part of the community's history had been overlooked: the story of its taverns, particularly its once-thriving saloon culture. He writes, "Virtually nothing exists in print or in manuscript about the way they looked, precisely what they served, or their place in the social life" (*Daily Mail* 1976). After National Prohibition, the tavern had slowly made a comeback in his community, but just over 40 years later, Warner conjectured, only very old people had any recollection of a time when, with a population of around 15,000, Hagerstown had entertained 40 saloons, or approximately one for every 375 residents. Many old-timers could recall the wild days of National Prohibition, but few could remember when the city's saloons "fulfilled a comradeship need and provided intellectual stimulation of sorts that man couldn't find elsewhere." Asking the remaining old-timers what the saloons were like, Warner opined, was problematic since their memories could be "distorted by the golden glow of nostalgia which makes good things in the distant past appear so much better" (*Daily Mail* 1976). In this statement, Warner assumed that those who could remember the saloon would remember it fondly as a place that with time was made ever better in the imagination. But if memory could not be fully trusted, then real research would be needed. The saloon age has long held a warm place in our collective imaginations, evoking both a sense of community and a sense of mayhem. Warner's call to better appreciate the history of taverns in his community reflects an understanding that one cannot know a community without examining where that community gathers. And throughout history, that place has been the tavern.

In 1831, 26-year-old Frenchman Alexis de Tocqueville arrived in the United States on an extensive tour that resulted in a two-volume study of American democracy and society. Tocqueville notes that one of the great strengths of American democracy was a proclivity for forming voluntary associations. In short, Americans, Tocqueville noted, loved to socialize (see especially Damrosch 2010). As the historian Robert Weir observes in his history of the Knights of Labor, Americans in the 19th century were joiners. They sought out voluntary associations and actively participated in them. Weir notes that by 1901 there were at least 600 societies, with the Masons alone having 6 million members (Weir 1996, 22–24). But in recent decades, much has changed. In *Bowling Alone*, Robert Putnam chronicles his groundbreaking study of American society as it entered the 21st century, noting that Americans are joiners no more and that they do not seek to associate with one another in the ways of yesteryear (Putnam 2000). Tocqueville saw the American proclivity for joining as a great strength of democracy, but Putnam argues that the recent American penchant for going it alone means that more Americans are having decreased face-to-face social interactions with people they do not already know well. Putnam's title makes the point that people still bowl, just not in leagues as they once did. Now they are more likely to either bowl alone or bowl with people they already know well. They are therefore less likely to interact with new people or those they might only know casually. Therefore, each person today is more likely to spend the majority of their time on their own metaphorical island.

One common place where people might meet and interact with those they do not already know well are houses of worship. But attendance at these institutions is way down across the country as well. As a recent Pew Research Center Study demonstrates, just 36 percent of Americans indicate that they attend a religious service at least once a week, and 30 percent indicate that they never or seldom attend (Pew Research Center 2015). Though, as public spaces are diminishing in many towns across the United States, and though they may have once had larger congregations, houses of worship remain in many communities one of the two most common places where people might interact with those they do not already know well; the other place is the tavern. And many communities have them in roughly equal numbers. Mount Carroll, Illinois, for example, is a quaint little city of around 2,000 people located in the northwestern part of the state. As with scores of small towns across the United States, many of the storefronts in its downtown are empty, but the small community nevertheless still contains seven churches and five thriving taverns. A drive through the downtowns of many communities in the United States will reveal that taverns continue to blend into Main Street, while many other businesses have shuttered their doors. In towns such as Mount Carroll, the tavern, like the church, operates as a semipublic space where people mingle. Of course, taverns are generally restricted to those over the age of 21, but in theory, the tavern, like the church, is open to everyone. And in taverns, as in churches, many patrons are looking for a sense of community and an escape from the pressures and cares of the workaday world. However, a big difference is that, in the tavern, this escape tends to be enhanced with intoxicants.

The consumption of intoxicants has been a central feature of societies since the dawn of humankind. As Friedrich Nietzsche put it in 1882, the history of intoxicants "is almost the history of 'culture,' of our so-called higher culture" (Nietzsche 1964, 122). Ancient societies sung the praises of alcohol as the driving force of creativity and brilliance. Homer, the eighth-century Greek poet and father of Greek literature, wrote, "No poems can please for long or live that are written by water-drinkers" (Ackerley 2010, 102). And Horace, a first century BCE Roman philosopher, asked, "Whom has not the inspiring bowl made eloquent?" (*New Dictionary of Quotations* 1874, 160). However, much has changed since the days of Homer and Horace regarding the potency of intoxicants. As David Courtwright has noted in what he terms the "psychoactive revolution," the ability to alter one's consciousness has greatly progressed in the last few centuries, and people have increasingly found more potent means for doing so (Courtwright 2001, 2). Many forms of intoxicants are illegal to sell and possess, and laws related to intoxicants vary across the United States and the world. In recent years, marijuana has become more acceptable, both socially and legally. In fact, some have worried that legal marijuana could become a drag on alcohol sales, which would be a blow to tavern keepers. It is too soon to tell if this is the case, but one thing is certain: Americans still consume very large quantities of alcoholic beverages, and many of them are still consumed in taverns, an industry that currently commands nearly $20 billion a year in sales in the United States (Statista 2017). As long as there has been society, there have been intoxicants, and as long as there have been businesses and customers, there have been taverns that have sold alcoholic beverages.

The tavern has been around as long as any other societal institution. It has always been, and it surely will always remain. Shortly after the landing of the first English settlers at Jamestown in 1608 and Plymouth Rock in 1620, the American tavern quickly took root. Along with the building of churches came the building of taverns, both seemingly springing organically from the soil as fast as English settlements multiplied. Nearly every early community had taverns, and they provided many important functions, serving for instance as inns and places of shelter for wayward travelers as well as meeting houses and places of revelry for locals. Into the next century, Americans were still drinking, and they were doing so heavily. Ben Franklin observed this fact when in 1737 he noted multiple terms for drunkenness in a publication he titled *The Drinkers Dictionary*. Franklin was no teetotaler, and he also liked to imbibe, and in verse he sang the praises of alcohol, but he was concerned about the incredible amount of drunkenness he witnessed around him, and he witnessed much of this in taverns (Szasz 1993, 83; Larson 1937). He must have spent a great deal of time around drinkers because he compiled a list of 228 terms that were used to describe intoxication. Phrases such as "has swallow'd a Tavern Token" and "He makes a Virginia Fence" are charming reminders that as long as alcohol has inhabited a central part of society, we have been coming up with euphemisms to describe drinking and drinkers. Fast-forward a couple more generations and Americans were drinking as much as ever. The historian W. J. Rorabaugh describes the early republic as containing a "nation of drunkards," in which profound changes in society created a period that Rorabaugh asserts witnessed the highest levels of alcohol consumption of any time before or since (Rorabaugh 1979). In this environment, taverns thrived and evolved.

In the latter half of the 19th century and into the first two decades of the 20th century, the golden age of the tavern emerged: the saloon period. Saloons became ubiquitous features in the many downtowns of the United

States. They also became the iconic symbol of the great American frontier. Unlike the earliest American taverns, saloons emerged as primarily working-class male institutions where many men whiled away their free time and their paychecks. For reformers, the saloon and its products came to pose one of the greatest threats to the well-being of the country, and as Jack Blocker notes, this belief resulted in the creation of one of the greatest social movements in American history, the temperance and anti-saloon crusades (Blocker 1989). On January 26, 1919, when the Eighteenth Amendment was ratified and added to the United States Constitution, many Americans rejoiced, believing that through the force of law they would finally remove the United States' oldest and most pronounced vice along with its many dispensers—taverns. Many other Americans, primarily working-class Americans who had been the saloons' primary customers, saw this moment as an incredible travesty. In their eyes, prohibitionists represented an effort to trample their rights and symbolized a nativist assault on their cultures. They could rightly point out that in the nation's 129-year history, only 17 amendments had been passed, and 10 of them, the Bill of Rights, had been added at the same time. But the first two decades of the 20th century were a time of rapid change. Progressives who had soldiered at the front lines of the Prohibition movement sought to wrest control of their country from both big business interests and a burgeoning immigrant-filled working class. Progressives had pushed through the Sixteenth Amendment, creating the income tax, and the Seventeenth Amendment, establishing the direct election of senators. These amendments were an attempt by a largely middle-class-led progressive movement to tame the power of the wealthy. The Eighteenth, the prohibition of the manufacture and sale of alcohol, was meant to tame the working class. It did not.

What had seemed like a good idea to many in 1919 no longer seemed like such a good idea a few years later. The nation came to realize that Prohibition did not in actuality prohibit. Americans seemed to be as obsessed with drinking alcohol and visiting taverns as they had ever been. In fact, as David Kyvig observes, many middle-class Americans discovered that the illicit nature of alcohol consumption had created a stronger temptation in their own young people to want to drink and frequent taverns (Kyvig 2000). During National Prohibition, people drank as they always had, sometimes alone, sometimes with others, but they continued to drink in establishments designed specifically for communal alcohol consumption. Commonly known as "speakeasies" because one had to quietly provide a passcode of some sort at the door before being allowed entry, these establishments sprang into being as quickly as each saloon closed its doors. Just as they had during the age of the legal saloon, Americans flocked to these new establishments, made even more alluring by the fact that their very existence was illegal (Lerner 2007). These new underground establishments contained many of the same elements that their once-legal predecessors had possessed. The structure, purpose, and form of taverns, even illegal ones, have remained timeless.

After Prohibition, the Gilded Age saloon did not make a comeback, and drinking and tavern-going entered the modern age, and Americans have continued to drink copiously. Alcohol is advertised on television and in many other mediums, and liquor stores, liquor aisles, and drinking establishments dot our landscape. The epic failure of National Prohibition very much continues to weigh on our collective psyche. While the Woman's Christian Temperance Union does in fact still exist, almost no one takes seriously the idea that alcohol or drinking establishments should once again be made illegal, though in fact there are still portions of the United States that prohibit the manufacture and sale of alcohol. As the *Economist* notes, 18 million Americans today live in communities where it is illegal to sell alcohol (*Economist* 2018). However, overall, we have accepted the idea that when it comes to alcohol, prohibition does not in fact prohibit. The tavern may face obstacles, and in some communities these obstacles are greater than in others, but the tavern is here to stay.

CHRONOLOGY

1750 BCE Hammurabi's Code contains first known dramshop laws.

1563 Spaniards make wine in Florida from wild grapes.

1587 Roanoke colony brews the first beer in an English colony in North America.

1619 First dramshop laws are passed in the English colonies. Jamestown enacts laws against drunkenness.

1620 Puritans carry more beer than water on the *Mayflower* on their trip across the Atlantic.

1623 First grapes for wine production are planted in English colonies.

1629 John Smith notes that Puritans are making alcoholic beverages.

1630s First "ordinaries" open in the English colonies in North America.

1634 First known tavern license in Boston is issued to Samuel Cole.

1784 Doctor Benjamin Rush argues that excessive alcohol consumption is a problem in the United States.

1791 Congress passes the Distilled Spirits Tax.

1829 David Yuengling, a German immigrant, establishes the Eagle Brewery in Pottsville, Pennsylvania. Yuengling claims to be the oldest brewery in the United States.

1840 John Wagner, an immigrant from Bavaria, brings lager yeast and is credited with brewing the first lager beer in the United States.

1840s Use of the term "saloon" to describe taverns begins to become commonplace in the United States.

1844 Jacob Best founds a brewery in Milwaukee.

1848 Massive unrest in Europe results in large numbers of immigrants arriving in the United States. Many of them bring their brewing knowhow with them.

1851 Maine adopts first statewide prohibition laws. Vermont follows in 1853.

1857 Lager beer begins outselling ale in the United States.

1870s Adolphus Busch becomes first brewer in the United States to use pasteurization in the brewing process. This allows for better storage and longer transportation of beer.

1872 Adolph Coors establishes a brewery in Golden, Colorado.

1873 The Woman's Christian Temperance Union is formed in Hillsboro, Ohio, on December 23.

1880s Several states adopt statewide prohibition, including Kansas, Iowa, North Dakota, and South Dakota.

1889 The first known use of the term "speakeasy" to describe an unlicensed drinking establishment appears in a newspaper.

1893 The Anti-Saloon League is formed in Oberlin, Ohio, on May 24.

1900s Several states adopt statewide prohibition, including Mississippi, Georgia, Oklahoma, North Carolina, and Tennessee.

1910s Several more states adopt statewide prohibition, including Alabama, Oregon, West Virginia, Washington, Montana, Nebraska, Indiana, Michigan, Florida, Kentucky, Texas, Virginia, South Carolina, Idaho, Colorado, Arkansas, and Arizona.

1913 Beer production stands at 2 billion gallons per year, an increase from 1.2 gallons in 1900.

1913 Congress passes the Webb-Kenyon Act, which bars the transportation of intoxicating liquors across state lines into dry states.

1919 Eighteenth Amendment banning the manufacture and sale of intoxicating liquors is ratified on January 16.

1920 National Prohibition goes into effect on January 16.

1920 First illegal drinking establishments, often referred to as "speakeasies," open in the United States

1933 President Roosevelt signs the Cullen-Harrison Act ("The Beer Bill") on March 22, 1933, which makes legal the brewing of beer with an alcohol content of 3.2 percent or lower.

1934 First Beer Day is celebrated on April 7 to recognize the day that the Cullen-Harrison Act officially went into effect.

1935 Alcoholics Anonymous is founded in Akron, Ohio.

1940 Beer production reaches pre-Prohibition levels.

1959 Coors Brewing Company introduces the aluminum can to the brewing industry.

1965 The "ring pull" is invented for beer cans.

1973 Mechanical refrigeration is invented by Carl von Linde, an employee of the Spaten Brewery in Munich, Germany.

1980 Mothers Against Drunk Driving is founded in California on September 5.

1980s Microbreweries begin growing in number.

1984 On July 18, President Reagan signs a law that links states' access to highway funds to raising the minimum drinking age to 21.

1988 Wyoming becomes the last state to raise its legal drinking age to 21 on July 1.

2012 Voters choose to make marijuana legal for recreational use in Washington State and Colorado on November 6. Many states have followed suit, and some worry that it could have an impact on the tavern industry.

Chapter 1

THE TAVERN: A BRIEF HISTORY

> There is nothing which has yet been contrived by man, by which so much happiness is produced as by a good tavern or inn.
>
> —James Boswell (Boswell 1830, 305)

James Boswell, an 18th-century Scottish biographer, observed in the above quotation a truism that captures the essence of the tavern, an institution that has been a consistent presence in the human experience since the beginning of civilization. Its importance as a mainstay in nearly all societies has been noted by archeologists, and it has frequently found its way into the narratives of the earliest forms of literature. Boswell explains the tavern's allure, but society has often found it to be a problematic presence as well. In ancient Babylon, for instance, we find evidence in Hammurabi's Code of the first known dramshop laws, some of which required the death penalty for vestals (nuns) caught in taverns (Harper 1904, 119). This draconian statute, part of the first known list of statutes ever produced by any civilization, represents some of the first rounds fired in society's long struggle to regulate this mirthful and yet problematic space. Though in most societies the tavern has been a consistent presence, and large numbers of citizens have partaken in the consumption of intoxicants in them, a paradox exists as demonstrated in Hammurabi's Code. The tavern is an inevitable presence, but it is one that is viewed with suspicion. What has troubled many about this space has not changed much over millennia, nor have the reasons these spaces are patronized. As a business and as a social space, taverns have always been sites where merriment and despair have comingled. Taverns are spaces that enhance community while also creating communal discord. This work will examine the American tavern from the outside in, but first we will consider in this chapter a brief history of this unique social space.

In ancient Greece the services provided by taverns were not much different than they would continue to be throughout Western history. Some catered to the respectable and the well-off, while others attracted a lower-class clientele. Some provided lodging for weary travelers, while others were merely spaces for drinking and carousing. Many provided sport of one kind or another, such as cockfighting and other forms of gambling. Others provided amusements for their patrons in shows put on by actors, musicians, and dancers (Gulick 1902, 255). The *taverna* or *kapeleion* was a ubiquitous presence in Greek towns and cities, with many private homes doubling as places that served this same function (Kelley-Blazeby 2001). Taverns were a constant presence throughout the Roman world as well. Through conquest and trade, the Roman world extended its reach throughout the Mediterranean region and beyond, creating vast sea lanes and road systems that carried weary travelers to the empire's farthest reaches. One of the things travelers could count on at day's end was the presence of taverns, where they could find rest and sustenance. (For more on life in the Roman world, see especially Aldrete 2008.) One of the earliest taverns to be discovered in Western Europe was recently unearthed in southern France at the former Roman town of Lattara. This roughly 2,100-year-old tavern served as both a restaurant and a barroom, occupying an enormous space that contained many rooms and large open spaces, where, on any evening, community members and travelers alike filled its large halls (Luley and Piques 2016, 184).

In the medieval period and beyond, taverns and their functions changed very little. (For more on the medieval tavern, see especially Cowell 2001.) They continued to provide refuge for weary travelers, and they served as community centers where people heard gossip and learned about the outside world from those passing through. However, as Hammurabi's proscription against nuns in taverns indicates, there has always been a gendered divide in the tavern. Historian A. Lynn Martin notes that taverns in the medieval world were primarily male spaces and that women found there risked being thought of as possessing low character, or even worse, being labeled as prostitutes. One theme that is eternal to drinking spaces, however, is that they have served as places where individuals can challenge the mores of society, as spaces where customers can take off the masks that the outside world imposes on them, and, after a few libations, feel uninhibited among their fellows. Martin notes that the medieval tavern sometimes served this purpose for women who sought to challenge the dictates that their society placed on them. By drinking in public, they could overcome the restrictions social norms typically imposed. Of course, such displays came with risks. Too much indulgence could lead to a loose tongue and behavior that might cause future problems. However, behind the tavern's doors, a patron could find a sort of "antichurch," with the tavern keeper serving as the "antipriest." In this sense, women were not the only ones defying society's mores. By drinking, swearing, and blaspheming, the medieval tavern patron could offer some level of resistance to institutions that sought total control over his or her spiritual and physical life (Martin 2008, 98–112).

While serving as spaces of ribaldry and arenas to deviate from expected cultural norms, taverns also served as meeting places for guilds, merchants, scientists, and politicians (Martin 2009, 90). Taverns have often been one of the preferred haunts of the creative class as well, as alcohol has long been a creative lubricant, and taverns have served as the primary centers of its disbursement. In the modern age, from Arthur Rimbaud to Ernest Hemingway, lovers of literature have often connected alcohol to the creative process. However, perhaps no tavern has witnessed such creative genius as the Elizabethan period's most famous dispenser of spirits, the Mermaid Tavern, which was located near Saint Paul's Cathedral in Central London. In the Mermaid, merriment makers drank alongside the likes of such literary greats as John Donne, Robert Bruce Cotton, Richard Carew, William Strachey, Ben Jonson, Francis Beaumont, and, some have contended, even William Shakespeare. This set styled themselves as members of the "Mermaid Club," and on many an evening they drank, argued, and shared ideas late into the night. In the early 17th century, Beaumont fondly described the nature of their meetings there in verse:

> What things have we seen
> Done at the Mermaid? Heard words that have been
> So nimble, and so full of subtle flame,
> As if that every one from whence they came
> Had meant to put his whole wit in a jest,
> And had resolved to live a fool the rest
> Of his dull life. (Lee 1904, 184; Ellis 2012, 95)

Sadly, the Mermaid perished in the Great London Fire of 1666, but its memory has lived on long after it did. In an 1819 poem titled "Lines on the Mermaid Tavern," the great English poet John Keats paid homage to the role it played in inspiring magnificent works of literature. In the opening lines of his dedicatory poem, Keats wondered if the heaven (Elysium) that these long-gone literary titans now inhabit could be as magnificent as the nights they spent in the Mermaid. Keats wondered through verse, "Souls of Poets dead and gone, what Elysium have you known, happy field or mossy cavern, choicier than the Mermaid Tavern?" (Keats 1909, 131).

Through such loving lines, it is clear from Keats's sweet and yearning homage to the Mermaid that he would have given much to have been able to travel back and spend an evening of drink and merriment in the presence of his literary forebears in their dedicated house of mirth.

ALCOHOL ARRIVES IN THE NEW WORLD

Around the same time that the Mermaid's evenings were being filled with libations and cheer, the first English colonists were establishing colonies in North America. With the establishment of Jamestown in 1607 and Plymouth Colony in 1620, English settlers fought to carve out a world in which they could first survive and ultimately thrive, and not long after arriving in this hostile environment, they established taverns at the same time they erected other social institutions, such as churches. Despite this, taverns had played a part in motivating the Pilgrims, the first Puritans in North America, to leave the relative comfort of their adopted home of Leiden, Holland, to risk their lives in the arduous voyage across the Atlantic. These former residents of Scrooby, located in the East Midlands of England, relocated to Leiden in 1608 in order to find relief from persecution in their mother country and to practice Christianity as they saw fit. They found refuge in Holland in part because the Dutch were fairly tolerant of diverse Christian beliefs. However, once the Pilgrims settled in the cosmopolitan city of Leiden, they discovered that Dutch religious tolerance extended to include a social atmosphere in which carousing in taverns played a large role. We can get a glimpse of this world from Dutch artists such as Jan Steen and Dirck Hals, who portrayed tavern life in paintings that captured the essence of the often rowdy, licentious, and freewheeling atmosphere of Dutch drinking establishments. Puritan elders soon came to realize that such an atmosphere was a threat to a community that was more focused on the rewards in the next life than the pleasures of this one. They worried about the effect such an environment was having on their young people, who might come to enjoy the city's free atmosphere, posing a threat to their eternal souls and the sanctity of their community. Pilgrim leader William Bradford observed that their children, due to the "great licentiousness of youth," found "manifold temptations of the place, were drawne away by evill examples into extravagante & dangerous courses" (Bradford 1856, 24). This threat, alongside other issues, ultimately became too much for the band of the faithful, so they decided that God's kingdom on earth would certainly not be created in Leiden. Instead, they elected to stake their fates and their faith on the months-long journey across the forbidding Atlantic.

Their disdain of Leiden's tavern life notwithstanding, the Pilgrims also drank alcohol, and they and their fellow Englishmen to the south in Jamestown created the first taverns in the New World. The Pilgrims, who arrived at Plymouth Rock in 1620 on the *Mayflower*, a claret ship, faced multiple difficulties and hardships on the 66-day voyage (Gately 2008, 122). They had originally intended to land in Virginia, but bad weather drove them farther north in the inauspicious month of November toward the coast of what would become Massachusetts. They could have pushed south down the coast, but they faced a problem. Their supplies had dwindled to dangerous levels, and for the passengers at least, there were no more stores of beer (Lender 1982, 2). This was a major problem because beer and other alcoholic beverages were seen as essential stores for any journey at sea. To illustrate this point, we can consider the store of intoxicating beverages that Puritan leader John Winthrop brought with him 10 years later when he led 11 ships of the faithful to Salem in June 1630. He recorded that when he and his followers set out, they were heavily stocked with intoxicants, bringing with them "42 tonnes of beere" (about 10,000 gallons), the same amount of wine, and only 3,000 gallons of water. To top it off, passengers brought their own stores. Certainly, the miserable cross-Atlantic voyage that lasted weeks and could bring death unexpectedly tempted some to overindulge along the way. Winthrop observed that during the voyage one girl got so drunk she nearly died. Looking back, Winthrop judged the incident the same way older generations have frequently judged their youth, stating, "We observed it a common fault in our young people that they gave themselves to drink hot waters very immoderately" (Winthrop 1996, 20).

Puritan leader Cotton Mather opined that rum is "a creature of God" (Rorabaugh 1979, 30). Perhaps rum's effects helped some Puritans feel closer to God at times. Of course, some Puritans drank in order to feel intoxicated, as was probably the case with Winthrop's young charge, but they also drank alcoholic beverages for practical purposes. In much of Europe, water was not trusted and was considered unhealthy, particularly in urban areas (Sallinger 2002, 3). As Ben Franklin quipped over 100 years later, "In wine there is wisdom, in beer there is freedom, in water there is bacteria" (Jacoby 2012, 1300). For the long journey across the Atlantic, then, fermented and distilled beverages were necessities, and the consumption of water was an absolute last resort. John Winthrop noted this about a family who had traveled for 26 weeks from London to Massachusetts, during which time they went through their store of beer and were forced to resort to drinking their store of "stinking water." Winthrop noted that it was only through "the providence of the Lord" that they had survived (Jameson 1908, 200). William Bradford observed that when the first party from the wayward *Mayflower* went ashore on November 11, 1620, in search of provisions, the bravest among them decided to test the water they found in a local spring. Fortunately, they found the water to be "as pleasant unto them as wine or beer had been in foretimes" (Bradford 2002, 65). Beer and wine are mentioned many times in Winthrop's journals and in Bradford's account as well, and though the New World provided plenty of clean water, these English colonists were not going to give up their beer, wine, and distilled spirits. One of the first tasks of importance for the newcomers, then, was to make sure they could continue making and dispensing these beverages.

THE EARLY COLONIAL TAVERN

John Smith of Jamestown fame noted that alcoholic beverages were present in abundance in the early English settlements, stating that from malt corn and barley, colonists were making "good ale, both strong and small, and such plenty thereof, few of the upper planters drink any water." A later observer noted the presence of at least six public brew houses, referred to as ordinaries, whose products were "strong and good" (De Bow 1858, 420). Early ordinaries tended to be simple affairs. As Gavin Nathan has noted in his history of Boston's taverns, in many instances early ordinaries were simply run out of small two-story homes, with the proprietor and his family living upstairs and running their business downstairs (Nathan 2006, 3). Behavior in Puritan taverns was tightly regulated, and a license to operate one had to be obtained by the court, and only those with good reputations needed apply. One such license, for instance, granted to Nathaniel Pierce, allowed him to "sell liquors unto such sober-minded neighbors as he shall think meet" (Brooks 1886, 387). Furthermore, even though alcohol would flow freely, customers were expected to behave in a manner befitting Puritan society. Therefore, Pierce's license proscribed customers from behaving "in a beastly manner" or acting "unseemly in the eyes of God." As this indicates, Puritans frowned on drunken behavior. John Winthrop noted the punishment, for instance, that befell a habitual drunkard named Robert Coles, who "having been oft punished for drunkenness, was now ordered to wear a red D around his neck for a year" (Winthrop 1996, 120). Tavern licenses also required their keepers to keep themselves in order. Tavern keeper Francis Sprague, who was granted his license in Duxbury, Massachusetts, on October 1, 1638, fell on the wrong side of the law when, in that same year, he was fined 40 shillings for "drinking overmuch," and the next year his license was taken away for a period. In 1641, he was ordered to no longer "drink any wyne or strong water until the next gen[er]al

[Court], without special lycence." Despite strict regulations, it seems that drunken behavior was a frequent problem because the Duxbury court decreed in 1671 that every ordinary keeper must turn in those who "doe not attend order, but carry themselves uncivilily by being importunately desirous of drink, when deneyed, and do not leave the house when required." To make sure that mischief was kept to a minimum, the court named two men "to have inspection of the ordinaries and other suspicious places" (Winsor 2001, 46–47).

By 1634, communities were required to have ordinaries, and that same year Samuel Cole opened the first tavern in Boston (Earle 1900, 180). Establishments such as Cole's served the necessary function of public houses where meetings and festivals could take place, but they also served travelers seeking a room for the night (Gately 2008, 127). Traveling between communities was common and sometimes hazardous, and taverns were a welcome stop. Medford, Massachusetts, was a typical New England community, sitting betwixt Maine and Boston, making it a frequent stop for travelers. A 19th-century history of Medford that looked back on this period explains that visitors were presented with an assortment of tavern options, all located on one street. Taverns such as those found in Medford were important way stations for the rapidly expanding colonial population, and as such, if they were to serve their proper social and economic function, they needed to serve all comers. In this way taverns often served both lower- and upper-class patrons under the same roof, helping to create a sense of shared community.

To illustrate this point, we can consider the amazing journey of Dr. Alexander Hamilton (not *the* Alexander Hamilton of Revolutionary War fame), a Scottish-born doctor who traveled in 1744 from Annapolis, Maryland, to York, Maine. His account of his journey, *Itinerarium*, reads like an adventure story, but most importantly it is one of the most vivid accounts of life and culture, including tavern life, in the American colonies before the Revolution. During his journey, Hamilton stayed at a variety of taverns, providing us with a vivid picture of how social classes brushed shoulders and tipped back drinks together in colonial taverns. For instance, early in his journey, Hamilton decided to stay at a tavern in Baltimore called Tradaways, and as he came on the establishment, he witnessed men departing who were quite drunk. According to Hamilton, this "drunken club" made quite the scene, leaving the establishment barely able to remain upright. Hamilton observed that such a state reminded him "why our heads overloaded with liquor become too ponderous for our heels." He further observed that these miscreants were not only stumbling drunk but also loud and obnoxious, uttering a mix of "oaths and Goddamnes." The innkeeper clearly knew that Hamilton was from a higher class because he hastily rushed to apologize for the behavior of his lower-class customers, claiming that it was not his wish to serve them. Instead, he insisted, he preferred to maintain a reputation "noted far and near for keeping a quiet house." In fact, he proffered that he preferred to have as customers upper-class gentlemen such as Hamilton. However, he lamented that he had no choice in serving such men because, he stated, "we that entertain travelers must strive to oblige everybody, for it is our daily bread" (Gray and Kamensky 2012, 15).

Hamilton stayed at various taverns and inns such as Tradaways each evening of his journey, and he frequently noted this mixing of classes within them, but he also noted other mixings as well. He noted several times the amazing discourse he found in tavern life as he mingled with his fellow countrymen, who represented a multitude of nationalities and religious persuasions. In Philadelphia, for instance, he noted spending his evening with a potpourri of "Scots, English, Dutch, Germans and Irish; there were Roman Catholicks, Churchmen, Presbyterians, Quakers, Newlightmen, Methodists, Seventhdaymen, Moravians, Anabaptists, and one Jew." He went on to describe how this mixed company of around 25 conversed into the evening, sometimes "divided into committees in conversation." Their conversations, though heated at times, fortunately did not lead to too much acrimony, though Hamilton observed that they came close to it when their course of conversation turned to religion. Then, "high words arose among some of the sectaries." Fortunately, such was the magic of the tavern and of the evening that "their blood was not hot enough to quarrel" (Gray and Kamensky 2012, 28–29; for further commentary on the significance of Dr. Hamilton's *Itinerarium*, see especially Imbarrato 1998, 40–85).

DISCONTENT AND THE TAVERN

Dr. Hamilton's evening among newfound friends demonstrates the sense of community that the tavern and its shared social glasses can produce. But, of course, while taverns have served as centers of community life for all classes and all sorts, they have also frequently been feared as places of mayhem and vice, particularly those establishments that attract society's lower classes. Observers throughout history have fretted over what might be going on behind the tavern's closed doors, where within activities ranging from debauchery to rebellion could be taking place. It was in John Hughson's New York tavern, for instance, where in 1741 a plan for violent rebellion was said to have been hatched by the lower classes of that city, which consisted primarily of African American slaves and poor whites. In the end, around 40 people were implicated in the plot and executed, some burned alive, while others were hanged. (For more on this event, see especially Lepore 2005.)

Half a century later in Virginia, it was in Richmond taverns where another plot by the enslaved was supposedly planned and almost brought to fruition. In 1800, Gabriel Prosser, an enslaved blacksmith and a natural-born leader, supposedly visited with and recruited other slaves in the Richmond area in order to encourage them to rise up and rebel against their condition. However, the plot was revealed before an uprising could be hatched. In the end, nearly 30 people were hanged. In both these near rebellions, taverns earned the ire of investigators and the public as details of these alleged plots played out in courtrooms and became well known. The fact that neither of these famous "uprisings" ever came to fruition has caused some historians to believe that perhaps they were simply imagined by paranoid individuals who feared those they enslaved and exploited. However, the message throughout the country was clear: it was in taverns that these conspirators had gathered and conspired, reinforcing in the public's mind that such establishments could be dangerous dens of defiance that lurked in their midst. (For a discussion about Prosser's rebellion, see especially Sidbury 1973 and Egerton 1993.) Such incidents strengthened the idea that taverns needed to be watched.

As the colonies moved closer to rebellion against Great Britain, taverns often served as centers that watered the seeds of growing sentiments of sedition. No tavern from this era is as famous or as important in American history as the Green Dragon in Boston, which served as an important epicenter of discord and plotting against Great Britain. In the years following the Revolution, Americans began to recount the events leading up to open hostilities, crediting the people and places that played their part. A century after these events, an 1871 history proudly noted that the Green Dragon was the site of "patriotic gatherings held within its somber walls during the darkest days of the American Revolution, when Samuel Adams, James Otis, Joseph Warren, Paul Revere, and other true sons of liberty in their secret councils planned the deliverance of their country from thralldom and the grievous oppressions of Great Britain" (Shurtleff 1871, 605). The Green Dragon was one of the oldest structures in Boston, tracing its lineage back to the mid-17th century, when it began life as an inn. It was also one of the largest structures in the city, taking up three-quarters of an acre. Within its confines, travelers could find a stable for their weary horses and beds for their weary bodies. The imposing structure was made of brick,

The Green Dragon Tavern, built in the early 18th century in Boston, has been called the "Headquarters of the Revolution." It was here that the Sons of Liberty met and planned the "Boston Tea Party." The Green Dragon was a typical early American tavern, providing lodging for travelers and space for public meetings. (Everett Collection Historical/Alamy Stock Photo)

with two stories in the front and three stories in the back, all covered by a pitched roof. Visitors were welcomed by a distinctive sign, a green copper dragon. It was here over pints that patriots held forth about the indignities they were suffering at the hands of Great Britain. And it was here that actual rebellion was planned. It was on the cold night of December 16, 1773, that the Boston Tea Party was planned by lantern light in the Green Dragon, and it was from its doors that the ginned-up perpetrators, calling themselves Mohawks and disguised as such, poured forth to carry out their destructive deed. The Green Dragon was also where Paul Revere began his famous ride toward Lexington on the night of April 18, 1775. For these reasons, the British rightly referred to the Green Dragon as a "nest of treason." During the war the well-known tavern continued to serve the emerging nation as a hospital and refuge for the aged (Nathan 2006, 66; Drake 1917, 46–48). Sadly, the Green Dragon was taken down in 1832, but several decades later a plaque was placed on the new structure in order to remember the tavern's importance to the birth of the young nation:

On this spot stood
THE GREEN DRAGON TAVERN
The secret meet place of the
Sons of Liberty,
And in the words of Webster, the
Headquarters of the Revolution.
To mark a site forever memorable as
the Birthplace of American Freedom,
this tablet is placed by the
Massachusetts Society of the Sons of the Revolution
August 19, 1892.
(Bacon 1893, 28)

While the Green Dragon played its part in helping bring on the revolution, another tavern, the Queen's Head, also played its part by serving as witness to the war's end. Its significance was noted in March 1920, just a couple of months after National Prohibition took effect. A New York City magazine dedicated to tourism looked back fondly on what it described as one of the oldest establishments in the city, the old Fraunces Tavern, located at the southeastern corner of Broad and Pearl Streets. It had been built as a residence in 1719 but was turned into a tavern called the Queen's Head in 1762. A description of the Queen's Head when it was put up for sale in 1775 provides an excellent glimpse into what a large tavern from that period was like: "The Queen's Head Tavern, near the exchange is three stories high with a tile and lead roof, has 14 fire places, a most excellent large kitchen, fine dry cellars, with good and convenient offices sufficient for a large trade, is a corner house very open and airy and in the most complete repair, near the fair" (Drowne 1919, 21). Just as with its cousin to the north, its patrons likewise grumbled about British indignities against the colonies, some of whom would pay for their treason against the crown with their lives. During the war, the Queen's Head was also assaulted, suffering a cannonball shot that pierced its roof. When the war ended, the Queen's Head hosted General Washington and his staff, and they said their goodbyes to one another within its walls (*Official Metropolitan Guide* 1920, 47). It had to have been a touching and heartfelt moment when after eight years of war, on the late fall evening of December 4, 1783, Washington raised a full glass of wine to those who had followed him through so many hardships and toasted, "With a heart full of love and gratitude, I now take leave of you, and most devoutly wish that your latter days may be as prosperous and happy as your former ones have been glorious and honorable." He then lifted his glass higher and continued, "I cannot come to each of you to take my leave; but I shall be obliged if each one will come and take my hand" (Lossing 1884, 45). Following the war, New York was the home of the nation's capital until 1789, and the Queen's Head served the new government by providing offices for the Department of Foreign Affairs under Secretary John Jay. By the opening of the 20th century, the tavern was nearly demolished, but due to the efforts of those who prized its place in American history, it was remodeled instead. Retaining the name Fraunces Tavern, it reopened in 1907 and continues to operate as a popular tavern and museum (Porterhouse Brewing Company n.d.).

TAVERNS IN THE EARLY REPUBLIC

Taverns in the early republic continued to play their role as centers of community life for all classes of people. Postwar Philadelphia was brimming with taverns wherein could be found patriots celebrating their revolutionary-fueled republican sentiments. Littered with taverns and houses of prostitution, Philadelphia was a large coastal trading hub tied to the Atlantic world. Sailors, merchants, and workers frequented the city, seeking a variety of comforts from the locale's many bawdy institutions. (For a discussion about Philadelphia culture in this period, see especially Lyons 2006.) During the long, hot summer of 1787, when the leading men of the new nation met at the Constitutional Convention in Philadelphia, their discussions spilled each evening from Constitution Hall to nearby taverns. In particular, heated political discourse took place at the Indian Queen Inn and Tavern, where several members were staying (Morton 2006, 299). The Indian Queen, built in 1759, was the largest tavern in Philadelphia and had a storied past, having previously served as the residence of Sir Richard Penn, the headquarters of General William Howe, and later the residence of George Washington and John Adams (Earle 1900, 52–53). It has also been rumored that Thomas Jefferson penned a draft of the Declaration of Independence at a desk on the second floor of the establishment (Watson 1857, 470; Smith 1990).

As the new republic developed, Americans continued their tavern-going traditions unabated. When the nation's capital relocated to the District of Columbia in the early 1790s, taverns grew at the same pace as government buildings. In 1903, W. B. Bryan, a member of the Columbia Historical Society, addressed the role of taverns in the nation's capital during the post-Revolution years. By the year Bryan gave his speech, taverns had long since transformed into saloons, entities that large numbers of Americans had come to see as a great source of problems in their communities. However, Bryan explained to his audience, taverns had once served as central actors in the Revolution's cause and in the early life of the republic. Bryan used the terms "hotel," "public house," and "tavern" interchangeably, demonstrating the diverse functions that the institution held in public life.

The first tavern of note in the nation's new capital was founded by John Tavers on August 24, 1793, and was known for holding "birthnight balls" to celebrate the birth of George Washington. As had been the case in Philadelphia and New York, the new capital's taverns were centers of political activity, serving as the locus for the day's political questions, as sites of nominating conventions for candidates, and as polling places for elections. Citing the founding of the Orphans Court in 1801 as well as meetings for the Circuit Court of the District in taverns, Bryan put forth that they also served as sites for the dispensation of justice. Finally, Bryan explained to his audience that individual taverns became such an intricate part of the social fabric of the Capitol that they served as landmarks to residents and visitors alike, providing "the key to much of the geography of the city" (Bryan 1904, 71–106).

On the new republic's frontiers, taverns sprang up organically within new communities, just as they had in New England and Virginia two centuries prior, and they continued to provide the same services. One typical frontier community, New Salem, Illinois, began life as a grist mill in 1828 and is famous for having provided a start to a young Abraham Lincoln, who found lodging in a New Salem tavern when he first arrived in that fledgling community in 1832, the same year when, at the age of 23, he unsuccessfully sought a seat in the Illinois state legislature. The one and only tavern in the new settlement was owned by James Rutledge, whose daughter Lincoln would fall madly in love with. (This young lady, named Ann Rutledge, was said to be quite a beauty. She died at the age of 22 in 1835, breaking young Lincoln's heart. See Charnwood 2009, 78–79.)

Rutledge's tavern was a five-room, two-story log tavern that served the same purposes taverns always had, providing rooms for rent and a place to eat and, of course, drink. Lincoln rented a room upstairs at first but quickly went into the tavern business himself when he and his business partner, William F. Berry, took out a license on March 6, 1833, placing the future 16th president into a tavern business of sorts. As in Puritan communities in New England, Lincoln and his partner had restrictions placed on them by their license, which set maximum prices that could be charged for alcohol: 18 cents for half a pint of rum and no more than 12 cents for the same amount of whiskey, for instance. Lodging was limited to 12 cents per night, while putting up a horse could cost a maximum of 25 cents. Furthermore, the business partners were required to pay a bond of $300 to Sangamon County to guarantee that the partners would keep an orderly establishment and that they would furthermore "observe all the laws of this State relative to tavern keepers" (Tarbell 1896, 227). Such regulations and restrictions demonstrate the important role that taverns played in frontier communities.

It seems that Lincoln's tavern was a fairly modest affair. Lincoln's establishment was the quintessential early tavern that provided a multitude of services. You could buy goods, but you could also buy drinks there. In this way, it was similar to the earliest ordinaries. One man who remembered it years later described it as a one-story, two-room affair that provided a bed and fireplace in the back for Lincoln. Some have contended that since Berry and Lincoln sold other goods, their establishment was more like a grocery store than a tavern. Perhaps people have made this claim because they have not liked the idea of equating Lincoln with the tavern business, a nefarious enterprise in the eyes of some. However, while Berry and Lincoln did in fact sell other goods, a contemporary observer remembered that they primarily sold liquor (Tarbell 1896). And even though state law forbade stores from selling liquor in anything less than half a pint, this was commonly ignored, and liquor was "sold by the dram." (For an excellent discussion about the Rutledge Tavern, see especially Mazrim 2007, 309–17.)

After leaving New Salem and moving to Springfield, Lincoln was not done with taverns. In 1843, he and his new wife, Mary Todd, found boarding in another tavern, the Globe, for $4 a week. It was in the Globe that their first son, Robert Todd, was born (Sandburg 1954, 78). It was in Springfield that Lincoln was launched toward greatness.

THE EARLY TEMPERANCE MOVEMENT AND THE TAVERN

By the time Lincoln got his start in New Salem, attitudes about taverns and their products were beginning to change in many quarters of American society. By any standards, drinkers in the early American republic drank heavily, very heavily, increasing to epic proportions over the first several decades of the 19th century (Rorabaugh 1979; Osborn 2014). W. J. Rorabaugh has estimated that during that period, Americans consumed about five gallons of distilled spirits annually per person, roughly half a pint of distilled spirits per day, around three times the amount consumed today (Rorabaugh 1979, 8–11; Osborn 2014, 90).

Ida Tarbell, one of the most famous journalists of the Gilded Age, paints a picture of American drinking habits in places such as rugged New

Salem and explains why such a revered figure as Lincoln would have been engaged in the liquor business:

> In a community in which liquor-drinking was practically universal, at a time when whiskey was as legitimate an article of merchandise as coffee or calico, when no family was without a jug, when the minister of the gospel could take his "dram" without any breach of propriety, it is not surprising that a reputable young man should have been found selling whiskey. (Tarbell 1896, 226–27)

While many Americans continued to believe that drinking was a normal routine of life and even provided healthful benefits, many people were changing their opinion, viewing such prodigious drinking as that described by Tarbell as having deleterious effects on the drinker and on American society. In the previous century, Benjamin Rush, a Philadelphia physician and founding father, commented frequently on the dangers related to immoderate drinking, something he noticed that far too many of his countrymen were engaging in. In 1784, he published a work that addressed alcohol consumption as a threat to the health of the new republic. In *An Inquiry of the Effects of Ardent Spirits upon the Human Body and Mind*, Rush noted that "drunkenness is a medical vice, which offends not only God, but man" (Schneider 2003, 21–22). Whereas Cotton Mather had once equated rum with God's beneficence, Rush argued against the long-perceived health benefits of distilled beverages, though he was fine with fermented drinks such as beer, as was most of society (Schneider 2003, 21–22; Rorabaugh 1979, 30; Pegram 1998, 14). During the first half of the 19th century, such sentiments were becoming more widespread and were forming a growing consensus among many that Americans were imbibing far too much and that this habit not only threatened the health of the drinker but also the very fabric of society and the future of the new republic. As a result, taverns, the primary dispensers of intoxicating beverages, were moving into the crosshairs of reformers who were bent on addressing the problem of alcohol consumption.

As large swaths of Americans began turning their attention toward the damaging effects of drink, other changes in society contributed to a growing sense of angst. During this period there was an uptick in immigration, and the arrival of large numbers of immigrants, particularly the Irish, played a significant role in changing public perceptions about drinking and taverns. As Paul Boyer points out, negative reactions to these immigrants came in part from the rapid increase in the size of cities that they began to fill. From 1790 to 1830, for instance, Philadelphia more than tripled in size, while New York went from 33,000 inhabitants to 215,000 (Boyer 1978, 3–4). As cities increased in size, large numbers of taverns that catered to immigrants became a mainstay in city centers. As immigrants flocked to large urban areas, they sought the solace of the tavern to ease their ills and to comport with their countrymen. In large cities the influx of immigrants drove up the cost of rent and forced them into unpleasant, crowded conditions. As some observers at the time noted, the tavern served as one of the only amusements for this burgeoning working class. (For a study about immigration and working-class life in New York during this period, see especially Stott 1990, 3, 216.) To make matters worse, Rorabaugh argues, in that same period, the price of rum dropped, making drinking cheaper and allowing for the opening of more lower-class taverns. As cities swelled, and taverns and mayhem flourished, many older-stock Americans felt they were losing control of cities, which were to them increasingly resembling foreign lands (Rorabaugh 1979, 32).

No city in the United States served as a better reminder of the threat this menace posed than the nation's largest community, New York City, which seemed to be bursting at the seams with immigrants, impoverished neighborhoods, crime, and plenty of taverns. Herbert Asbury, in his 1928 classic, *Gangs of New York*, describes some of the dive saloons found there, particularly in the Five Points district in Manhattan. Many taverns were home to well-known gangs, such as the Whyos, who made their headquarters in a tavern called the Morgue. Scores of other gangs with names such as the Dead Rabbits, the Roach Guards, the Plug Uglies, and many more also made taverns their headquarters, making hooliganism and taverns synonymous in the minds of many (Asbury 1927b). Asbury estimated that Five Points had at least 270 saloons "and several times that number of blind tigers, dance halls, houses of prostitution and green-groceries which sold more wet goods than vegetables." Charles Dickens, during his visit there, remarked that the neighborhood was "reeking everywhere with dirt and filth," and "nearly every house is a low tavern" (Asbury 1927a, 9–10). In places like Five Points, a brand of hooligan, nicknamed B'hoys, had taken control of the streets, issuing from and retreating into taverns. As residents knew, many parts of the city were not safe, as the streets were filled with gangs, pickpockets, prostitutes, and other lower-class sorts. From the point of view of old-stock New Yorkers, the B'hoys had taken control, and their headquarters were the taverns from which these colorful miscreants streamed forth to commit mayhem. (For an excellent study about the culture of New York street toughs in this period, see especially Cohen 1998.)

Another issue that heightened angst regarding immigrants and taverns was the threat that many Americans felt they posed to young people.

Immigrants contributed to the growth of cities, and some contributed to the growth of gangs, but many new residents of the United States' growing urban areas were youths from the countryside and smaller towns who were drawn to large cities by the allure of opportunity and excitement, sparking a strong concern about the evils that threatened them there. Stories of houses of ill repute, dens of thieves, and bawdy taverns were not without merit. Older-stock Americans increasingly sought to protect young men and women from such places that they might be inevitably drawn to. As a result, while simultaneously attacking alcohol and taverns, some reformers also sought to provide sober alternatives to the tavern. Many lonely young city dwellers were tempted to seek out taverns in order to warm themselves by the fire among cheery friends who were imbibing their blues away. In response, reformers created organizations such as the Young Men's Christian Association (YMCA) in order to provide a warm, welcoming place to obtain a meal and a room for boarding. The YMCA and similar organizations provided young people with these amenities in a safe, often Christian-oriented environment that was very different from what the tavern had to offer (Boyer 1978). These changes meant that the tavern was ceasing to be the natural destination for weary travelers in the ways it had been in the time of Dr. Hamilton's sojourn. It was instead becoming a place to avoid for larger swaths of American society. For many, it was becoming a problem that needed to be dealt with through regulation and reform.

For most immigrant and native-born workers, however, the tavern was the preferred home away from home. Many workers frequented taverns in the evenings, but by day most labored as part of a changing economy and society that shaped the market revolution. (For an excellent study on the market revolution and its effect on American life, see especially Sellers 1991.) Workers sought employment at a myriad of new business enterprises that increasingly demanded that they eschew older work habits that had often allowed on-the-job drinking. Changing work patterns were accompanied by changing employer expectations that demanded that workers show up on time and sober and remain that way throughout their very long workdays. But after the workday ended, many workers took their drinking to nearby taverns. Taverns often witnessed a large uptick in business on Saturday evenings that continued late into the night on Sundays, as many workers ended their six-day workweek on Saturday with pay in their pockets and a desire to blow off some steam until the new week commenced. Such carousing often resulted in the inability or at least lack of desire to show up for work early on Monday mornings, a remnant of an Old World tradition. An 1858 encyclopedia explains that for centuries many workers routinely avoided work on Mondays, a habit known as "blue Mondays"

(Ripley and Dana 1858; Rosenzweig 1983). American employers sought to destroy such traditions. As Roy Rosenzweig explains in his study of factory life in Worcester in this period, the tavern was a major impediment to the ability of employers to command a new work ethic that the emerging industrial age required. In the market revolution, small, more familial workshops were transforming into larger industrial operations. Employers demanded that workers obey the clock and the new work ethic that demanded obedience and eschewed drinking. While the tavern promoted camaraderie, sociability, and equality before the glass, employers demanded discipline and promoted individualistic competition. The market revolution demanded sober workers who operated machinery in factory operations that were much less conducive to older forms of behavior (Blocker 1989, 8–9; Rosenzweig 1983, 61). Employers who sought to shape their workers to meet the demands of the new economy were aided by increasing numbers of immigrants who formed armies of often desperate job seekers willing to fill the ranks of those who could not or would not adapt.

As the nation progressed toward the mid-19th century, more and more Americans separated themselves from the tavern and its products. Whereas, from the first English settlements in North America the tavern had served as an egalitarian institution performing important social functions, by the age of Andrew Jackson the tavern's benign presence was increasingly in doubt. As a result, the first few decades of the 19th century witnessed the rise of a myriad of temperance societies that sought to convince drinkers to leave the tavern and abstain from drinking. Early temperance movements urged people to drink less, but by the early 1830s a new movement called teetotalism pushed drinkers to abstain completely and become members of an emerging "cold water army" (Baron 1962, 193). This push for total abstinence occurred at the same time that the Second Great Awakening, an evangelical movement that encouraged Americans to clean up their lives and get right with God, swept the nation (for more, see Hatch 1989). Multiple temperance societies, such as the Washingtonians, the Order of Good Templars, and the American Temperance Society, emerged across the land, each using posters and pamphlets, pulpits and street corners to get out their message. Pastors frequently preached a temperance message from the pulpit, asking attendees to come to the front of the room and pledge to stay sober. The bravest among this movement even went straight into taverns to appeal to the customers within (Blocker 1989, 21–25). These encounters did not always go well, but such displays of bravery by the growing army of the tavern's foes demonstrate a commitment to a cause that was increasingly bringing more Americans onto the antidrink and antitavern bandwagon.

Reformers portrayed drinking and tavern-going as a form of abnormal or even immoral behavior that threatened the home and even the nation. The term "demon rum" became a catchall term to describe the curse of drink, a curse so powerful that it could ensnare anyone in its clutches, quickly removing the choice to drink from the individual's control. In this period hysteria against drink and tavern-going reached epic proportions. Scores of Americans reported that they or someone they knew suffered from drink-induced hallucinations known as *delirium tremens*. For many, drinking was no longer a simple pastime; it had become a pathological disease (see Osborn 2014). Stories abounded of out-of-control drinkers who had often taken their first drink in a tavern, quickly leading them down a path toward habitual drinking and ruin. These drunkards' narratives typically featured young men with bright futures who were tempted to step into a tavern and try a first drink. From there this individual rapidly descended down a path that led to his ruin and the ruin of those around him. This apocryphal story was told by word of mouth and from the pulpit, but it was also effectively relayed in literature and theater. One such tale was one of the most widely read books and most oft-seen plays of the 19th century. Written by Timothy Shay Arthur in 1854, *Ten Nights in a Barroom* told the sad story of Joe Morgan, a man who came under the control of alcohol as a result of his visit to the saloon of the villainous Simon Slade, who ultimately kills Morgan's daughter when she comes to beg her drunken father to leave the tavern and come home. The book appeared in the same decade as Harriet Beecher Stowe's antislavery tale, *Uncle Tom's Cabin*, and Arthur likened the drinker to the slave in that both were held in bondage by tyrannical forces. Arthur described taverns as places where "souls are destroyed by thousands every year," with tavern keepers being "corrupt men who are scattering disease, ruin, and death . . . over the land!" (Arthur 1854, 161; Pegram 1998, 55; Parsons 2003).

Of course, none of this was good for tavern keepers and their businesses, and they certainly had cause to be nervous. As a result of temperance reformers' unrelenting crusades against the tavern and its products, Americans did begin to drink less. Rorabaugh estimates that due to antidrink agitation, per-capita alcohol consumption prior to the Civil War fell a great deal. Furthermore, not only were Americans choosing to drink less due to persuasion but also the temperance movement was successful in restricting access to alcohol through the law, an effort that was boosted by the rise of a nativist political movement in the 1850s, the American Party, that earned the nickname "Know Nothingism" due to its members' desire to keep their inner workings secret. In an atmosphere that targeted immigration and immorality as the root causes of the nation's ills, alcohol and taverns were viewed by large swaths of anxious Americans, many of them Know Nothings, as the nexus of both problems (for more, see Holt 1999). As a result, some towns, counties, and states turned to outlawing the manufacture and sale of alcohol altogether. In 1851, the mayor of Portland, Maine, and head of the Maine Temperance Union, Neal Dow, became the nation's leading general in this fight when he successfully pushed for passage of a law in his state that banned the sale of alcohol except for "medicinal, mechanical, or manufacturing purposes." As Dow explained many years later, this effort came to fruition after many years of work by thousands of Maine citizens who "had cheerfully contributed time and labor and money in an effort to end its [alcohol's] pernicious influence and effects" (Dow 1898, 360). And, asserted Dow, the primary spring from which alcohol flowed was the tavern, the "source of many ills, too numerous to be counted, too multiform to be described" (Dow 1898, 182). Within a few years, 15 more states followed Maine's lead (Blocker 1989, 51–60). For many observers, it appeared that the tavern's days were truly numbered.

THE TAVERN SURVIVES

By the 1850s, temperance was fast becoming one of the defining political issues of the 19th century. However, two events averted the tavern's demise. The first was the coming Civil War. By the 1850s, attention turned increasingly to the tensions between slaveholding and free states and away from the drink issue. Temperance movements would ultimately revive, but they would have to bide their time until the war ended. And second, the 1840s and 1850s witnessed a large influx of German immigrants who popularized a type of beer that would revolutionize drinking in the United States and lead to the rise of the great American saloon. Previously, English ales dominated the American beer-drinking palate. This newcomer, lager beer, which, unlike ales, is a light-colored, crisp, pale beverage, is produced through a process in which the yeast ferments at the bottom of the brew instead of at the top, and it rapidly became the preferred beer for the American palate, soon overtaking ales and Weiss brews (Blum 1999, 44–45).

Prior to the popularity of lager, many Americans did not drink beer at all, as many drinkers preferred distilled beverages such as whiskey and rum. Many establishments did not even sell beer. Abraham Lincoln's liquor license, taken out in 1833, for instance, does not even list it (Tarbell

1896, 226). But this frothy newcomer, which seemed to come straight from the hand of Radegast, would persuade a lot of Americans to take up the beer-drinking habit, with many becoming convinced that drinking lager beer was not even the same as drinking alcohol. An 1860 contributor to the journal *Scientific American* praised lager beer, referring to it as the "milk of men" for its nutritional value and superiority to ales in terms of its lower alcohol content, which contributed to greater levels of sobriety. He went on to write, "The lager bier war is at present 'all the rage;' nevertheless that drink will fulfill its great moral and social mission against brandy, whiskey—in short, against every species of *aqua vitae*" (Riedel 1860, 85). This sentiment, that lager beer was nutritional and contributed to sobriety, was one that would become a mainstay of beer defenders throughout the saloon period, with lager beer becoming labeled "the temperance drink" in advertisements and a great deal of commentary. In a short time, German brewers became the new beer barons, replacing those of English stock who produced darker and heavier ales. As the nation concluded the Civil War and entered the Gilded Age, lager beer and the saloon formed a partnership that would help define the era. By the end of the Civil War, lager beer was the king of drinks, and with its rise the saloon exploded on the American landscape.

THE RISE OF THE SALOON

Looking back, the saloon period is often represented as the golden age of the tavern, but at the time it was seen by many as a scourge on the communities in which the institution proliferated. The saloon represented the complete break of the tavern from mainstream civic life. Whereas at one time travelers such as Dr. Alexander Hamilton, a representative of the upper class, had sought out the comfort of the tavern alongside other classes of citizen each evening during his journey, the postbellum tavern, the saloon, largely served a more specialized clientele, primarily made up of working-class men. This gave rise to monikers such as the "working-man's club" and the "poor man's club" to describe the institution. During the Gilded Age, the saloon became a ubiquitous sight on Main Street, becoming so common that in many towns it was an unavoidable presence and, for many, it was a scourge that lurked on every corner and oftentimes in between, a scourge that needed to be destroyed. However, millions of American men who patronized the saloon saw it as a refuge from the plague of industrial capitalism that dominated and devoured working-class life. As Jack London so eloquently explained in his semiautobiographical *John Barleycorn*, "All ways led to the saloon. The thousand roads of romance and adventure drew together in the saloon, and thence led out and on over the world" (London 1913, 5). For many working-class men, the saloon became their church and the saloon keeper their pastor.

The late-19th-century industrial revolution demanded a never-ending supply of bodies to fuel the mercurial expansion of the industrial United States after the Civil War. This army of labor was fed by a steady and massive influx of immigrants to U.S. shores, an influx that did not taper off until the outbreak of World War I in 1914. Cities in many parts of the nation experienced large population increases, with large percentages of newcomers being immigrant workers, and along with them came a corresponding increase in the number of saloons. Just after the Civil War, the American population stood at under 39 million; then it exploded. By 1890, it had increased to nearly 63 million, and then it increased even more, not slowing until war in Europe cut the flow of immigrants to a trickle during the second decade of the 20th century. By 1910, the U.S. population stood at nearly 92 million. This rapid and never-ceasing influx of immigrants changed the texture of the American body (Hunt 1910, 24). In Illinois, for instance, the 1910 census reveals a land saturated with immigrants, with over half of its population that year being either foreign-born or having at least one parent who was (Hunt 1912). The influx of such large numbers of immigrants fed a backlash as communities struggled with rapid growth and industrialization (see Wiebe 1967). In many communities, citizens experienced a dizzying amount of development and growth characterized by larger factory operations that belched pollutants into their environment. Along with the factories, downtowns were transformed, and saloons seemed to sprout from the very earth, like weeds. Inside the saloons, workers, many of them foreign-born, whiled away their evenings and stumbled out into the streets, making life uncomfortable for the original inhabitants of their newfound communities. For many, these weeds were consuming all the plants around them.

Bloomington, Illinois, located around 135 miles to the southwest of Chicago, serves as an excellent example of this phenomenon. In 1850, Bloomington was a quaint farming community with the census showing just 1,594 inhabitants (*Seventh Census* 1853, 712). Its upstanding citizens were proud of the fact that, since the community sprang forth from the prairie just a few decades prior, they had been able to keep their town clean of drinking establishments. An 1879 history of Bloomington claimed that temperance forces had been so effective there prior to the half-century mark that "in the year 1850, there was not a saloon in the city of Bloomington, showing us they were up and doing" (Le Baron 1879, 378). However, this changed radically over the course of the decade as thousands of immigrants poured in to take railroad-related jobs. By 1860, the population of Bloomington exploded to over 7,000 residents, a fivefold increase (*Pantagraph* 1898; *Eighth Census* 1864, 97). And with them came saloons, lots of them. By 1910, Bloomington's population increased to 25,768 (Hunt 1912, 636, 644). In that year, this prairie community had over 70 saloons (*Street Number Directory* 1909, 693–95).

In much of the United States, stories similar to that of Bloomington were the rule and not the exception, as saloons proliferated in American cities large and small. For instance, Thomas J. Noel, in his study of Denver's saloons, found 478 of them operating there in 1890 (Noel 1982, 75). Little Galena, Illinois, with a population of only around 4,800 people, had 28 saloons in 1914, around one saloon for every 170 inhabitants. Chicago, Illinois, the queen of all saloon cities, with a population of just over 2.1 million in 1910, had over 7,000 saloons (Hunt 1912, 636, 644). An 1895 investigation into Boston's saloon-going habits estimated that a quarter of a million residents, about half the population, visited that city's saloons each day, while an 1898 study of the saloon issue in Chicago estimated that a similar percentage of the Windy City's inhabitants imbibed each day in the city's many saloons (Billings et al. 1905, 147). These numbers largely reflect patronage at legal drinking establishments. There were large numbers of illegal drinking establishments as well, which were described by such colorful titles as "blind pigs," "blind tigers," and "speakeasies." Perry Duis notes that 1870s Boston was estimated to have over 2,500 of them, or one for every 97 people (Duis 1999 [1983], 29). Nearly every community could tell the same story: the saloon and its armies of intoxicated patrons seemed to be everywhere.

The rise of the saloon coincided with slightly decreasing work hours, not for all workers but for many, allowing for more leisure time to spend imbibing in saloons. Roy Rosenzweig notes that in 1830 the standard workday was 11 hours, but by the 1880s the average workday had dropped to 10 hours at a majority of business establishments. This came about to a large extent because workers demanded it, and many of the labor battles that took place in this period were in part over excessive work hours. As a result, the "eight hour movement" gained a great deal of steam in the late 19th century with the motto "Eight hours for work, eight hours for rest, eight hours for what we will" (see Roediger and Foner 1989; Rosenzweig 1983). More leisure time meant more time for saloon-going. And at the same time that workers decreased the amount of time they spent at work, their employers increasingly demanded that they no longer drink on the job. Drinking on the job had long been a normal part of the work routine as many workers enjoyed mixing socializing with work. In fact, at many job locations in an earlier United States, employers were expected to provide alcohol throughout the workday. However, many factors began to change this, including temperance movements, employers' attitudes, and increased levels of automation (Rosenzweig 1983, 36). (Rosenzweig's study of Worcester, Massachusetts, reveals that the records pertaining to the building of the town hall in 1820 show that salaries for the workers included payments in alcohol. Rosenzweig further notes that Irish laborers who built the nation's canals received four to six breaks a day for drinking.) For many workers, then, the sounding of the bell at the end of the workday meant a chance to finally imbibe in a friendly and familiar atmosphere.

THE SALOON'S APPEAL

So as the saloon proliferated, reformers condemned it, but many also wondered just what was so appealing about the institution that it was drawing so many workers to spend so much of their free time and hard-earned pay behind its swinging doors. In 1931, George Ade, a Chicago native and Gilded Age humorist, looked back nostalgically on the age of the saloon, seeking to explain its myriad of appealing features to a public that after 10 years had grown tired of National Prohibition. Ade commented on the class divide that the saloon represented by explaining that every city had at least one "gilt edge" club that was frequented by "the socially elect" who "could become pickled under polite auspices." The saloon, on the other hand, was not such "a savory resort." Instead, Ade explained, it was an establishment that served working-class men in a familiar atmosphere, so that "when you had visited one of the old-time saloons you had seen a thousand" (Ade 1931, 27–28). It was, as anti-saloon reformer Raymond Caulkins described it, "the poor man's club," a place where for a nickel beer, a workingman could feel like he belonged, like he had dignity, in a world that on a daily basis served up the emasculating and soul-crushing hardships of Gilded Age industrial capitalism outside of the saloon's proverbial swinging doors. While the church could have provided an outlet for the workingman, it seemed that the saloon was winning that role. In 1901, Rev. Charles Stetze sent letters to labor leaders to find out why workingmen were not more interested in church. From the many replies he received, he concluded in part that workingmen found more solace and camaraderie in three institutions (all places where alcohol was more than likely consumed): the lodge, the labor union hall, and the saloon. But it was mostly the latter institution that earned the workingman's allegiance. Stetze discovered to his chagrin that "the place of the church is being actually taken by the saloon, for it is mostly here that the workingman finds occasion to become enthusiastic. The saloon offers many attractions in the way of billiards, pool, reading-rooms, gymnasium, etc." (*Public Opinion* 1901, 178). All these attractions were of course enhanced with each downed alcoholic beverage. The church just could not compete in this realm.

For the armies of the working class, the saloon was much more than a social club. New arrivals to a city were often sure to make the saloon one of their first stops. Many came with the name of a particular saloon etched in their memory, having been told by others to make a stop there. On entering the saloon, the working-class man quickly found a familiar environment filled with others like him. The typical saloon was smoke-filled, somewhat dark, and oftentimes reeked from the smells emitted by the hard-working and hard-drinking men gathered within. The walls were adorned by imagery that spoke to working-class masculinity, featuring, for instance, posters of famous prize fighters and signs advertising the house beer mixed in with titillating pictures of scantily clad women. Within, the newcomer might find those who shared his trade or his ethnicity. And then there was the "free lunch." Many a saloon, hoping to entice customers, offered a wide fare of foods, ranging from pickled meats to eggs and breads. Oftentimes a saloon owner's family spent much of their morning preparing that day's spread, hoping that it would entice much-needed customers. It was an all-you-can-eat paradise, offered for the price of a beer (see Melendy 1900). With a beer in one hand and a plate of food in the other, the newly arrived could now focus on his other reasons for visiting the saloon.

A good barkeep was sure to welcome the newcomer, hoping to make him a regular. The newcomer hoped that the barkeep might know of possible jobs or rooms for rent; or perhaps he might know about local fraternal organizations or unions to which he could turn for assistance. Workers without fixed addresses sometimes had their mail forwarded to the saloon, making the saloon keeper a quasipostman. Saloon keepers often cashed workingmen's checks and kept safes on the premises, serving as quasibanks, providing safe places to keep men's cash and perhaps their valuables. Saloons also hosted events ranging from union meetings to weddings that brought communities together and made newcomers feel welcome. Saloon keepers themselves were in many ways, if not the kings, at least the princes of the working class. They themselves typically derived from working-class ranks, often having left behind their laboring profession in order to chance their place behind the bar. They understood what it was like to be a worker in the Gilded Age, and they understood how to create an environment that appealed to their working-class customers (see Ade 1931; Duis 1999 [1983]). Their lived experiences meant that they could provide a sympathetic ear in an unsympathetic age.

While many observers noted that saloons took on an increasingly homogenized appearance over time, saloons in fact catered to various clientele. As Madelon Powers has noted, one way to break down saloon types is that some were based on occupation, some were based on neighborhood, and still others were based on ethnicity (Powers 1998, 26). For instance, Peter Cole, in his study of an Industrial Workers of the World local in Philadelphia, demonstrates how neighborhood and occupation formed the basis for saloon patronage for longshoremen who, in an effort to find work, often whiled away their days in saloons near the docks that catered to them (Cole 2007, 14). Tom Goyens has chronicled the saloons of New York in the Gilded Age that became the haunts of the German anarchist movement. In these welcoming spaces, workers with an eye toward liberating their fellow workers from the ravages of Gilded Age capitalism met, debated, and planned for a better future, all over tall pints of lager (Goyens 2014). In this period of sharp ethnic differences brought on by mass immigration and competition for employment, individual saloons frequently catered to particular ethnicities. In many cases, Irishmen tended toward Irish saloons, Germans to German saloons, and so on. And sometimes woe be unto those who wandered into a saloon in which they did not belong. An Aurora, Illinois, saloon-goer reminisced years after Prohibition closed that city's saloons that one of the city's favorite haunts, Turner's Beer Garden, a haven for Aurora's large German population, was not friendly to non-Germans:

> The German population drank there, in great numbers, during the summer months, drank their beer, danced the old time waltzes, rolled ten pins, and had a fine time, when left alone, but now and then a bunch of Yankees and Irish lads would horn in and the result was apt to be black eyes and bloody noses. (*Aurora Daily Beacon* 1932)

The ethnic saloon was usually staffed by one's own countrymen, and the walls were adorned with mementos of home. Musical acts frequently played folk music from home, and perhaps a song or two from a village or town left behind might be heard. But perhaps sweeter than the frostiest, coldest mug of beer was the sound of one's own mother tongue as it rolled from the lips of the saloon keeper and his army of faithful customers paying homage along the bar to a distant motherland.

As the saloon period wore on, competition between them became increasingly cutthroat. Just as there were large numbers of saloons, there were also large numbers of breweries, and over time the two became inextricably intertwined. Originating in England, a business relationship, known as the tied-house system, emerged because saloons served as the primary vehicles for brewers to get their products to customers, so they found that fronting saloons and requiring their owners to only sell their products was an effective method of business. Breweries often provided everything the prospective saloon keeper would need, from the stereotypical mahogany bar to the large mirrors behind it to the storefront itself. As will be discussed in the following chapters, they even began constructing their own saloons. For this reason, many observers noted that saloons took on a look of being mass produced. As George Ade pointed out, it often seemed that if you set foot in one, you felt you had set foot in a hundred, and the tied-house system certainly furthered this trend. Finding a prospective saloon keeper was easy. For many a workingman, the prospect of trading in one's tools and smock for an apron and a place behind the bar in one's own saloon was enticing, as many a workingman must have sat in saloons night after night thinking, "I could do this." For some workers,

O'Leary's saloon, 1906. The saloon was located at 4183 South Halsted and was owned by "Big Jim" O'Leary, one of Chicago's most famous saloon keepers. O'Leary's, as with many saloons, was a tied-house establishment. In many tied-house saloons a brewery exercised a great deal of control over the establishment by providing sponsorship and financing. (Chicago Sun-Times/Chicago Daily News collection/Chicago History Museum/Getty Images)

the saloon served as a sort of a retirement plan in an age when there were no old-age pensions. For others, the saloon served as a second income, as some kept their jobs by day, while wives and other family members pitched in to keep the saloon up and running. In some cases, widows found that the saloon offered them a living in a harsh world with few prospects once a breadwinning husband had passed on. For many saloon keepers, the dream was short-lived. Turnover in the saloon business was high, and oftentimes the saloon keeper found that he had spent a couple of years behind the bar, getting deeper and deeper in the red, only to find that he had to turn his keys over to the next owner selected by his sponsor brewery once he could no longer keep up with his payments (see Duis 1999 [1983], Higgins et al. 2017, Mendelson 2009, and Powers 1998).

Another form of competition for the saloon came from refrigeration and the advent of bottled beer. Throughout much of the life of the saloon, the primary way to get alcohol was through the saloon keeper. Families or individuals who wanted to drink at home did so by bringing a pail, often known as a "growler," to a saloon. Women and children often brought their growlers through a side door in order to avoid the potential debauchery happening inside. Many workingmen brought their pails or sent a boy or girl with one in order to have it filled so beer could be enjoyed on the job. Many saloon keepers disliked the growler trade because they believed they lost money on it. Competition was so fierce in the saloon business that filled growlers sometimes cost about the same as a single pint of beer consumed on the premises, usually a nickel or a dime (see Powers 1998). In the first couple of decades of the 20th century, advancements in beer bottling meant that beer could commonly be purchased at stores. In fact, many stores offered delivery service, and with the increasingly common home telephone, those desiring spirits could simply phone in their orders. Many predicted that this would lead to the demise of the saloon, since it would be cheaper and more convenient to consume beer this way (see Duis 1999 [1983]). However, these changes did not bring down the saloon. Saloon keepers discovered then as now that people do not frequent drinking establishments simply because they are looking for the best deal. If this were the case, then indeed taverns would be in serious trouble. Instead, some enjoyed drinking at home while also continuing to frequent saloons.

THE SALOON UNDER ATTACK

The saloon certainly served many positive functions in working-class communities, and for many working-class people, it provided the gathering place of their class, a poor man's club within which everyone raising a social glass was an equal. But this mainstay of working-class life was under constant attack. As discussed above, in the first half of the 19th century, the drink issue had been forced to take a backseat to the expansion of slavery and the coming Civil War, but after the war ended, antidrink fervor had a resurgence as a major moral cause (see Tracy 2005). As had been the case with previous generations, those who opposed the saloon frequently portrayed it as a malignant influence that threatened the fabric of society while preying on the next generation. Francis E. Clark, president of the Christian Endeavor Society, voiced what many anti-saloon zealots felt when he addressed 10,000 of his members in 1901, telling them that "the Saloon-keeper and the distiller are closing up their ranks and combining their evil geniuses to debauch the youth of our land" (*Public Opinion* 1901, 81).

The proliferation of temperance movements can be traced back to the early decades of the new republic when notable organizations such as the Washingtonians and the Sons of Temperance sought to entice drinkers to pledge to give up drinking for good. However, coinciding with a massive wave of immigration in the 1870s, an effective anti-saloon army, the Woman's Christian Temperance Union (WCTU), emerged out of Ohio. As its name indicates, it was a female-led and largely middle-class organization that through moral force encouraged temperance while at the same time seeking to destroy the saloon by any means available to them. On the morning of December 16, 1873, a group of women emerged from a church in Fredonia, Ohio, marched into a nearby saloon, and demanded that its owners cease selling alcohol. Over the next several months, this scene was repeated in scores of communities as armies of women physically protested the saloon. Some entered saloons singing hymns and praying, while others gathered in front doing the same thing. In some cases, the male patrons merely laughed at these women, while in others they poured invectives and even beer on them. However, for those who earned a living in connection to the saloon and those who visited it, this was no laughing matter. What may have looked like a short-lived and frantic movement at first soon coalesced into a powerful and permanent network of women who were determined to put the saloon out of business (see Blocker 1985).

While the WCTU quickly became a visible scourge of the saloon-going public, an even more effective anti-saloon movement, also erupting from Ohio, emerged nearly two decades later in Oberlin in 1893. Styling itself the Anti-Saloon League (ASL), this organization quickly became, according to Jack S. Blocker Jr., the most effective political pressure organization in the history of the United States. The ASL skipped relying on persuasion and the moral righteousness of the women's cause of the WCTU and went straight for the power of the reins of government in its efforts to destroy the saloon and deny Americans the right to drink. Focusing on city halls, state governments, and even the national government, the ASL waged war on the saloon business and the suppliers of its products. The 1917 ASL annual yearbook was able to brag that by March of that year, due to the efforts of the league, "25 states with an aggregate population of 35,380, 568 . . . had adopted prohibition of the sale of intoxicating liquors for beverage purposes" (Cherrington 1917, 5–6). Furthermore, within states that still had wet territory, large swaths had been turned dry by local option elections. These elections allowed local municipalities and counties to oust their saloons by letting voters decide the issue at the ballot box. Sometimes whole states went dry though state legislatures, as did Maine in 1851, and in other instances communities and counties voted to oust saloons and declare themselves dry territory.

As a result of these efforts, the ASL could brag that by March 1, 1917, more than 55 million Americans, occupying over 60 percent of the land mass of the nation, lived in dry territory. So when National Prohibition arrived, much of the country was already dry. The ASL frequently produced maps of the United States that showed dry territory colored in white and wet territory covered in black. Any glance at such maps in the run-up years to National Prohibition showed a country that seemed to largely be dry. However, these white areas on the map represented the areas of the country that were largely rural. Nearly the entire South appeared to be white, for instance. The holdout areas were largely urban. Industrial cities with large working-class and immigrant populations thwarted local option efforts through their support of the saloon. This led the ASL to conclude that for it to be successful it would need to take its fight national once it became obvious that large areas of the country, particularly cities with large working-class populations, would never vote themselves dry. So, with World War I as a backdrop, the ASL successfully lobbied Congress for National Prohibition, achieving success when the Eighteenth Amendment was ratified on January 16, 1919. Now the nation would be able to answer the question on a national scale: Would prohibition actually prohibit? During the long, slow road that led to National Prohibition, those who opposed local option and the closing of saloons had often couched their language in that of liberty, forming organizations with names such as the Liberty League to oppose anti-saloon forces. One New York magazine warned in the waning days of the legal saloon that prohibition "amounts to the imposition of a tyranny on a free people" (*Official Metropolitan Guide* 1921, 17). Such sentiments were especially common among working-class people, who perceived the effort to eradicate the saloon as an effort to control working-class and immigrant behavior.

PROHIBITION AND THE SPEAKEASY

Though the Eighteenth Amendment was ratified on January 16, 1919, it was not scheduled to go into effect until the following year. So for saloon-goers and saloon keepers, a strange pall hung over their shared world. Saloon keepers grappled with what to do next. Many of them had left working-class professions to establish a more comfortable living serving alcohol and holding court with their fellow working-class compatriots. Many American cities contained scores of saloons, and tens of thousands of people depended on the saloon business for their livelihood. Some saloon keepers decided they would keep their storefronts and fixtures and convert to soda fountains or restaurants. However, as many of them would discover, there would soon be an oversaturated market of such businesses because prior to National Prohibition the marketplace had already sorted out how many restaurants and soda fountains were viable. But January 17, 1920, loomed, and choices had to be made. Janesville, Wisconsin, was typical of the many communities across the nation that experienced this transition. By July 1920, it was reported that 12 of that city's 19 saloons had been replaced by other businesses. H. S. Thometzt's saloon had transformed into States Restaurant. Myers' Bar was now Myers' Restaurant. A new billiard hall called the Coliseum replaced another saloon. William Lawyer's saloon had now become a stationery and office supply store. John Hemmings's saloon was now a bank, while Maurice Dalton stopped wetting whistles with beer in order to satisfy sweet tooths with a sweet shop (*Janesville Daily Gazette* 1920). How quickly saloons made the conversion, or if they did at all, was determined in part by local attitudes about the wisdom of Prohibition. For instance, a survey conducted in the five boroughs of New York City in 1924 sought to determine what had become of the former saloons that had heavily populated the king of American cities. Comparing saloons up and running in 1916 with 1924, the survey found that of 3,800 saloons surveyed, the majority had become restaurants, followed by clothing stores. However, the report claimed that 461 of them were still operating in the open as saloons (*Saloon Survey* 1924, 12). Such blatant disregard for the law often did occur in cities such as New York, where the majority of its inhabitants despised Prohibition (see Lerner 2007).

For saloon-goers and drinkers of all sorts, the next year became a scramble. For the Eighteenth Amendment and its enforcement mechanism, the Volstead Act, did not prohibit the possession of alcohol, just its sale and manufacture. Therefore, alcohol procured before National Prohibition went into effect was not illegal to possess after January 1920. Drinkers therefore stocked up, ensuring that despite there being no legal drinking establishments there would still be a healthy stockpile of alcohol. There were plenty of other ways to cheat the system as well. For instance, alcohol could still be procured for religious purposes, so suddenly many noted that there were priests and rabbis galore who seemed to need prodigious amounts of alcohol for their religious rites. Others simply made alcohol at home, in warehouses, and in the woods. Stories of bathtub gin, stills in the woods, and fake factories that were actually booze-making business operations abounded, and so did stories of deadly alcohol concoctions. For instance, newspapers frequently featured tales of those killed by drinking wood alcohol, a problem that was on the rise even before Prohibition took effect. Others procured alcohol from abroad, and a booming black-market business with Mexico and Canada flourished. Prohibition did not prohibit. The dry nation on paper remained, in reality, quite wet.

The Prohibition era has long been revered as one of the most fascinating periods in American history. We associate many exciting things with the 1920s, known affectionately as the Roaring Twenties, and flappers, jalopies, jazz, and mobsters are part of our collective memory. Prohibition, the defining feature of the age, is understood by most as a failed and yet perhaps a noble experiment. Even after nearly 100 years, the failure of that experiment is etched deeply in the American psyche, and few today propose outlawing alcohol again, even though the WCTU does still exist. From the beginning, National Prohibition was destined to fail. Anyone who had long lived in a dry part of the United States knew that Prohibition there had not stopped people from obtaining alcohol. Residents of Maine, a dry state since 1851, had known this for nearly 70 years. To have actually tried to eradicate alcohol from the American public would have been an expensive and herculean effort that would have turned the United States into a police state. Fortunately, Congress did not go in that direction when it established mechanisms for enforcing the Eighteenth Amendment. Instead, it went in the opposite direction, allocating too little in funds and resources toward enforcement. The Bureau of Prohibition, which came into being as a result of the Volstead Act, the enforcement mechanism of National Prohibition, was placed under the Treasury Department and from the beginning was allocated too few resources and provided with too few poorly paid agents. These agents quickly learned they were outmanned and outgunned and that they served a public that increasingly despised their mission. Many of them also learned that working for the other side tended to be a more lucrative prospect (see especially McGirr 2015).

As a result, enforcement of National Prohibition was weak from the start. A 1923 newspaper headline in the *Cleveland Plain Dealer* lamented, "Dry Forces Labor Day and Night But Rum Still Flows," while the subtitle read, "Enforcement Machinery, Going Full Tilt, Fails to Cope with Booze Flood in Cuyahoga." Highlighting the problem, this article claimed that Cuyahoga County, which contains Cleveland, was plagued with at least 10,000 stills and 30,000 bootleggers (*Cleveland Plain Dealer* 1923). Those living in cities like New York where anti-Prohibition sentiment was widespread found that alcohol was as plentiful after 1920 as it had been before. As a consequence, a night out at a nightclub or other establishment could be just as booze-filled as it had previously been when drinking was legal and taverns had been allowed to operate openly. Raids of illegal drinking establishments frequently made headlines, and those who drank in them risked run-ins with the law. Of course, the amount of risk also depended in part on local law enforcement's attitudes about Prohibition, attitudes that were sometimes influenced by payoffs from gangsters or those who ran illegal establishments. Despite the risks, social drinking endured as people continued to seek out places where they could enjoy their libations with friends and strangers.

In order to serve this enduring need, a new type of tavern was born and proliferated: the Prohibition speakeasy. The term "speakeasy" predates the National Prohibition era, and it can be found in use as far back as the early 19th century. Prior to the 1920s, it had long stood for any drinking establishment that was operating outside of the law and existed alongside other terms such as "blind pig" and "blind tiger." An account from 1889 in a Philadelphia newspaper, for instance, describes a "War On Speakeasies" resulting from a combined effort of licensed saloon keepers helping law enforcement root out those serving alcohol without a license (*Philadelphia Inquirer* 1889). Speakeasies varied in many ways, but the Prohibition-era speakeasy was often simply a tavern like any other. Some were dives that served poorer customers, while others were lavish, catering to wealthy thrill seekers. However, one thing they all had in common was that owners, alcohol suppliers, and customers were all breaking the law. Legal tavern-going has always been a bit of a rebellious act, each patron engaging in a little rebellion against the mores and customs of a society that exists outside of the tavern's walls. However, add the illegality of drinking, and the act becomes even more exciting, more of a rebellion. That excitement often began before one even entered the speakeasy. These establishments had long ago earned their name, "speakeasy," because a potential customer might be challenged by a doorman to identify him or herself and, of course, to do so in a quiet (easy) voice. So being admitted meant that one was, in a sense, in the "in crowd," having been cleared as an acceptable customer. Finding a particular speakeasy could also be part of the thrill. The legendary caricaturist Al Hirschfeld described the quest for a New York speakeasy known as the 44th Street Club: "Take the stairs if you'd rather, but the elevator boy will cheerfully take you up the three stories and tell you which door in this office building, housing music publishers, small-time booking agents, and mail order promoters leads to the club" (Hirschfeld 2003). Once one entered, he or she could then revel with fellow lawbreakers. Theoretically, the police could show up at any moment. Someone might yell "raid," at which people might scramble out of secret passages that led to hidden basements and tunnels, some leading down the block or perhaps to a legitimate business next door. Even what one was drinking could be a bit of a mystery, and many terrible and even dangerous alcohol concoctions abounded during Prohibition.

Not every establishment that served alcohol operated like the speakeasy of legend, with customers having to know which door to knock on and what password to use to get in. Many establishments engaged in various legal businesses, such as restaurants and soda fountains, but also kept alcohol on hand for trusted customers. Such was the case in the conservative and idyllic little farming community of Mount Carroll, located in the rolling hills of northwestern Illinois. Mount Carroll's residents had already voted the city dry in 1908, so local Prohibition had existed there for 12 years before the entire nation took the plunge (*Centralia Evening Sentinel* 1908). In 1923, at the height of National Prohibition, 38-year-old lifelong resident Frank Poffenberger purchased an already established pool hall, but pool fees were not his only source of income. Instead, for trusted customers, he kept alcohol in the back, ice cold, in his walk-in coolers. In a small town, such business practices were sure to eventually get the attention of local law enforcement. And such was Poffenberger's bad luck when in 1923 Carroll County sheriff Henry Shiley paid him a visit, catching him red-handed. The bold lawbreaker was then required to pay a hefty fine of $700 for flouting National Prohibition, but it seems that this did not stop him from continuing to serve alcohol. Several years later, claiming that "we only got knocked off once," his son Walter bragged that Shiley's visit was the only time his father was caught. Poffenberger apparently continued to serve alcohol in secret, but he was never caught nor fined again (Emerson 1921, 509). It is safe to assume that in a town as small as Mount Carroll with a population of less than 2,000, many had to have been aware of what Poffenberger was doing. Perhaps the visit from the local sheriff and the resulting fine had merely been a warning to be more discreet about the practice. After all, many Americans scoffed at National Prohibition and enjoyed defying what they saw as a ridiculous law when they could (*Mount Carroll Mirror Democrat* 1973).

THE END OF PROHIBITION AND THE RETURN OF THE LEGAL TAVERN

Many Americans despised National Prohibition from the start. This was certainly true for most of the working class, who largely saw the Prohibition movement as part of a larger war on their culture and an assault on their personal liberty. The push for Prohibition had largely been a middle-class cause. However, as Prohibition went on, many middle-class parents began to notice that the culture that sprang up as a result of the illegality of drinking made it an enticing activity for the sons and daughters of the middle class, and it was the latter who gained a great deal of attention for their newfound tavern-going habit. As one writer complained in 1928, "Saloons which permitted unescorted women to enter their doors were far less numerous than the present night clubs and speakeasies" (*Canton Daily News* 1928). In fact, gangsters such as Al Capone were noted for their penchant for brazenly flouting the law, but many noted that lots of Americans did not seem to care since Capone was in part flouting a law they increasingly did not believe in anyway (Rose 1996). One magistrate in Trenton, New Jersey, lamented in 1923 that Prohibition had done nothing to curb drinking. Speakeasies there operated in the open. In fact, claimed the magistrate, one convent near him was filled with nuns who complained that they were kept awake at night by all the noise from nearby speakeasies that served boys as young as 15 (*Trenton Evening Times* 1923).

Therefore, by the late 1920s, the desire to end the failed experiment gained steam, and across the nation citizens began to organize against National Prohibition. In 1929, a New York socialite named Paula Sabine created the Women's Organization for National Prohibition Reform, and she used her status as a member of one of the United States' leading families to gain the ears of members of Congress, many of whom had never stopped imbibing anyway. From the start of National Prohibition, the ASL and the WCTU would not admit that their long sought-after goal was flawed, and as the 1920s progressed, they continued to dig in their heels, always meeting evidence of Prohibition's failure with the argument that more time and lots more enforcement was what was needed. With time theirs proved to be a losing cause.

In the early 1930s, National Prohibition was more than a decade old, and the Great Depression stalked the land, bringing greater portions of misery each day. Some argued that since people were clearly drinking anyway, would it not be better to bring back the breweries and the distilleries and the dispensers of their products so they could be regulated and taxed. The argument continued that these taxes could help strained governments and so would the thousands of alcohol-related jobs that would be created. The new president, Franklin Delano Roosevelt, offered a path forward to legal alcohol early in his presidency. In fact, his campaign had supported an end to Prohibition. Shortly after taking office, on March 13, 1933, Roosevelt asked Congress to make beer legal by rewriting the Volstead Act to recategorize what would be considered as alcoholic beverages, and raise the standard higher than 0.5 percent alcohol by volume. So by requiring that beer contain no more than 3.2 percent alcohol, producing or serving it did not violate the Eighteenth Amendment (Ogle 2006, 194). On March 22, Roosevelt signed into law the Cullen-Harrison Act, also known as the Beer Bill, and immediately beer began to flow across most of the nation as thousands of brewery workers and bartenders returned to work. However, demand for beer was such that many communities were caught short, dry due to lack of supply but certainly not to lack of demand (Lender 1982, 172–76). Now that beer was legal again, places to serve alcohol legally would begin to make a comeback.

As legal beer began to flow again, the nation prepared for the end of National Prohibition, which came with the ratification of the Twenty-First Amendment on December 5, 1933. The long, strange experiment with National Prohibition was over, and the tavern was set to make a comeback, but in many parts of the United States communities agreed that the saloon as it had been would not be making a comeback. Whereas saloons had once filled, or littered, depending on perspective, downtowns across the United States, most communities returned to legal drinking establishments slowly and cautiously, desiring to keep their communities from returning to the saloon era. President Roosevelt warned the nation that repeal of the Eighteenth Amendment did not mean that communities would return to pre-1920 conditions, which he called "repugnant," and by this he meant a return to the saloons that had been prominent features of much of the nation's downtowns. He admonished that "no state shall, by law or otherwise, authorize the return of the saloon either in its old form or in some modern guise" (*Telegraph Herald* 1933). In fact, some communities barred businesses from even using the term "saloon" to describe their establishments. The terms most commonly used in the post–National Prohibition age were "bar" and "tavern," and in many cases these new taverns were shadows of what the once-raucous saloon had been. There was a consensus in the nation that Prohibition clearly had not worked, so drinking establishments would be allowed to once again open their doors, but there was also a consensus that communities across the nation would not return to a time of saloon-fueled mayhem.

The alcohol industry and taverns faced many challenges in 1934. While Prohibition had not prohibited, it certainly had discouraged. Americans drank heavily during the saloon period, and alcohol-related profits were accordingly high, but consumption changed as a result of National Prohibition. As Jack Blocker notes, many have assumed that drinking either stayed consistent during Prohibition or even increased. Perhaps this perception comes from the imagery that is associated with the Roaring Twenties with its speakeasies, jazz clubs, and gangsters. However, Americans drank much more during the saloon period and tapered off their drinking during Prohibition. For instance, as Blocker notes, from 1900 to 1913, the amount of beer produced increased from 1.2 billion gallons to 2 billion gallons, and the amount of distilled beverages jumped from 97 million gallons to 147 million gallons. However, by the end of Prohibition, Americans had cut their alcohol consumption in half (Blocker 2006). Prior to Prohibition there were hundreds of breweries, distilleries, and wineries that dispensed a large portion of their products in tens of thousands of saloons. Americans were thirsty for legal intoxicants after the 13 long years of Prohibition, but for those in the business, the question was how thirsty would they be?

Taverns also faced multiple forms of new competition. One of the first was simply home drinking. It is true that during Prohibition many enjoyed going to speakeasies, but these could also be dangerous and unsavory places. Patrons also put themselves at risk of being caught there by law enforcement. Therefore, home drinking had become the safest way to consume alcohol, and during Prohibition many Americans sipped their alcoholic beverages behind the closed doors and drawn curtains of their homes. Another factor to consider was a great many things had changed about the American home during Prohibition that made staying at home and drinking a more entertaining prospect. Radios, which did not exist during the saloon age, had become common, and refrigerators that could keep beer cold were also becoming common in American homes. Of course, despite these advances, people still went out for entertainment, and many amusements outside the home did not necessarily involve alcohol. One such common form of mass entertainment was the great American movie theater. Prior to Prohibition movies were a relatively new phenomenon, and then films were silent. During Prohibition the first "talkies" were introduced with *The Jazz Singer* in 1927, and Americans went to the movies in droves.

Even though when Prohibition ended one out of every four workers was out of work, and a movie ticket generally cost around 35 cents, roughly 60 to 70 million Americans packed movie houses each week (Ross 1998). Essentially, during National Prohibition Americans had had to find many public leisure activities that did not involve drinking, and many had. The question was, would they now come back to the tavern?

Taverns did begin trickling back into the mainstream United States. In Dubuque, Iowa, for instance, a city that had boasted 124 saloons in 1900, a mere 19 taverns were listed in the city directory that was published on January 1, 1934 (*Telegraph's Dubuque City Directory* 1899–1900, 674–75; *Telegraph's Dubuque City Directory* 1934). However, by 1937, 126 taverns could be found in the community, and by 1939, that number had risen to 150 in that iconic Mississippi River community of around 40,000 residents (*Dubuque City Directory* 1939, 657–58). Despite the tavern's return, it took several decades for Americans to increase their consumption of alcoholic beverages. A poll taken in 1939 indicated that 42 percent of respondents did not drink. Prohibition had decreased the United States' overall alcohol consumption, but in the decades following the repeal of the Eighteenth Amendment, consumption did begin to rise once again. However, it was not until the 1970s that Americans caught up to pre-Prohibition levels of consumption (Blocker 1989, 240).

Whereas before Prohibition thousands of breweries flourished, the trend after Prohibition was for a few to gobble up the marketplace, and with little competition came little in the way of innovation. This meant that for decades the average tavern customer had few beer choices, and most choices tasted pretty much the same anyway. By the 1970s, this began to change as more small operations went into the craft beer business. One of the changes this has wrought in recent decades is the advent of the microbrewery. While many customers of these establishments certainly did drink to get drunk, the microbrewery customer often believes that he or she is engaging in an authentic experience that is as much about sampling the beer as it is about feeling its intoxicating effects. Hence, the sampler. Samplers provide customers with a tray of a few, typically two-ounce, samples of the various beers brewed on the premises. The Brewers Association estimates that by 2015 there were 4,225 craft breweries with 1,650 being brewpubs (Brewers Association n.d.).

Today, the increasingly ubiquitous microbrewery is but one tavern choice. There are many. In 2013, North Dakota beat every other state for the number of taverns per capita at one tavern for each 1,580 residents, while Virginia has the fewest taverns per capita with one tavern for every 63,410 residents (*Capital Times* 2013). While the North Dakota ratio of taverns to residents may seem high, it is low compared to the saloon era, when many communities saw ratios of saloons to residents below 200. Today, Americans enjoy a variety of tavern options, and the industry thrives. This is despite the fact that there are more forms of competition in terms of entertainment than ever before. It is cheaper and safer to drink at home, but it seems that the tavern offers something that is worth leaving the comfort of one's home for. Today taverns thrive, and in many communities there are as many taverns as churches. The following chapters will consider the space of the tavern and its functions in order to provide a better understanding of its enduring allure.

Chapter 2

THE TAVERN AND THE COMMUNITY

> And always and everywhere I found saloons, on highway and byway, up narrow alleys and on busy thoroughfares, bright-lighted and cheerful, warm in winter, and in summer dark and cool. Yes, the saloon was a mighty fine place, and it was more than that.
>
> —Jack London (London 1913, 33)

As with many working-class youths of his generation, Jack London found his way to the tavern at a young age. In his semiautobiographical *John Barleycorn*, London claims that his first encounters with the institution began at the age of five when he was frequently sent by his father to fetch beer by the pail. In this way, London learned early of the tavern and of its intoxicating products. He reveals that during one of his can-rushing trips, he tried beer for the first time and went on to live a life of alcoholic ruin (London 1913, 12–14). When London was a youth in the last two decades of the 19th century, taverns had become more commonly referred to as saloons, and to the chagrin of many they were a prominent feature of American life, dotting the landscape of many American cities. Many children were sent by their working-class parents to fetch beer by the pail, most commonly referred to as a growler, at nearby saloons, and in most working-class neighborhoods, there was always one nearby. In some cases, children simply entered through the front door and sauntered up to the bar. At many saloons there was a side entrance or window for children engaged in this chore. Once inside, the child offered his or her pail to the bartender to be filled. The saloon keeper instantly knew why the child was there. In fact, he probably saw the child regularly and knew the child's father as a steady customer. He may have known the child's mother as well, as she too may have been a regular growler customer. In this way, the saloon presented itself as an organic part of the working-class community, serving and interacting with all members of the family. But this practice also incurred the wrath of its opponents.

Many decried the institution and the access it granted to women and children as further proof that the saloon was ruining working-class families We can see middle-class attitudes about the practice in an 1892 drawing that appeared in *Harper's Weekly*, titled "Working the Growler on a Saturday Night," which displays the image of a young boy exiting a saloon with a growler of beer cradled in both hands. As in young London's case, this pail was more than likely on its way to an impatient father waiting at home for the child's return. Behind the boy we can see the open doors of the saloon, revealing a lively male crowd within, as a sinisterly shadowed customer is sauntering toward its corner entrance while casting a furtive glance at the child. The boy seems timid as he glances backward toward the saloon as if afraid that he could be followed by a ne'er-do-well. In the street, watching the boy exit while carrying his shame in his hands, are two respectably dressed ladies and a young girl. Their countenances imply both concern for the welfare of the child and perhaps also scorn for the father who sent him there and the saloon keeper who served him (*Harper's Weekly* 1892).

Today, it is taboo (and of course illegal) to send one's child to a tavern to procure its products, but in London's day this was common, and most working-class communities saw nothing wrong with it. Many in the United States did, however, and the practice earned much commentary from pulpits, tracts, and newspapers, and, as a result, there were efforts to curb the tradition by law. For numerous Americans, children going into and out of saloons further demonstrated negligent parenting practices, which, they believed, were a problem for working-class communities. Such behavior was also a sign of what was wrong with the institution itself and a visible example of its pernicious influence on the working-class families that were its primary sponsors. Reformers were also frustrated that local law enforcement seemingly turned a blind eye to the practice in many neighborhoods. In 1894, a Boston Baptist church was the site of a mass meeting by the League for Enforcement of Law in Boston. The crowd, which had gathered to learn about the evils of can rushing, witnessed, "with the aid of a stereopticon," a vision on the screen of pictures taken the previous Sunday of the exterior of a saloon. Pictured in the photographs were "uniformed policemen standing idly in front of the doors, while children with beer cans [pails] were entering by the side doors" (*Daily Arkansas Gazette* 1894). This story was reported in newspapers throughout the country, with some claiming that these pictures were from New York and other cities as well, reflecting the ubiquity of the saloon question. From the point of view of these concerned citizens, can rushing was a way that taverns chose to visibly represent themselves in their communities, a way of seemingly thumbing their collective noses at those who worried about the deleterious effects of saloons in their communities. Such practices were used as ammunition by reformers who ultimately drove the nation toward the disastrous Eighteenth Amendment and the end of the saloon.

After the saloon period, can rushing was a thing of the past, and today is a charming anecdote from another age, but it serves as a reminder of the complicated relationship that taverns have often had with the communities in which they reside. For many, the tavern is an integral part of their lives, and just seeing its welcoming facade and signage creates a sense of warmth and community. As passersby see drinkers enjoying a cigarette on the sidewalk in front of a tavern while loud music seeps out, mixing with the night air and the smell of tobacco, some are enticed and drawn in. For others, such scenes affirm that taverns are a blight on their communities and are places to be avoided—and regulated. Throughout American history, tavern keepers have had to balance between attracting and keeping customers and avoiding running too far afoul of the standards of the communities in which they operate. They have always been dependent on local government for the licenses they need to stay in business: run too far afoul of community standards, and a tavern keeper could lose his license quickly or, even worse, wind up in jail. Proprietors desire to create a fun and in many cases even a salacious atmosphere, but they must do so while walking a fine line between attracting customers and attracting problems with their communities. But staying in business first and foremost means attracting customers.

Letting potential customers know what to expect in the barroom and entice them to come find out begins on the outside. For instance, Poopy's, a famous tavern in the northwestern Illinois community of Savanna, provides no mystery as to what type of customer would be attracted to the establishment. Savanna is a rather economically depressed community that has many of the hallmarks of scores of postindustrial Midwest communities. The town, however, attracts one group of visitors to the community in large numbers: bikers. When the weather permits, the thunderous roar of motorcycles, mostly Harley-Davidsons, is frequently heard around town. Some of these riders are serious enthusiasts who sport the biker look and ride whenever they can. Others are weekend riders out to get away from the workaday world and transport themselves through their high-powered machines into a world where camaraderie is built around

"Poopy's," a famous tavern located in Savanna, Illinois, draws motorcycle enthusiasts ("bikers") from far and wide. The large and distinctive signage (which is the same on both sides) in front of the bar's parking lot lets them know they have arrived. From photos in restrooms to paintings on the wall, titillating images that sexualize women have long served to promote male homosociality in taverns.

powerful American-built motorcycles. Poopy's has been successful at getting the business of both types of riders by personifying the culture that they are seeking, and as a result the establishment proudly claims that it is "Illinois's biggest biker destination." One can know immediately that he or she is stepping into this world simply by riding up to Poopy's vast parking lot, which on a warm weekend day is filled with motorcycles. Customers roaring down highway 84 toward Poopy's are greeted by a massive sign featuring on both sides two larger-than-life, scantily clad women draped across motorcycles. Poopy's sign leaves little doubt about the customer base that the tavern is trying to attract. Those seeking a quiet evening or those who are not enamored with the culture that surrounds the Harley-Davidson mystique and all that goes along with it know immediately that Poopy's is not for them (Swenson 2017).While this tavern might thrive and be welcomed in a town such as Savanna, where bikers spend money at Poopy's and other bars that cater to them, such an establishment and clientele would not be as welcomed in other types of communities. Poopy's is not for everyone, but one thing that can assuredly be said about the place is that it is authentic, and from past to present, Americans have sought authenticity in their tavern choices.

EARLY COMMUNITY TAVERNS

As discussed in chapter one, early taverns, often called ordinaries, in colonial America were important centers for community, doubling as meetings places for community business and even as centers of worship. In 1900, at the height of the saloon age, author Alice Morse considered the early American tavern and the draw it had for the community, writing, "They were for the comfort of the townspeople, for the interchange of news and opinions, the sale of solacing liquors, and the incidental sociability" (Earle 1900, 3). The first taverns in the English colonies served both as community gathering centers and as way stations for weary travelers. Traveling between communities in colonies such as Massachusetts was arduous, and travelers counted on taverns to be in each community and to be ready for their arrival. At a tavern a weary customer could expect to stable and feed his horse as well as obtain a meal and room for the night. All, of course, for a fee, but fees that were often set by law so that travelers knew what to expect in terms of prices. Such a system worked well to allow agents of commerce, ministers, messengers, and others to be able to move around the colonies. A century and a half after the first English settlers arrived in North America, not much had changed.

Nicholas Cresswell was an English immigrant who was typical of the energetic colonists who sought financial opportunity in the New World and were willing to endure discomfort and put forth great effort to achieve it. As with many colonists, Cresswell sought to make his fortune in land speculation, and he traveled far and wide in the colonies between 1774 and 1777 in an effort to do so. Fortunately for future generations, Cresswell kept a fairly detailed journal (Gill and Curtis 2009). One consistent theme that occurs frequently in Cresswell's journal is his interactions with taverns, places he welcomed as refuges from the difficulties of travel in that period, and readers of his journal can sense the relief that he felt each time he sighted a welcoming tavern after a hard journey. For instance, on one occasion, Cresswell recounts a cold, difficult night spent sleeping on the ground in the Appalachians, with "water frozen in kettle about 10 foot from the fire." After traveling 30 miles the next day, relief was had at Runnel's Tavern, where he and his party dined and slept well. The next day he crossed a mountain and then "called at Creig's Tavern for a supply of Rum, then over the Devil's Hunting Ground to Tittle's tavern." For travelers such as Cresswell, the tavern was a lifeline, an oasis along the journey. Knowing where taverns were located and how to identify them was of the utmost importance (Macveach 1924, 45).

In smaller communities there might have been one or two taverns that would have been easy to find, and in larger cities there were typically several, and they were certainly not hard to find either. Then as now, taverns had a distinctive presence that let passersby know what they were, and in larger communities their presence would have been easily noted. As Mark Edward Lender estimates regarding Boston, there were a handful of licensed ordinaries in the 1630s, but by the 1680s there were dozens in that iconic city with few checks on their ability to multiply (Lender 1982, 12). As Peter Thompson points out in his study of taverns in the Revolutionary period, many cities had tolerant licensing protocols and had done little to limit the number of taverns. At the same time, many cities set maximum prices that could be charged to customers (Thompson 1999, 24–25). Charging predictable and reasonable prices was one way that taverns presented themselves to their communities as essential way stations for travelers, while at the same time serving as organic parts of their communities, where all could gather for communal purposes. As a result of liberal policies aided by general community approval, cities such as Philadelphia had scores of taverns that ranged from respectable establishments to bawdyhouses (see Lyons 2006). The city's openness in the granting of tavern licenses meant that those citizens who wanted to go into the tavern business encountered few barriers, but the double-edged sword that allowed one this opportunity meant that those who chose to engage in the business faced stiff competition (Thompson 1999, 67–68). Because the number of taverns in Philadelphia was so high, the ratio of denizens to taverns was extraordinarily low, even rivaling wild mining communities a century later. Such fierce competition would have pushed tavern keepers to desperately seek to attract and retain customers. Thompson estimates that in 1763, there were 12 taverns for a population of 2,100 residents, for a ratio of one tavern per 175 residents. By 1769, the number of taverns had ballooned to 178 for a population of just over 28,000, for a ratio of one tavern per 158 residents.

Of course, many customers who whiled away their hours in the city's watering holes were not residents of Philadelphia but were instead simply passing through that busy seaport city. However, in order to have kept so many establishments in business, it is clear that tavern-going was a mainstay of entertainment for the city's residents, many of whom spent their evenings engaged in drinking, discourse, and carousing (Thompson 1999, 27). Residents might have spent money on food and drink but were likely to go to their own homes at the end of an evening. Of course, there were more services provided in Philadelphia's taverns than simply the pouring of libations and the serving of supper. Many of the city's taverns also served as inns. According to a survey conducted in 1756 that was commissioned to determine how many troops could be billeted in the city during the crisis of the French and Indian War, an initial count concluded that there were 101 taverns that contained a total of 400 beds. This number may not have represented all the tavern beds available and may reflect a desire to purposefully hide the availability of accommodations for troops, but it is still a high number (Thompson 1999, 57).

Walking down any thoroughfare in much of colonial America, one could not help but notice the obvious presence of taverns, sometimes appearing side by side in a row and sometimes appearing intermittently between other businesses, providing travelers and locals many choices of establishments. One iconic tavern from the period that provides some perspective for how taverns appeared to passersby and potential customers is Philadelphia's iconic Old Tun Tavern, which is reputed to be the birthplace of the United States Marine Corps and the site of the first Free Masons lodge that was established in North America. The term "tun" found its way into the naming of many taverns from the period. "Tun" refers to a measure of alcohol or a cask that contains alcohol. The Old Tun was built in 1685 by two brothers, Samuel and Joshua Carpenter, and it had a long and storied existence before it burned down in 1781 near the end of the American Revolution. It was there that the United States Marine Corps was established on November 10, 1775, when a Quaker named Samuel Nichols was commissioned by the Continental Congress to form two battalions of marines. It says a lot about the reputation of the Old Tun that it was chosen as the headquarters for this important purpose. This event ensured that the Old Tun would never be forgotten, as keepers of Marine Corps lore have kept the tavern alive in memory, so that on each November 10, current and former marines raise a social glass to their beloved corps and to the Old Tun where she was born. The formation of the first Masonic Lodge in North America was said to have happened there as well. No one is sure of the exact date when the lodge came into existence, but the earliest known existence of the Tun Tavern Lodge is from a document dated June 24, 1731. Later, Benjamin Franklin presided as the lodge's grandmaster when it moved its location to another Philadelphia tavern, the Royal Standard Tavern, in 1749 (Kyriakodis 2011, 212; Adamson and Segan 2008, 500; *Pennsylvania Magazine of History and Biography* 1896, 116).

A sketch of the Old Tun, produced in 1904, provides modern observers an opportunity to imagine the exterior of a popular Philadelphia tavern as colonists walking past might have experienced it. We can see that the Old

Tun was a large three-story building packed tightly between the establishments that surrounded it. It contained a large porch surrounded by railing. The top floor was covered by a steep gabled roof that had several dormer windows facing the street, denoting likely guest accommodations. Rising from each end of the establishment were two large chimneys. The sign in front of the Old Tun was rectangular and modest in size and design, perhaps denoting the tavern's already famous reputation. In the center of the sign was a cask representing the "tun" in the tavern's name. This would tell passersby that a master brewer was on the premises. The sign was held fast on a pole that extended vertically from the center of the structure out into the street. In the illustration, men can be seen milling about in front of the tavern, engaged in conversation, with one man sitting confidently astride a horse engaging in conversation with another man standing on the establishment's ample porch while holding on to the railing (Department of the Navy 1946). Those gathered around the outside of the Old Tun reflect the public nature of the tavern, which served as a conduit for sociability that blurred the liminal space between its interior and exterior.

Philadelphia had other large taverns with names that evoke the glory of a bygone age of wooden ships and pirates and rebels. Some of the largest in that storied city were the Indian King, Three Tuns, the Blue Anchor, and the Indian Queen. The Indian Queen is described as a three-story brick structure that was 21 feet wide and 40 feet deep. Peter Thompson describes it as having contained "five large rooms on the first floor . . . Four of these rooms could be converted to form two even larger rooms capable of seating up to hundred 'gentlemen.' There were two large kitchens, sixteen lodging rooms, and four rooms for servants" (Thompson 1999, 59). To the modern observer, such buildings would seem small in comparison to most modern city structures. But in the 18th century, these establishments would have greatly impressed visitors to a community that had around 40,000 residents.

Many taverns had common names. Indian Queen also appears to have been a popular tavern name, and taverns with that moniker were to be found in cities up and down the colonies. An early tavern with the same name from this period that we can still visit and enjoy as a historic landmark is the Indian Queen Tavern in New Brunswick, which was built in the early 17th century as a residence that later became a tavern. Indian Queen may have been a common tavern name, but this was no common tavern. It was an upscale establishment that was visited by George Washington, Ben Franklin, and John Adams in 1783 for a dinner given in the general's honor (Middlesex County Government n.d.). The tavern was moved in 1971 to its current location about seven miles away in Piscataway. However, much of the original tavern was left intact, so visitors today are able to get a good feel for the colonial-era tavern (Mokarry 2009). There is nothing about the Indian Queen that would indicate to most that this was a tavern other than a modest sign in front. In fact, the casual passerby might assume that this historic landmark is merely a lovely, two-storied family home. One thing that would alert a modern observer that this is a historic structure, however, are two chimneys extending boldly toward the heavens at each end of a pitched gable roof. The homelike nature of this Indian Queen reflects exactly what its proprietor would have wanted to project, that his establishment would serve as a temporary home for those traveling through, a place where they could warm their feet by a toasty fire while sharing in libations and conversation, followed by a welcoming bed upstairs where they could obtain rest after a day's long journey and perhaps an evening of imbibing with new friends.

Another famous Indian Queen, located in Bladensburg, Maryland, also claims a George Washington visit. In fact, it is alternatively known today as the George Washington House. This Indian Queen was built in 1732 in the gorgeous Georgian design. An application to the National Park Service in 1973 to have it put on the National Register of Historic Places provides us with an excellent description of the structure before it was restored:

> The George Washington House is a fairly simple but, impressive in contrast to its surroundings, two and one-half story brick structure with basic mid- and late eighteenth century characteristics. The principal facade is five bays in width, with wide centrally located doors at both first and second levels. . . . At each end of the building is a single exterior chimney, each matching in detail. . . . There are three dormer windows with classical detailing on the main façade. (Owens 1973)

TAVERN SIGNAGE

Since many tavern structures resembled the homes and businesses around them, signage would have been important to let passersby know that they were passing a tavern and perhaps entice them in. In fact, signs were not always optional. For instance, by 1672, innkeepers in Connecticut were required to erect "some suitable Signe set up in the view of all Passengers for the direction of Strangers where to go, where they may have merriment" (Schoelwer n.d.). Those who failed to put up a proper sign faced a fine. As Martin Treu has noted in his study of early American signage, American colonists followed the English custom of fixing a large pole in the ground in front of a business establishment and then affixing a pole along the top, so that the whole contraption resembled a large upside-down L. Then a wooden sign with the name of the tavern and usually some sort of picture was affixed to the horizontal pole. Treu notes that to get a good sense of a proper English tavern sign that American colonists would have based their designs on, one should observe William Hogarth's famous 1751 artwork titled *Beer Street*, where one can find Hogarth's satirical portrait of the virtues of drinking beer over gin and other hard liquors. In *Beer Street* one finds happy and productive revelers basking in the glow of beer consumption. A central feature of the piece is a sign painter working on the type of wooden signage that was a staple of the period. As Treu notes, proper signage was essential to ensure that passersby would not mistake a tavern for just another residence. As one 1780s traveler noted, this type of signage gave taverns a distinctive look on approach: "The taverns in the country are recognizable, even at distance, by a sort of gallows arrangement, which stands out over the road and exhibits the patron of the house" (Treu 2012, 18).

One 1907 observer, J. Howard Wert, recorded in a Harrisburg, Pennsylvania, newspaper a nostalgic reflection about taverns of old, providing readers with a glimpse of a time when taverns were central, integrated features of nearly every community. By 1907, the tavern, then in the form of saloons, was under serious assault by reformers who were waging a relentless war against alcohol and the very existence of the tavern itself. As is common in many pieces where the observer is remembering the past, there is a nostalgic longing for a lost period—in this case a remembrance of a time when the tavern was a cherished, normal part of the community. Wert noted that these establishments advertised by means of "an enormous wooden post sunk firmly in the ground to a depth that would enable it to defy the fiercest tempests and rising above the surface twenty-five to thirty-five feet." Attached to this large post, Wert claimed, was a large oval sign "suspended by huge and tightly riveted grappling irons." On such signs, passersby would see an image of "the particular individual, animal or article that gave its name to the house" (Wert 1907, 10). The enormity of some of these signs, described by Wert, can be attested to in an 1836 drawing by John Warner Barber, an engraver, who produced a plethora of quaint scenes of early American life. In his *South View of Southington, Ct.*, we witness a street scene that features what appear to be at least two churches on one side of the street and a tavern on the other. One wonders if Barber meant to evoke the duality that the tavern and the church provided in American communities. In front of the tavern are two tall timbers with a cross timber along the top, holding a large sign by two chains (Malley 2000). Most tavern signs were probably not as large as the one shown in this artwork. There are plenty of other images and descriptions of taverns that denote smaller signage. Clearly some larger establishments invested in very large signs, while smaller establishments and those located in more crowded sections of cities would not have had the ability to display such towering edifices.

Most taverns provide comparable products and services, so which tavern one chooses has a great deal to do with reputation or initial observations. Tavern signage has always played an influential role in appealing to customers' tastes. The images on a tavern's sign and the name of the establishment are meant to evoke an emotion in the observer. And as Shakespeare quipped, "What's in a name?" As always, early taverns displayed their names on their signage, and many of the names were common. For instance, many taverns had animal names and used images of animals in their signage. As Henry Wadsworth Longfellow wrote in 1863 in his epic poem "The Wayside Inn," travelers were greeted to that tavern by a marker "half effaced by rain and shine . . . The Red Horse Prances on the Sign" (Longfellow 1863, 2). Horses appeared frequently in tavern names and on tavern signs. As Wert remembers, many establishments had names referring to "the white bear, the black bear, the white horse, the black horse, the buck, the beaver, the eagle, the white swan, the black swan, [and] the duck." Other examples of common tavern names were derived from war, such as "the sheaf, the sickle, the bold dragoon, the anvil and hammer, the compass, the crossed keys and the like." After the American Revolution, in a sign of patriotic republicanism, many taverns displayed the names of heroic Americans on their signage, such as "Washington, Jefferson, Adams, Franklin, Lafayette, Baron Steuben, Pulaski, Wayne, Putnam, Starke, and a hundred other heroes and statesmen of the period that tried men's souls" (Wert 1907, 10). These names are reflected in the tavern names of Harrisburg where Wert hailed from, including the following: "Black Horse, Spread Eagle, Seven Stars, Swan, Washington, Baron Steuben, Lafayette, Duck, Fox, Golden Lamb, Cross Keys, Compass, Red Lion, Ship, William Tell, Pennsylvania Arms, Green Tree, Ben Franklin, Bull Head, William Penn, Rising Sun, Eagle, King of Prussia, Sheaf, [and] Black Bear" (Wert 1907, 10).

Norman Rockwell captured the spirit of tavern naming and its intersection with patriotism perfectly in his 1936 painting titled *The Tavern Sign*. In this iconic painting, we see three curious onlookers dressed in the attire of the Revolutionary War period watching with awe as a tavern painter works in earnest to complete a sign for a tavern that is to be called George Washington Inn. In its center is a large portrait of the great general himself. To the side of the painter lies the former sign that is to be replaced by the new one that is in the throes of creation. The old sign contains a portrait of King George III, advertising, of course, the King George III Inn (Rockwell 1936). It goes without saying that at the birth of the new republic, no patriotic drinker would have set foot in a tavern under the original name. Ten years earlier, in 1926, in yet another homage to patriotic, tavern-sign painters in the early American republic, Rockwell portrayed a postcolonial artist hard at work in 1785, just after the country had gained its independence, creating a tavern sign for the whimsically named Ye Pipe and Bowl Tavern. This painting features an older craftsman who is intensely and lovingly creating a bright and colorful portrait of Washington with a face that contains much rouge and a long pipe extending from ruby-red lips. Interestingly, Rockwell chose to portray the great founding father with a red military coat, attire equated with the British who he had so recently vanquished on the field of battle (Solomon 2013, 127).

It seems, however, that not all taverns chose to jettison their British antecedents after the Revolutionary War. Such was the case with the Wolfe Tavern, located in Newburyport, Massachusetts. The Wolfe began its life as a tavern three years after the famous British general James Wolfe fell at the age of 32 in 1759 at the most famous battle of the French and Indian War, the Battle of Quebec. It seems that the founder of the Wolfe sought to honor the famous general by naming his tavern after him. He featured him prominently on a sign that was fixed to a pole in the ground in front of the tavern. On the sign, Wolfe appears in semiprofile, looking into the distance. Honoring a British general made sense in 1759 because most American colonists were still loyal and patriotic British citizens. As the relationship between mother country and colonies deteriorated, the Wolfe was reputed to have been a meeting place of the Sons of Liberty, and it is said that at one point General Lafayette had his headquarters there. It seems, however, that after the war one of the Wolfe's proprietors did not take to the idea of having his tavern named after the storied general, so he took down the pole and sign, but it was put up again later, and the Wolfe lived on. Unfortunately, the original Wolfe Tavern burned down in 1811, and allegedly the fire took the sign that bore General Wolfe's image with it, but the proprietor rebuilt and carried on the storied tavern's traditions. Over the next several years, the Wolfe Tavern went through a series of failed proprietors and different names. Finally, a new proprietor found the original sign that proudly displayed General Wolfe and fixed it to the ground with a ship's spar. As legend has it, the tavern finally began to prosper again. It would be great to say that the Wolfe Tavern prospers to this day, but unfortunately, as proof that modernity often tramples upon the gems of history, the historic building that housed the Wolfe was demolished in 1951. However, the famous sign of the Wolfe Tavern has lived on in memorabilia, displayed on postcards and wooden signs (Berry 2015).

The Connecticut Historical Society boasts the largest collection of tavern signage from the early American period. The society asserts that between 1750 and 1850, there were somewhere around 50,000 taverns up and down the Eastern Seaboard. In general, tavern signs were made from wood and therefore have generally not survived the ravages of time. However, the historical society hosts an impressive collection of 65 original tavern signs that provide us a glimpse into the everyday world of the early United States. Susan Schoelwer, the director of the museum collections at the society, argues that such signs were a type of folk art at a time when average people did not have much in the way of art in their homes. However, they could appreciate these signs as a form of "everyman's common art" in a time when people lacked "access to the variety of visual images that we have today"(Schoelwer 2001). While many signs were simple affairs, somewhat crude and hastily constructed, others were much more elaborate. The most famous sign artist of his day was William Rice from Hartford, who put a great deal of care and artistic talent into his work, sometimes adorning it with lead glass flakes and gold leaf. Many of his creations were in the style of *trompe l'oeil*, a type of artwork that literally means "fool the eye," a technique that creates 3-D illusions for the viewer. His signs varied widely in design, and he traveled up and down the Eastern Seaboard supplying samples of his craft to tavern keepers who then hired him to make something special for their place of business. All who saw a Rice sign knew who had produced it since he was one of the few artists to put his name on his work (Liebenson 2001). One of his earliest known signs, created in 1807, was for Tarbox's Inn in East Windsor, Connecticut, and features the iconic American eagle with arrows in one talon and an olive branch in the other and a shield painted with the colors of the American flag. A later sign, created in 1824, also features the patriotic eagle theme, but on a much more elaborate scale. This sign is adorned with a golden frame and a fairly gaudy amount of gold throughout. Another sign features a vibrantly painted subdued lion with a chain around its neck, perhaps signifying the United States' victory over Great Britain. Lions were a popular subject matter for Rice, and on another sign for a tavern called A. Phelps Inn in Colebrook, New Hampshire, a bold lion stares at the viewer with a look of hungry anticipation as if it may pounce from the sign and onto the street at any moment. For Wadsworth's Inn in Hartford, Rice produced a regal lion that also appears as if it could walk off the sign immediately and command all the beasts of the earth. Yet another piece for Dyer's Inn takes a much different direction from eagles and lions and instead features a beehive and a plow, both symbols of industriousness. It is outlined with the motto "Hold or Drive," a Ben Franklin saying that was meant to encourage industriousness. Why the tavern keeper who commissioned the sign, Zenas Dyer, would want to encourage such thoughts among his drinking customers is a mystery (Malley 2000).

THE TAVERN GOES WEST

By the 19th century, conditions along the Eastern Seaboard had changed so that the tavern no longer served as the essential way station for the weary traveler. Communities had spread, had grown in size and population, and increasingly offered a variety of options for the traveler. However, as the nation continued to expand, many of the conditions that had favored the tavern as an oasis in an otherwise wild land continued. Further west, frontier conditions would persist until late into the 19th century. Small western communities in many ways mirrored their 18th-century predecessors along the Eastern Seaboard. Locals sought central meeting places, and weary travelers sought a warm bed and succor. To get a good sense of this, one need only read Mark Twain's semiautobiographical account of his trip west by stagecoach in 1861 from Missouri to Nevada. This account is an excellent narrative of what travel was like in the years before the transcontinental railroad. From stop to stop, Twain looked forward to alighting along the way at "stations," which served a similar role to that of the earliest ordinaries. These were crude affairs and appropriately matched the rough conditions around them. Twain describes them as "long, low huts, made of sundried, mud-colored bricks, laid up without mortar. . . . The roofs, which had no slant to them worth speaking of, were thatched and then sodded or covered with a thick layer of earth, and from this sprung a pretty rank growth of weeds and grass." They may have been homely in appearance, and Twain describes them as being just as crude within, but after a long day's or several days' journey, such a sight would have warmed the soul (Twain 1872, 18). From such humble origins the Old West saloon was often born.

The Old West conjures up images of wide-open spaces and travelers traversing great distances under harrowing circumstances. Certainly, the sight of a community of any kind and the visage of a tavern where one might find relief after a hard journey were welcome. Of course, the Old West saloon is also famous for its reputation for violence and mayhem. Perhaps some of the tales that have built this reputation are exaggerated, but for a large part of the 19th century, tales of the Western saloon, told in dime novels, newspapers, and by word-of-mouth, fueled the imagination and created consternation in a growing number of Americans. Attitudes about the tavern had begun to change and harden as more and more Americans, particularly those of older stock and the middle class, began to view the institution as a menace, a semi-foreign space within their communities. This was in part a reaction to immigration and the changing nature of the clientele of the tavern that increasingly became more working-class male and often foreign-born. An 1872 editorial titled "Our Whiskey Holes," from a Colorado newspaper, lamented that by that time taverns, then commonly referred to as saloons, had become unwieldy things that threatened the future of the state. Answering the question, "When is something to be done about our whiskey holes, lager and beer saloons and gambling halls?" the editorial went on to demand that the law be applied to get the saloon menace under control, arguing, "These things have been left alone too long; they will be firmly rooted and hard to get rid of, unless they are taken in hand at once" (*Weekly Gazette* 1872).

Perhaps no city has a more iconic connection to the many memes of the violent West than Tombstone, Arizona. There, on a mid-October Friday night, 47-year-old James Edward Roberson wandered into the famous Doc Holliday's Saloon and checked in his gun with the bartender before beginning to imbibe. In the heyday of the Old West, some saloons posted signs on their exteriors that informed passersby that they would have to surrender their weapons before they would be allowed to patronize the establishment. Such signs were necessary because violence in many western communities was indeed epidemic. Lots of working-class bachelors and others away from their families often created atmospheres of freewheeling masculinity that produced men with short fuses who often had access to guns (see Johnson 2009). Roberson seems to have wanted to carry on the tradition. At some point after midnight, he got his gun back from the bartender and proceeded to shoot another patron (Associated Press 2017). In communities such as Tombstone, this would not have been such an odd occurrence in the late 19th century. Tombstone was well known for such lawlessness, hosting one of the most famous violent events in western history, the shootout at the O.K. Corral in 1881, forever making the Earps and Clantons iconic American families. Roberson, however, had never met the Earps nor the Clantons, and his feud had nothing to do with them. In fact, his "shootout" in Tombstone took place in 2017, 136 years after the Earps and Clantons ensured that Tombstone would live forever in American folklore as the archetype of the Wild West. The reason this story had purchase as a newsworthy story outside of Tombstone is because of the violence that took place there and the violence associated with the taverns of the Old West, an image, welcome or unwelcome, that the region portrayed well.

Charles Marion Russell (1864–1926) produced some of the most iconic paintings about the American West. In *Smoke of a .45* Russell captures the violence and mayhem many associate with the Old West and the saloon. Note the trumped-up name of the humble saloon. (Alamy Stock Photo)

Images of western violence have lived on in movies, folklore, and art. In the paintings of Charles Marion Russell (1864–1926), a legendary chronicler of the West, we can catch an artist's rendition of the raw, violent culture that existed inside and outside saloons. We can consider Russell to have been a firsthand observer to the types of events he sought to capture, as he was a true bona fide man of the West. Having arrived in Montana as a teenager in the 1880s, he found work as a hunter and a cowboy (see Taliaferro 1996). A great many of the more than 2,000 paintings Russell produced feature the interior and exterior of saloons. Many depict the institution as a violent place where life was as cheap as a glass of whiskey. In his 1907 *Smoke of a .45*, for instance, we see men being gunned down in a shootout in front of a saloon by riders fleeing the scene on horseback. What prompted the shootout is left to the imagination. Russell's saloon is a simple, single-story log cabin with a small wooden porch, a customer entrance with a large rack of antlers over it, and two windows that face the street. This stark little building is gilded with elaborate signage that ironically announces the name of this simple structure as the Palace, a joke that would not have been lost on its rough-and-tumble patrons. In his 1908 *In*

Without Knocking, we can witness the lawlessness and wildness of some western cowboys who are portrayed aggressively riding their horses right into a simple saloon, guns drawn, firing into the air, while playing cards litter the ground all around. This little saloon, called the Hoffman, was similar to the Palace in its simplicity but was constructed of boards rather than logs. Card playing and death were frequent subjects of Russell's western saloon art. Finally, *Death of a Gambler*, depicts a shootout taking place in front of a hardscrabble saloon whose owner did not put effort into a trumped-up name for his tavern, instead simply displaying a run-down sign over his run-down establishment that reads "Saloon." In front of this simple wooden structure, two men with playing cards strewn around them are losing their lives in a gunfight. Onlookers casually observe the scene, and through their nonchalant demeanors, we can infer that Russell wants us to believe that such scenes were merely a normal part of their daily lives.

By the mid-19th century, the Pacific Northwest was as wild and as untamed as any place on earth. Those who ventured there knew hardship. Stephen W. Silver hoped to profit by providing refuge from hardship, so he took out an advertisement in 1851 hoping to draw attention to his establishment, aptly named Silver House, located in Oregon City, a small community just south of Portland, then the capital of the Oregon Territory. Just two years after Oregon had become a territory, the 1850 census recorded just over 13,000 inhabitants living there, in an area that included present-day Oregon, Washington, Idaho, and part of Montana and Wyoming. By 1860, that number would grow to over 52,000, and by 1870 to over 90,000 (United States Census n.d.). The Oregon Trail brought thousands of new settlers who willed themselves across an unforgiving continent or over dangerous oceans in search of a better life, and Silver hoped that a portion of them would want to stay at his Silver House, which he advertised as designed for the "accommodation of the boarding and traveling community." As proprietor, he sought to attract and retain customers "by strict attention to his table, beds, and whatever may conduce to the comforts of his guests, to merit a liberal share of their patronage." He promised that the hungry traveler could expect "the table [to be] furnished with the best the market affords, and not surpassed by any in the Territory." For the drinking customer, the Silver House bragged that it had a "bar [that] will always be found bountifully supplied with the most choice liquors." For amusement, the advertisement assured the traveler that he could enjoy the Silver House's "bowling saloon." And of course no establishment for the weary traveler would be complete without "good stabling and horses for hire" (*Weekly Oregon Statesmen* 1851). For one who came across such an advertisement and had endured much, Silver's must have evoked visions of Shangri-La. Whether it lived up to its promotion is unknown.

As Silver's advertisement demonstrates, the desires of travelers in the West were not much different from those of travelers in the American colonial period. Travelers sought all-purpose accommodations and comforts after long and arduous journeys (West 1979, 27). While the tavern is certainly linked in the American imagination with the early history of the nation, the tavern and the Old West have a strong connection. It is impossible to consider one without the other. As has been noted by numerous historians, the number of saloons in the West was truly amazing. In many communities, their façades were seemingly everywhere. For instance, Bodie, California, located on the Nevada border, boasted 65 saloons and no churches in the late 19th century. Today, Bodie is a ghost town that attracts visitors who want to experience the Old West, and by the late 1990s the number of annual visitors to Bodie had grown to around 200,000. Visitors must use their imagination to understand what the Bodie of the gold-rush period was like as they take in a ghost town filled with dilapidated structures upon which nature continues to take its toll. It is estimated that in Bodie's heyday there were around 2,000 structures, and many of them were saloons, along with dance halls and brothels that also would have served alcohol. As the geographer Dydia DeLyser notes, one of the most common interests of the ghost town's many annual visitors is to find the old saloons (DeLyser 1999; DeLyser 2006, 283–84). Guessing may be difficult, as buildings that might once have been saloons would today look similar to the other businesses that thrived there. But it is easy to understand why visitors would be more interested in figuring out which establishments were saloons rather than, say, retailers of dry goods. As Elliot West notes, "The Western saloon remains an indelible part of the popular image of the American Frontier. As part of our national mythology, the barroom of the celluloid images and pulp fiction novels is an exciting place, peopled with steely-eyed heroes [and] oily villains" (West 1979, 142–43). Its proverbial swinging doors marked a liminal space, a border between civilization and anarchy, order and freedom.

Western saloons varied greatly in terms of size and quality, ranging from two-bit watering holes and gambling dens to extravagant resorts that included theaters and bowling alleys. Saloon #10 (aka Nuttal & Mann's) in the mining camp of Deadwood in the Dakota territory, named for the placer claim it was sitting on, was the former, and it became one of history's most famous saloons in 1876 when Wild Bill Hickok was shot down there by the scoundrel Jack McCall. Today, Saloon #10 is a tourist attraction and a regular hangout for locals. Visitors come to experience a brush with the Old West, but its main draw is, of course, the assassination of Hickok; in fact, visitors to the famous tavern's website are first greeted with a reenactment of that event (Old Style Saloon No. 10 2015). When Hickok met his fate, #10 was a simple watering hole, but other establishments in the mining camp were much nicer, catering to upscale visitors as well as those willing to spend their hard-earned money on lavish entertainments. Contrasting Saloon #10 were more opulent resorts such as the Bella Union, which has been described as a saloon, theater, and house of prostitution. There patrons could gamble, carouse with prostitutes, and witness stage performances of Gilbert and Sullivan theatrical works (Erdoes 1979, 175).

As with many western communities, Deadwood sprang into existence rapidly, and the saloons sprang forth with it. Elliot West describes how western saloons that were connected to mining communities grew from rough rustic establishments to permanent well-established fixtures as communities sprouted from the earth and matured in rapid succession. West describes this as a three-stage transition that started with a strike. Once word got out that a strike had happened, miners seeking wealth and glory descended on the fledgling community, and entrepreneurs hoping to sell them things arrived simultaneously. What quickly emerged was a chaotic camp that one miner described as "in its most primitive mold, the streets being undefined, the business center uncertain, and the habitations of the crudest build" (West 1979, 28). Leadville, Colorado, for instance, exploded into being in 1877 after a silver strike. West provides an eyewitness account of a traveler to Leadville just two years later:

> Tents; wigwams of boughs; wigwams of bare poles, with a blackened spot in front, where somebody slept last night, but will never sleep again; cabins wedged in between stumps; cabins with chimneys made of flowerpots or bits of stove pipe.—I am not sure but out of old hats; cabins half roofed; cabins with sail cloth-roofs; cabins with no roof at all,—this represented the architecture of the Leadville homes. (West 1979, 28)

These crude camps changed rapidly, seemingly before one's eyes, as homes and businesses abounded. But no business flourished as quickly as the saloon. In Leadville, for instance, an 1882 city directory indicates that just five years after silver had been found, there were at least 110 saloons up and running (*Corbett & Ballenger's* 1882, 323–24).

In these budding camps, the erection of taverns seems to have been at least as, if not more important than the creation of other establishments. As Thomas J. Noel notes, many early saloons doubled and tripled as churches, banks, hotels, restaurants, meeting houses, seats of government, and so forth, serving many of the same functions that their 17th-century predecessors had on the Eastern Seaboard (Noel 1982, 11–20). For this reason, newcomers to western communities would often first seek out a tavern for any number of needs, if not to simply get the lay of the land. As Richard Erdoes chronicles in his study of western saloons, newcomers often found that in appearance the earliest saloons matched their primitive surroundings. For instance, if a tavern opened on the prairie where wood was scarce, it was constructed of sod or stones. In the Southwest, early saloons were often adobe structures, made of bricks constructed from earth, clay, and straw and baked in the sun. These were actually quite sturdy and enduring and comprise some of the oldest existing structures on earth. But the majority of early western taverns were constructed of wood, and many of them were later replaced by brick as communities matured (Erdoes 1997, 38). J. D. Borthwick, a traveler to California, noted the appearance of camp saloons in the heyday of the 1849 gold rush. In his travels, Borthwick came on the town of Mokelumne Hill in northern California, located roughly 120 miles from San Francisco. There he found a wild community that he describes as a mixture of "equal proportions of French, Mexicans, and Americans, with a few stray Chinamen, Chilians, and suchlike." The town, he claims, including the saloons, "was all of canvas." Of course, such accommodations quickly upgraded as communities grew and prospered (Borthwick 1857, 179). Structures were composed of whatever the builder could get his hands on immediately. Borthwick provides an excellent eyewitness account of how such camps appeared:

> Some were mere tents, with perhaps a wooden front sufficiently strong to support the sign of the occupant; some were composed of sheets of zinc on a wooden framework; there were a number of corrugated iron houses, the most unsightly things possible, and generally painted brown; there were many imported American houses, all, of course, painted white, with green shutters; also dingy-looking Chinese houses, and occasionally some substantial brick buildings; but the great majority were nondescript, shapeless, patchwork concerns, in the fabrication of which, sheet-iron, wood, zinc, and canvass seemed to have been employed indiscriminately.

As Borthwick noted, San Francisco itself was a small community that "consisted merely of a few small houses occupied by native Californians." The discovery of gold in 1848 changed all that, bringing rapid growth. Borthwick observed that by 1851, "hardly a vestige remained of the original village." The town grew so quickly that "the city represented a makeshift and temporary appearance, being composed of the most motley collection of edifices." A large number of these crude and hastily slapped-together structures were taverns, scattered haphazardly throughout the community, As Borthwick witnessed, the city's main street was littered with "numerous drinking and gambling saloons" (Borthwick 1857, 44–45).

A decade after the gold rush hit California, a journalist named Elliot Lord observed firsthand the rush of miners to the first massive silver discovery in the nation, the Comstock Lode strike. The resilience and tendency toward risk taking that typified the miners astounded Lord as he observed a people who could live hard, work hard, and drink hard (Peck 1993). After news of the strike became public in 1859, Lord noted that the communities that sprang up in the Nevada mountains were "wretched huts of canvas, wood, and cobble stones . . . forming a shapeless city traversed by three main lanes styled streets." However, Lord contrasted these humble dwellings with the saloons: from the outside they appeared to be lighted and welcoming, and compared to the crude hovels in which many of the miners resided, Lord asserted that the saloons served as "the real homes of the citizens" (Lord 1883, 73).

On another occasion, Lord provides an outstanding description of the first saloon in an isolated, mining camp that sprang forth in March 1860. Lord recounts the tale of a party in San Francisco who heard about a camp located 239 miles away through the rugged Sierra Nevada Mountains in the Washoe Valley, a camp that would later become Virginia City. Many pack teams set out in early March but found themselves bogged down in Placerville, a mining camp at the foot of the Sierras. On arrival many believed that pushing on and trying to get through the daunting Sierras to the camp would be an impossible endeavor at that time. One intrepid entrepreneur, John L. Moore, however, decided that if he could make it, he would reap a mountain of profits by selling his wares to desperate miners. So Moore, who had set out with the party from San Francisco on March 9, pushed on with a load that consisted of necessary goods such as blankets and tin plates as well as other essentials, such as 10 gallons each of brandy, gin, and rum; 30 gallons of whiskey; and 70 gallons of "wines and liquors of various kinds." Moore must have counted his blessings when he emerged from the formidable mountains into the camp on March 31. The miners must have also counted their blessings when they learned of the arrival of supplies, particularly the "liquor-laden mules," which "were welcomed by the thirsty miners as well-springs in a desert are hailed by weary travelers." Lord reported that the thirsty miners "could scarcely wait while he unpacked his stores." And so, the first saloon in Virginia City was erected. It was a crude and simple structure but probably seemed like a palace to men who had been so long deprived of life's basic comforts. Lord describes this makeshift saloon as consisting of a canvas tent that was 15 by 52 feet in size and housed an establishment that boasted that "the first carpet laid in Virginia City was spread upon its floor." This makeshift watering hole also proudly erected an American flag on its roof, the first in the camp. The new proprietor used a canvas sheet to divide his establishment into a tavern area for drinking and a separate area for lodging. The sideboard of a wagon served as his first bar (Lord 1883, 66).

Simple canvas structures were often followed by simple wooden ones. In a typical Western community, the most commonly viewed architectural style of the time were humble wooden structures with false fronts, a visage that has become as synonymous with the western saloon as those legendary swinging doors. However, as one historian notes, false-front architecture was common throughout the United States during the late 19th century, particularly where rapid construction took place, and few communities witnessed such rapid construction as those in the West. For many communities, the cheap wooden false-front structures were simply hasty markers that town building had begun (Francaviglia 1991, 151–52). False fronts were flat, tall structures that fronted a building, perhaps to make the building appear grander and larger than it actually was. Some building owners decorated their false fronts with cornices or latticework. Still others used false fronts to give the appearance that their building had a second story, going so far as to make a false window or two on their false front (West 1979, 37). And of course the false front provided space for signage, which was often painted in large letters, sometimes using cursive lettering to give the impression that the saloon was fancier than it was. Another reason for false-front architecture in the Old West may have been to make remote and hastily constructed communities seem more permanent, grand, and urban than they actually were (Treu 2012, 28). In time, as communities developed, many of these structures were replaced by brick, typifying the turn-of-the-century downtowns that are still found in many communities that today tend to house small shops, restaurants, and of course taverns. One of the most famous of the false-front saloons of the Old West is the Mint, which was built in Silverthorne, Colorado, in 1862 and continues to serve as a saloon today. It is also the oldest building in Summit County. Other than the neon signs in the front window that advertise various beers and announce that the establishment is open, the Mint looks more or less as it did when, as the false-front signage indicates, it opened during the Civil War (*Summit Daily* 2016).

In Western parlance, saloons were often described as one-bit or two-bit establishments, and potential customers knew this by reputation, but appearance could certainly tell the tale as well. A saloon earned one of these two titles based on the amount that the establishment charged for whiskey and beer. One-bit establishments were much more common, and one could expect to pay no more than one bit or 12.5 cents for whiskey or beer. Two-bit establishments charged 25 cents for a whiskey or beer and were less frequently encountered than one-bit establishments, but an individual of means or perhaps a miner or a cowboy who had recently experienced good fortune would seek out the better surroundings of the two-bit establishment (James 2012, 57; Lord 1883, 377; Monahan 2017, 25). Saloon keepers, whose establishments in the Old West often existed on the edge of society in crude communities, peopled with those who endured the most hardscrabble and challenging existences, seemed to relish urbane and fanciful names for their establishments. This is in keeping with the spirit of the origin of the word "saloon" itself, which was derived from the French *salon* (Worth 2009, 47).

Saloon keepers tried to re-create the comforts and familiar scenes of the places that many had left behind in the East, where fancier fare could be easily had. Perhaps some saloon keepers chose names that deliberately mocked the harsh conditions that surrounded them. One can speculate about this possibility by viewing a remarkable photo of a 19th-century Oklahoma saloon, the Bijou. In French, *bijou* implies that an establishment, particularly a restaurant, is small and elegant. From this late-19th-century photograph, it is obvious that the Bijou is certainly small but probably not elegant. Unfortunately, the visual evidence that remains of the Bijou only allows us to see its exterior, but judging from the photo, it is probably a safe guess that the Bijou was no fancier on the inside than it was on the outside. Perhaps the Bijou's owner, a man named Kelley, named his establishment with a bit of tongue-in-cheek humor, an act of thumbing his nose at the stark surroundings in which he threw up his simple structure. Pictured in the photograph is a front and side view of the Bijou that reveals a small, wooden, one-story structure with a sharply pitched gable roof and a single chimney at the rear. The front of the Bijou is a tall, square false front that gives the impression of a larger, more sophisticated structure, exactly as was intended. On each side of the wide entrance (unfortunately, we cannot see if the Bijou sported swinging doors) are two tall windows, allowing any passerby to see the good times happening inside, perhaps enticing him to enter. On the false front in large and flamboyant cursive lettering, we see "The Bijou." Thanks to the sign, no passerby from any distance would mistake this structure for anything other than a saloon. The occasion for the photograph is the delivery of kegs of alcohol, probably beer, which appears on a wagon in front of the saloon. Several men are in front, holding what appear to be glasses of beer at the ready to toast for photograph poses. Two men directly in front of the wagon each have

Gathered around the kegs at Kelley's saloon. This photograph, from the late 19th century in the Oklahoma Territory, of a saloon keeper and his customers gathered to welcome a new shipment of beer perfectly captures the Old West saloon. Note the false front architecture and the fancy lettering, which demonstrates the tongue-in-cheek humor that proprietors used to trump up their humble establishments. (National Archives)

one foot on a keg, glasses held high. The proud saloon keeper stands in the middle of his large flock, sporting a bit of paunch under his spotless white apron, arms akimbo, proudly staring into the camera as lord of his small manor and court (U.S. House of Representatives 1894).

While the Bijou played at being fancier than it was, many establishments indeed were and offered better accommodations. In an age before movie houses, many Americans enjoyed live theater, a chance to watch plays on stage. As Watson Parker notes in his history of Deadwood, the line between saloons and theaters was thin to nonexistent (Parker 1981, 73). So while a patron might be seeking to see a play, rent a room, or have dinner, he could usually also imbibe. In theaters, patrons could catch a production of *Macbeth* or *Uncle Tom's Cabin*, starring actors and actresses already known in the East, such as John Wilkes Booth's father, Junius Brutus Booth, and his brother, Edwin Booth. The first theater of reputation to open in California after the discovery of gold was the Eagle. Richard Erdoes notes that at the Eagle, patrons had to get to their seats by climbing a ladder that was attached to the outer part of the wooden building. The bottom part of the ladder had canvas affixed to it to prevent men from looking up women's skirts (Erdoes 1979, 174–76). The famous Palace Theater in Denver was another of many establishments where actors and actresses alighted the stage to the amusement of miners, cowboys, and middle-class patrons alike. The Palace Theatre was constructed in 1864 at the corner of 15th and Blake Streets by a gambling titan named Ed Chase and would later be purchased by Bat Masterson, one of the West's most famous lawmen. The Palace was a well-known establishment that catered to all comers, including high-class customers such as U.S. senators. A photograph of the Palace from the 1870s reveals a remarkable large brick structure. Several patrons, including men and women, proudly pose for the camera in front of the two-story building, many of them on the second-floor balcony. Highlighting the mixing of the theater and the tavern, a beer hall featuring Tivoli beer, a brewery that went into operation in 1859, takes up a portion of the right side of the first story, advertising that inside customers could find "Billiards and Pool" and enjoy "Lunch All Day." On the left side of the first story a billiard hall that included a "ten pin" bowling alley called Lange & Hance boasted on its signage that customers could purchase "imported wines, liquors, and cigars," as well as PH. Zang & Company's Lager Beer (Pierson 2006; Tivoli Brewing Company 2018; Denver Public Library [1870–1880?]). From accommodations that included food and drink to theater and sporting amusements, the Palace had it all.

THE SALOON MATURES

As the Old West matured and towns transitioned from hardscrabble camps to more permanent settlements, saloons and their role in the community transformed with them. Thomas J. Noel and others have argued that when towns made this transition in the late 19th century, saloon-going diminished in importance. One reason for this, they note, is that many of these communities changed from being male-filled camps to towns and cities primarily consisting of families. In other words, the arrival of women and family life brought a domesticating presence that caused men to spend less time saloon-going (Noel 1982, 113; West 1979, 142). This analysis, however, does not explain the remarkably high number of saloons found east of the Mississippi, where settled communities preceded many of the Western towns and camps that have become so famous for their rough-and-tumble atmosphere and large numbers of taverns. In the Midwest and East, many communities with fairly equal numbers of men and women had similar ratios of saloons to citizens as those found in more primitive Western settlements.

Between the Civil War and World War I, the United States witnessed a massive migration of people from Europe who settled in communities that as a result witnessed rapid change. During this period, many immigrants went West, but most settled in cities east of the Mississippi River, taking jobs in the multitude of industries that were bounding forth. As in the West, the taverns multiplied with the population and came to dominate the downtown landscapes of scores of cities. When we think of explosive growth in this period, cities such as Chicago first come to mind. However, many communities in the Midwest witnessed a similar birth and growth, and many had origin stories similar to those of their counterparts west of the Mississippi. Typical of these were towns such as Streator, located in northern Illinois, which was incorporated in 1868 and was recorded in the 1870 census as having nearly 1,500 residents. Ten years later, the population more than tripled, and then 10 years after that it doubled to well over 11,000 residents. Just nine years after its founding, a history of LaSalle County, in which Streator is located, was produced, recounting the rapid changes that took place there. The writer compares his city's growth to that of Chicago, located about 90 miles away, claiming that both sprang forth seemingly overnight. Originally, Streator was called Scrabble, denoting the hard work the mining community engaged in to get the community up and running in the early years. Just a decade later, this writer recorded with pride that now

> churches, school-houses, large, substantial business houses and handsome residences, with elegant grounds and surroundings, now beautify the waste of ten years ago, while the hum of machinery and thronged streets are unmistakable evidence of business importance and prosperity. (*Past and Present* 1877, 323)

Among the businesses was, of course, a large number of saloons. It was noted in a nearby newspaper that in 1883, with a population of just over 5,000, Streator already had 33 saloons (*Daily Republican* 1883). As attested to in the history of La Salle County, in nearby Mendota, "a man named Cheek opened a saloon, a shop or two was added and the town was becoming a reality" (*Past and Present* 1877, 314). As this passage suggests, the erection of a saloon was seen as a sign that a town had been established and was as important as any other business in the birthing of a community. In nearby Leland, it was noted that "Leland now contains several good stores, quite a number of shops, two good elevators, several saloons, and one or two hotels. The Population is about eight hundred" (*Past and Present* 1877, 343). As in the West, the taverns were as organic to early Midwestern communities as any other establishment, just as they had been on the Eastern Seaboard during the earliest days of English settlement and just as they quickly became in the West.

THE "CORNER SALOON" AND THE TIED HOUSE

Today "corner saloon" is a well-known reference that brings to mind a period when the neighborhood tavern was a central part of communities across the United States. The term continues to dwell in our collective memory, and a simple internet search demonstrates that it is also a popular name for a large number of taverns throughout the nation. The American realist Edward Hopper (1882–1967) captured this omnipresent American landmark in his 1913 "*New York Corner*," a beautiful oil on canvas interpretation of a New York moment, a street scene that features several pedestrians passing a prominent corner saloon. In this painting, Hopper captures two worlds that every day rubbed shoulders in Gilded-Age Gotham. The saloon, which dominates the foreground, represents a place of community and leisure. Behind it, however, are factories and their large smoke stacks spewing the products of industry into the New York skyline. In these Dickensian monuments to "progress," multitudes labored and longed for something else. We cannot make out the words above the saloon's entrance on the prominent signage that wraps around the entire corner, but it screams Gilded Age. Like the saloon itself, the sign is large, golden, and flamboyant. It demands that passersby acknowledge its larger-than-life presence. Upon close inspection, the signage appears ethereal, floating almost ghostlike above the saloon it represents, a harbinger that it might soon depart, which it soon would.

As the saloon period wore on, the corner saloon became a cliché and in many cases was a reality. As a 1960 Oklahoma story about an old man recalling his saloon days was titled, "Oldtimer Recalls Wild Days of Corner Saloon" (*Ada Weekly News* 1960). For the writer of this article simply recalling the "Wild Days of the Saloon" just did not seem to capture the feeling of the period as much as he thought could be conveyed when the word "Corner" was added. While not all saloons were located on corners, many were. The term "corner saloon" featured so frequently in advertisements for saloons for sale that one could get the impression that every corner in the United States had a saloon on it. In fact, in the classified section of a San Francisco newspaper on September 12, 1904, under "Business Chances," there were 13 saloons offered for sale. Nine of them were listed as "Corner Saloon" (*San Francisco Call* 1904). Of course, this let potential buyers know that this location was the highest sought after and would get the highest possible traffic. Milwaukee was and remains one of the kings of the beer world, and remnants of that world still abound throughout the city. Unfortunately, development has cast asunder many of the historic and beautiful brick buildings that defined the community 100 years ago. Many have been replaced by cold, utilitarian box-shaped behemoths made of glass and steel. One establishment that has fortunately been spared the modern builder's merciless wrecking ball is a beautiful corner saloon. At 2249 North Humboldt Avenue stands a large three-story structure built in 1890 in the beautiful Romanesque style. On the ground floor, it has large half-moon windows that allowed potential customers to look in and see what they were missing. As with many such corner saloons, the top of the building contains a large turret with impressive detailing and deep-set windows facing the corner. This castle-like corner saloon bore the moniker "Joseph Schlitz Brewing Co. Saloon." It was saddled with this very unoriginal name because the saloon was built by the famous brewery in order to sell its products directly to customers. It stands on its corner as a lonely sentinel from the past to remind passersby that beautiful architecture was once the norm in "Brew City." Today, it is surrounded by the blight of the modern age—a gas station on one opposing corner, a vacant lot on another, and a strip mall on the third. It would certainly be preferable if this beautiful building were to once again be made into a saloon, but it is not to be. Instead, the developers who bought this rundown building are going to turn it into condominiums (*BizTimes* 2018). Hopefully the new tenants will think to raise a social glass, say "*prost*" to the former occupants, and, as they down their toasts, listen carefully for the sounds of the building's spirits.

George Ade said that if you had seen one saloon, you had seen them all. While it is true that the famed "corner saloon" took on a look, it is also true that this was a wonderful look. In the modern age, from coffee shops to convenience stores, corporate America has been responsible for homogenizing many public spaces as they seek to create uniform brands. This has led to bland, utilitarian buildings and stores that lack beauty and charm. But in the saloon era, this conforming trend had at least one positive outcome—beautiful monuments to Gambrinus. The tied-house system, discussed in the previous chapter, led breweries to find direct outlets for their products. By the last few decades of the saloon era, this process had accelerated, and more and more breweries took over saloons, and in many cases they even got into the business of building them themselves, and, of course, they most often acquired spaces on corners. Before the proliferation of the tied-house system, saloons were not necessarily distinguishable from the stores and other buildings that surrounded them. Today's taverns tend to be like that. They are housed in a mishmash of structures and designs. Some are beautiful establishments, while many others inhabit strip malls or warehouse-like buildings. Many are in fact only definable as taverns by signage out front and the neon beer signs that typically light up their windows.

As Perry Duis demonstrates, the tied-house system was in many ways a bad deal for the saloonkeeper, but it was a great gift for architecture, and if one knows where to look, it is a gift that continues to give. Unfortunately, many tied-house saloons have been torn down, but in cities across the United States, many of these buildings still stand. For instance, when one thinks of historic Omaha, Nebraska, beef probably comes to mind before saloons, but in the city styling itself the "Gateway to the West," architectural historian Patrick Thompson has identified at least 66 structures that were once tied to brewers. Today, one can tour Omaha and see those that remain. Not all former tied-house saloons are obvious, but once one gets a feel for what such a saloon looked like, many beautiful old buildings come into a new focus. Thompson points out that brewers sought their own architectural styles. For example, he writes, "Schlitz saloons used the bartizan (an overhanging corner turret that projected over the building's entrance) and Romanesque arched windows, while the Pabst saloons had square towers, crenellated parapets and Gothic—revival arched windows" (Thompson 2017). Some former tied-house saloons operate today as taverns. One is Schubas Tavern, built in 1903 on the southeast corner of an intersection in the West Lakeview neighborhood in Chicago. The tavern describes itself as a "neo-Gothic treasure," and it certainly is. The former saloon has beautiful brickwork, a lovely corner turret, and it still sports a large globe with the Schlitz logo boldly proclaimed on it. Currently, as in times past, Schubas continues to serve up beer, food, and mirth. But today it is also a noted venue for live bands (Schubas Tavern 2019).

Of course, Chicago, perhaps the king of saloon towns, had an incredibly large number of tied-house saloons, and as with Schubas, many of them still stand and are identifiable. After the great Chicago Fire in 1871, the city rapidly emerged from the ashes, and many saloonkeepers turned to brewers for help. Schlitz led the way, first providing the thirsty city with both beer and water in the immediate aftermath of the tragedy and then going on to play the largest role in the tied-house system in the Windy City. By the last couple of decades of the nineteenth century, the number of breweries competing for business in Chicago reached very high numbers. The same was true for saloons, and competition coupled with increased license fees pushed saloon keepers into the arms of brewers who were eager for the relationship. A 2011 landmark recommendation study commissioned for the City of Chicago identified 41 former tied-house structures that remain throughout the city. The breweries, especially the prominent ones, had deep pockets, and they sought to make establishments that were appealing and easily accessible to customers, so they were built in or near working-class neighborhoods and workplaces. Those that remain share several characteristics. First, many are of the Queen Anne style or reflect the German Renaissance Revival and tend to either be stand-alone structures or most often inhabit corners. Most have a first-floor storefront that faces the street, with the primary entrance facing the corner. They are typically two to three stories, with the saloon being on the first story, and the floors above being apartments, often housing the saloon keeper and his family. Above the entrance, once can usually find a turret with windows that faces the corner (Duis 1998, and City of Chicago Landmark Designation Report 2011).

It is certainly possible to pass some of these beauties and not realize that it had once been a saloon, but we can be thankful that many others still bear the logos of their former owners. Many are covered in ornately carved limestone, and the brewery logos of many of them are still visible. One such example is a former Schlitz tied-house saloon that is located in the North Center neighborhood. This magnificent former saloon is today a Starbucks, and that company's corporate signage is very prominently displayed, but above the corner-facing turret is a prominent large globe made of pressed metal with the Western Hemisphere displayed in vibrant painted colors. A large ribbon, cutting across Central America, spans the globe and boldly proclaims the Schiltz logo. Around the sign is beautifully carved stonework with ornate patterns. Many former tied-house saloons still display such signs, so if passersby in cities across the United States remember to look up, they might, by chance, be reminded of another age when beer and beauty mixed with architectural design and was brought to life by the amazing skills of working-class builders who made the urban world a more beautiful place.

Chapter 3

THE SOCIAL SPACE

> There was only one solution: the saloon, the congregating place of men, the place where men hobnobbed with John Barleycorn.
>
> —Jack London (London 1913, 163–64)

A "DIME A DOZEN"

In 1931, Chicago humorist George Ade reminisced about the saloon, which had not long ago been an integral part of the landscape in the storied "Windy City." But by the time of his account in the early years of the Great Depression, the legal saloon had been shuttered for just over a decade. Born in 1866, Ade had grown up in the great age of the saloon, and in 1931, when he was halfway through his sixties, he was reflecting as a man who had spent most of his adult life in the shadow of the great institution in perhaps the greatest saloon city in the world. He remembered a time when "saloons [were] everywhere and many of them open all night and all day Sunday" (Ade 1931, 8). During the great saloon age, the institution frequently made appearances in works of fiction and nonfiction as a space where sorrows were drowned, camaraderie was confirmed, and where some lives were ruined, and during his long career as a writer and observer of human nature, Ade had his share of things to say about the institution as well. Looking back, Ade remembered the social space of the saloon fondly for the most part and described it as a place of mirth and fellowship that had served as a center of community for generations of Chicagoans. Millions had once passed in and out of its swinging doors when thousands of saloons had filled his city, making their influence strongly felt, in a time, as he remembered, "when every shifting breeze of a city street was laden with a malty aroma" (*Past and Present* 1877, 20).

Chicago's saloons had indeed been a powerful presence. The muckraking journalist George Kibbe Turner wrote in 1907 that, regarding the Windy City's estimated 7,300 saloons, "the sale of dissipation is not only a great business; it is among the few greatest businesses of Chicago" (Turner 1907). With so many saloons up and running, Chicagoans had a wide variety of choices when considering where to do their fellowshipping around a social glass with their imbibing brethren. So, with so many to choose from, how was one to decide where to spend his precious nickels and free time? How did so many saloons distinguish themselves, one from another? Ade remembered that despite the saloon's profligate presence as it stretched across the American landscape, this "great business" was largely homogenous in nature, each saloon barely differing from another. Ade contended that if you had visited one, you had seen them all.

Sure, he pointed out, there were some well-known high-end establishments with unique features. For instance, many Americans knew of legendary saloons such as Chicago's great Workingman's Exchange, Ramos' Imperial Cabinet in New Orleans, or the Palace in San Francisco. The latter, which opened in 1875, was a tavern in the Palace Hotel that was touted as occupying the tallest building in the West at seven stories high and covering an entire block (*China Daily* 2015; Harned 2009). It was wildly famous in Ade's day, and it is still serving customers today. Visiting its tavern is a trip through time, and customers can still sit at its long, beautiful mahogany bar and drink in its Gilded-Age surroundings. Behind the bar, patrons can still admire a massive, more than a century-old painting of the Pied Piper of Hamelin that measures 16 feet long and 6 feet high and weighs over 250 pounds. Its detail is exquisite, and its colors are vibrant and stunning (Nolte 2013). Perhaps it was placed as a tongue-in-cheek jab at the oft-proffered assertion during the saloon age that saloon keepers were leading their customers to ruin. Tales of renowned institutions such as these made their way into newspapers and publications across the land. Some saloon-goers bragged to their fellow imbibers that during their travels they had visited them, and that yes they had indeed lived up to their storied reputations. But these "gilt-edge and exceptional places," as Ade called them, were the exception, not the rule. Most drinking establishments in the saloon period were simple working-class watering holes with customer spaces that were generally homogeneous in appearance and function. As Ade wrote, "For every one of the *de luxe* establishments there were a thousand boozing kens all of the same conventional pattern . . . When you had visited one of the old-time saloons you had seen a thousand" (Ade 1931, 27–28).

Not all taverns in the saloon period were quaint working-class establishments. The Palace Hotel in San Francisco, built in 1909 to replace the original that was built in 1875 but was destroyed in the 1906 earthquake, contained a high-class saloon. It is still enjoyed by patrons today. (Library of Congress)

As discussed in the previous chapter, the tied-house system fostered uniformity in the exteriors of saloons, and this was also true of interiors as well. But this was just one factor. As Perry Duis chronicles, as the Gilded Age wore on and the number of saloons in American cities grew at an almost frenetic pace, more and more individuals took their chances as saloon owners in a business opportunity that increasingly balanced upon a revolving door through which many working-class men entered with the hope of becoming their own masters behind the bar. But all too frequently they quickly exited the business in failure, forced to return to the difficulties and indignities of the workaday world. So the very factors that made it easy to go into business also drove many saloon keepers out of business in a relatively short time. As Duis writes, "Unlimited and relatively cheap licenses, along with the extensive help provided by the brewers, made it easy—too easy—to enter the business" (Duis 1999 [1983], 84). Those going into the business often relied on fixtures that were provided by breweries that often had their own fixture plants. Others relied on purchasing fixtures from those who were exiting the business and hoping to recoup some of their losses. "Saloon Fixtures" was a common heading in the classified sections of many newspapers. One such advertisement in a Buffalo, New York, newspaper in 1890, for instance, was typical, offering, "For Sale—saloon fixtures, everything that is required in the business, including beer pumps" (*Buffalo Evening News* 1890). Such advertisements told two-sided tales: a tale of failure for one leaving the business and hope for the one entering it. For the customer, this meant barrooms that tended to be familiar, just as Ade described them.

Such sameness makes one wonder if a customer leaving one saloon and sauntering up the street to another might sometimes forget that he had even left the last place, particularly if he had been drinking for a while. Ade provides a vivid description of what a typical saloon-goer could expect on his sojourn in pursuit of the next saloon, one that fits our collective memory of how saloons appeared. First, he writes that many establishments actually sought to mask from the outside what was happening inside, so many saloons had shutters or other means of blocking the view, using devices such as "grille work, potted ferns, one-sheet posters and a fly-specked array of fancy bottles." Ade describes the reason for such subterfuge this way: "The saloon business was furtive and ashamed of itself, hiding behind curtains, blinds and screens and providing alley entrances for those who wished to slip in without being observed." It was true that saloon keepers often wanted to hide what was occurring in their saloons from the view of the general public and the police. But it can also be argued that such furtiveness created a sense of curiosity for the initiate who passed by and wondered what interesting things might be happening inside. Should he decide to find out, Ade notes, he would typically pass through swinging doors that brought him into a darkened interior. On entering, he would see the ubiquitous bar, often made of mahogany or another hardwood, which "always had a brass foot-rail in front of it." Many a saloon floor was festooned with sawdust that Ade conjectured "was supposed to absorb the drippings." Standing at the bar were the customers arrayed in various states of intoxication, some talking loudly and jovially, others staring forlornly into their beer. A large mirror usually stood behind the bar, and under the mirror Ade remembered a typical layout as containing "a tasteful medley of lemons, assorted glasses and containers brightly labeled to advertise champagne, muscatel, port, sweet, Catawba, sauterne and that sovereign remedy for bad colds, Rock and Rye." If one looked up, he would usually see a tin ceiling. Upon the walls there were more than likely sexually titillating or sports-themed paintings and photographs. Once could count on witty sayings such as "Free Beer Tomorrow" posted near the cash register or on the backbar mirror. Behind the bar, perhaps polishing glasses while telling a dirty joke, one could expect to see a pot-bellied, aproned, and mustachioed saloon keeper who stood ready to greet the new initiate. This chap behind the bar was ready to slap a customer on the back and offer a bawdy joke or a sympathetic ear and sometimes important services and advice (Ade 1931, 30–31 and Powers 1998). If it was not unique décor that would bring a customer back to the same saloon, perhaps it was the social gifts of its keeper. As Jack London put it, "Saloonkeepers are notoriously good fellows. On an average they perform vastly greater generosities than do business men" (London 1913, 183).

Did saloon-goers mind this festive uniformity? Were they looking for a unique experience, or were they looking for the familiar? Perhaps the sameness in atmosphere and décor described by Ade provided a saloon customer some comfort, particularly if he was a bit intoxicated on entering an unfamiliar establishment. But was this tendency toward homogeneity only true of the great Gilded Age tavern of Ade's day? Today there is a certain predictable sameness in most drinking establishments in the same way that coffee houses or convenience stores have typically common features. People tend to be more comfortable with the familiar, and the typical tavern feels familiar today just as it always has. Throughout the long history of the tavern, an alikeness has prevailed in the function and structure of the institution's common space, the customer space. Tavern keeping has long been a cutthroat business, and many factors, including competition, can push a tavern keeper over the edge. In advertising their establishments, tavern keepers have touted their services and products in order to set themselves apart and attract customers. A glance at the front page of an edition of the 1875 *Oakland Tribune* contains standard Gilded Age advertisements for several drinking establishments promoting their wares and amenities. For instance, Herman Drucker's Capitol Saloon boasted "Foreign and Domestic Wines and Liquors," while its competitor, Becht's Saloon, claimed that "the best wines, liquors, and cigars will be found at the bar." WM. S. Searing promised potential customers that his establishment contained "Choice Wines and Liquors." Cronin's promised customers "Wines, Liquors, and Cigars of the choicest brands," but also touted "Billiards, Etc., Etc." What the two "Etc."s were about the customer would apparently have had to learn by visiting (*Oakland Daily Evening Tribune* 1875). But did customers really assume that any one of these establishments contained beverages or amenities that were much different from the others?

This chapter will consider what has comprised the typical features of barrooms, examining what has traditionally lured customers in and what keeps them coming back. In chapter 2, we considered the exterior of the tavern and its place in the community, but it is the interior that the customer is seeking. To understand the draw of the tavern's customer space, we must also consider why people frequent taverns in the first place. Today it is of course much less expensive to purchase alcohol in a store and drink at home. While the typical six-pack of beer might cost between $6 and $9 at the store, many taverns charge between $2 and $4 or more for a single beer. People can, of course, drink at home for a fraction of what it costs to do so in a tavern, and yet the tavern stands as a popular semipublic space that continues to lure customers in and keep them coming back. In 2011, in the midst of the worst economic crisis since the Great Depression, some concerned Nevada tavern owners expressed anxiety about the continued allegiance of their own customers should they decide that drinking elsewhere makes more sense. One tavern proprietor, Randy Miller, expressed that "a tavern is a unique animal," and he believed that many of his customers were starting to look for more than what he was used to providing. Miller lamented that in times past, a successful Nevada tavern was "simply a bar with 15 slot machines and a bowl of peanuts." But now Miller expressed concern that a recently enacted smoking ban and a sluggish economy might discourage his customer base from frequenting his establishment (Stutz 2011). Tavern keepers strive to create the atmosphere and amenities that lure customers to pay for drinks and other services in their establishments. They must also attract the type of customers that create an atmosphere that matches the theme and style of the establishment. Upscale taverns want to attract a different customer base than a corner sports bar, for instance. Many tavern customers talk in terms of a tavern's "crowd," the aura or personality created by the people who frequent an establishment. It is the tavern keeper and his staff, the atmosphere and amenities, and the customer base itself that creates the tavern's customer space. The features that Ade found to be so common in the Gilded Age barroom are not much different from the features that have been common to barrooms throughout time. The barroom is timeless.

EARLY TAVERN INTERIORS

Samuel Johnson, the 18th-century English writer and tavern patron, summed up well the immortal lure of the English tavern's interior, that which draws frequent customers to while away their free time and earnings, when he quipped in 1787,

> As I enter the door of a tavern, I experience an oblivion of care, and a freedom from solicitude: when I am seated, I find the master courteous, and the servants obsequious to my call; anxious to know and ready to supply my

> wants: wine there exhilarates my spirits, and prompts me to free conversation and an interchange of discourse with those whom I most love: I dogmatise and am contradicted, and in this conflict of opinion and sentiments I find delight. (Hawkins 1787, 777)

So if it is not the uniqueness of the products dispensed within, products that today are cheaper and easily accessible at the corner market, then tavern-going must be, as Johnson claims, a matter of seeking to comport with one's peers in the "free conversation and interchange of discourse" (Hawkins 1787, 777). By the early 20th century, not much had changed in terms of why saloon-goers sought out any one of thousands of New York saloons. In 1911, one observer, F. C. Laubach, concluded that "the vast majority of young men and boys come to the saloon for social purposes alone." As far as the drinking habit was concerned, Laubach believed that "the drink habit grew out of the innocent search for the satisfaction of the social instinct" (Laubach 1911, 3). Likewise, as Jack London remembered, during times of loneliness as he wandered across the American landscape, "I could go into a saloon and talk with any man. In the strange towns and cities I wandered through, the only place for me to go was the saloon. I was no longer a stranger in any town the moment I had entered a saloon" (London 1913, 106). In their quest for companionship around a social glass, it would seem that neither London nor Laubach's New York saloon patrons were in search of unique surroundings. They were instead in search of the common: the inside of a tavern in all its simplistic and uniform glory.

As has been discussed in previous chapters, the first taverns in the English colonies opened not many years after the first settlers arrived. Because of their importance and popularity as community centers, the colonial tavern and its familiar interior abounded. Bruce C. Daniels notes that in 1697, in the 274-mile distance between New York City and Boston, there were at least 26 taverns, which averages one tavern per 10 miles. These numbers increased with the population. By 1725, along a 54-mile stretch between Springfield and New Haven, 12 taverns could be found (Daniels 1995, 145). The very name "ordinary" denotes the fellowship that took place in them, originating in England and describing the serving of "ordinaries" or meals that were generally served on a common table (Forbes and Eastman 1954, 85). Weary and hungry travelers in the English colonies came from all social strata, and colonial taverns were therefore less likely to have class distinctions than those that would develop in 19th-century taverns. This was especially true in more rural communities that might only have one or two taverns (Sallinger 2002, 63). Such conditions helped confirm community as well-off and less-well-off colonists were likely to rub shoulders in the same establishments. Of course, some taverns developed reputations as being finer establishments and attracted more upscale customers, while others were known as rowdy or even licentious establishments, thereby attracting a rougher, more working-class crowd (Daniels 1995, 151–52).

To appreciate the early tavern's interior, we can consider one that has stood the test of time from the 17th century to the present, the Wayside Inn in Sudbury, Massachusetts. The Wayside Inn started life as the How Tavern in 1716 when David How petitioned for the right to "keep a hous [*sic*] of entertainment for travelers." How had chosen an excellent location, and the tavern would soon thrive due to coach traffic that took travelers between key cities such as Boston and Worcester, with passersby seeking food and shelter for the night. As with many New England communities, Sudbury itself had been established along an already existing Native American trail that would then be used by colonial travelers (Plumb 2011, 1–10). The tavern and inn has been kept in continuous operation to the present day, and though it was badly damaged by fire in 1955, the inn has been restored and somewhat modernized. However, pictures of its interior dating back to the 19th century provide us with a realistic view of what New England travelers experienced in the common room of the Wayside Inn. One 19th-century photograph reveals a large, cozy, and rustic common room with a low ceiling that contained heavy exposed beams. The entire interior has the look of crudely treated lumber, which makes for a cozy and earthy feel. The tables are small and round and surrounded by wooden, high-backed Windsor armchairs. In the center of the room is an exceptionally large fireplace surrounded by wooden rocking chairs. It is easy to imagine a scene featuring weary travelers on a winter evening sitting in the chairs in front of a roaring fire, with quilts in their laps and stocking caps upon their heads, pipes in hand, recounting the day's difficult and cold journey, one that would resume in the morning. But for now, they are engaged with new acquaintances in conversations concerning where they had just traveled from and where they are going to, perhaps followed by some discourse about the news of the day and the world at large. Above the fireplace can be seen large crossed cavalry sabers and a musket. It is likely that some of these travelers would have been veterans of the many conflicts 18th-century British subjects found themselves involved in, not to mention the many skirmishes with Native Americans. Many would have wielded such weapons and would have been comforted by their presence as they remembered past acts of glory (Earle 1900, 19).

Henry Wadsworth Longfellow, one of the United States' greatest poets, has immortalized the Wayside Inn in verse in his epic poem "Tales of a Wayside Inn." Longfellow lived relatively close to the famous inn and likely knew it well. Through his lyrical poem, we can see the tavern as it was in his time and how he imagined its past through his portrayal of a group of revelers frequenting and enjoying its barroom. At the time he wrote the poem in 1863, Longfellow was approaching 60 years of age, so he was reminiscing about an institution nearly a hundred years older than he. Therefore, his characters could have been contemporaries, or they could have been ghosts. We see the tavern through their eyes as they sought out its comfort "one autumn night," as they came on the welcoming visage of "the Windows of the wayside inn [which] gleamed red with fire-light" and stepped into a tavern "built in the old Colonial day, When men lived in a grander way, With ampler hospitality." Within they found what all have always sought in a tavern as they wrap themselves in its familiar sights and sounds:

> But from the parlor of the inn
> A pleasant murmur smote the ear,
> Like water rushing through a weir:
> Oft interrupted by the din of laughter and of loud applause,
> And, in each intervening pause,
> The music of a violin.
> The fire-light, shedding over all
> The splendor of its ruddy glow,
> Filled the whole parlor large and low. (Longfellow 1863, 1–10)

Soon the friends found comfort around the fire and seemingly left their cares outside in the autumn night air. They settled in, warmed with a glass of spirits in their hands, as Longfellow continues to tell their tale and set the scene:

> Around the fireside at their ease
> There sat a group of friends, entranced
> With the delicious melodies;
> Who from far-off noisy town
> Had to the wayside inn come down,
> To rest beneath its old oak trees,
> The fire-light on their faces glanced,
> Their shadows on the wainscot danced,
> And, though of different lands and speech,
> Each had his tale to tell, and each
> Was anxious to be pleased and please. (Longfellow 1863, 1–10)

As has been discussed earlier, the common space of the colonial tavern served a wide variety of purposes other than as a space for spirits and sociability for locals. Taverns hosted local government meetings, trials, weddings, and even church services (Daniels 1995, 117–20). They were the places where many community members and travelers came together to discuss local news and the wider world. Taverns served as way stations for weary travelers, providing an assured stopping point at the end of a long day's journey. There a traveler could expect to find a place to stable his horse and then receive a hot meal before turning in for the night. Colonial leaders understood the necessary functions that the tavern served and encouraged their establishment and regulated their services and prices. However, Puritan leaders expressed concern about problems associated with spending too much time in a tavern. The mixing of free time and alcohol in the barroom could lead, as Cotton Mather remarked in 1726, to "an evil Practice growing among us," which was "the needless resorting to Taverns, and spending much precious Time (particularly the Evening) in Publick Houses." This habit, warned Mather, was a "dangerous Tendency, of a criminal Aspect" (Mather 1726, 1). Because of these concerns, many New England communities heavily regulated their local taverns. As recounted in chapter 1, some such as Robert Coles were fined and shamed into better behavior. It was recorded in the early 1630s in Boston that Coles was "fined ten pounds and enjoined to stand with a white sheet of paper on his back whereon drunkard shall be written in great letters so long as the Court shall think best for abusing himself shamefully with drink" (Eshleman 1904, 216). We cannot know how bad Coles's drinking problem was or if he even actually had one, but it is possible that Coles may have just enjoyed spending some of his free time in the local tavern a bit more than others, earning him a reputation as a drunkard, or he may have run afoul of his Puritan community for some other reason, causing him to be singled out. The early New England tavern was a place where it was acceptable to spend some time, perhaps in the evenings after a hard day's labor, perhaps discussing God and local happenings with one's neighbors and those passing through. However, one was expected to maintain the outward appearance of sobriety and control. Perhaps Coles failed to do so on one too many occasions (Daniels 1995, 146). Fear of punishments such as the one handed down to Coles had an effect on the atmosphere of the tavern by controlling patron behavior. The community's watchful eye would have reinforced the feeling that it was in one's best interest to avoid loud and boisterous behavior and the appearance of intoxication. Such policing would have had a strong influence on tamping down the sort of ribaldry and boisterous behavior one typically associates with the tavern.

Puritans were concerned about not only excessive drinking and boisterous behavior but also controlling leisure time—idle time. One Massachusetts law regarding "idlers" decreed the following: "It is ordered that no person, householder or others, shall spend his time unprofitably, under pain of such punishment as the county court shall think meet to inflict." The law went on to require that constables "take notice of offenders . . . especially common coasters, tobacco takers, and unprofitable fowlers" (Eshleman 1904, 216). Communities therefore regulated the tavern-going habits of local residents, limiting the amount of time they were allowed to spend in their local tavern to, in some cases, an hour or less a day. In other cases, certain classes of persons such as servants, Indians, known inebriates, and others were not allowed to frequent taverns at all (Daniels 1995, 150–51). The problem, of course, with the Puritan fixation on idle time was that it was at odds with the very concept of the tavern. Having and enjoying idle time is the whole point of entering a tavern. We can see this dichotomy in an admonishment given by Mather regarding a congregant who seems to have enjoyed himself in the tavern a bit too much for Mather's liking the night before the Sabbath, "making himself troublesome to his other Neighbors by impertinent visit and Discourse, until near midnight" (Mather 1911, 310).

By the early 18th century, it was becoming apparent that Puritan mores were no match for the draw of the tavern and the spirit of revelry one could find within. As New England took on more immigrants and port cities such as Boston became integral nodes in the trade and movement of peoples in the Atlantic world, it became harder to police behavior and require pious outward appearances. Bruce Daniels's description of tavern culture in his study of leisure in late Puritan society describes an atmosphere that was not too different from what it would become as colonial populations continued to grow. Daniels found that in Newport, Rhode Island, with its 20 taverns by the mid-1720s, one could find all the hallmarks of tavern behavior that would exist in any period of American society. For leisure activities, taverns there and elsewhere contained pastimes that are common in many taverns today, such as darts, bowling, shuffleboard, gaming, and even prostitution (Daniels 1995, 151–53). Of course, many of these features of tavern life in Newport could be attributed to its position as a seaport city, attracting sailors from around the Atlantic world. New York, Boston, Philadelphia, and other seaport towns were similar in this regard. One of these Newport establishments, the White Horse, claims to be the United States' oldest tavern, having been constructed in 1673. Today's version of the White Horse, however, bears little resemblance to its origins as a community tavern that would have attracted the kind of rough crowd that Daniels describes. Today the White Horse boasts on its website that "we strive to create a fresh, contemporary culinary experience in America's Oldest Restaurant," also requiring diners to obey a business-casual dress code (White Horse Tavern n.d.). The White Horse has clearly become something different today from it was when it opened its doors nearly 350 years ago. Nonetheless, the White Horse is a time capsule that still contains some of the look and feel of the original tavern. In an application to the Department of the Interior to have the establishment placed on the National Register of Historic Places in the 1950s, the application's author boasted that much of the interior of the spacious two-and-one-half-story building still retained its original character. The heavy timber framing and overhead beams are exposed, and large brick fireplaces and chimneys still lend 17th-century charm (National Register of Historic Places 1971). While upscale diners in their business-casual dress and genteel manners now grace the White Horse, the original establishment would have catered to a much more mixed clientele of locals and sailors passing through, whiling away their time with heavy drinking and drunken boasts, accented by lanterns and candlelight that cast shadows of a bygone age on its timbered walls.

While the tavern may have served a necessary function in colonial society, making it an important pillar in the community, tavern interiors greatly differed in quality. Some such as the storied City Tavern in Philadelphia were known far and wide for their quality, hosting customers including many of the nation's signers of the Declaration of Independence and crafters of the Constitution. George Washington frequently recorded in his diary that he dined and entertained at the City Tavern during the hot and auspicious Philadelphia summer of 1787 (Washington 1887). Demonstrating the central place of the tavern in colonial society, the founders of City Tavern declared when they sought a charter for the tavern that "the Proprietors have built this tavern without any view of profit, but merely for the convenience and credit of the city." However, this claim belies the fact that the designers of City Tavern clearly had an upscale clientele in mind when they erected the 50-by-46-foot, two-story brick structure. A decade before the Convention, William Ellery, a signer of the Declaration of Independence and attendee to the Constitutional Convention from Rhode Island, provided in his diary an excellent description of the tavern where he along with around 80 attendees celebrated the Fourth of July in 1778. Their celebration was also bolstered by news of the defeat of General Clinton at Monmouth by Washington's army. Ellery's description of the evening provides an excellent glimpse of the social space of an upscale tavern. It would have taken a huge hall to entertain such a large party of celebrating men, and the City Tavern certainly could have supplied it. The party probably met on the second floor because it was there that two already large rooms could be altered to become one expansive

An accurate reconstruction of City Tavern, located in Philadelphia, Pennsylvania. City Tavern is one of the most famous historic taverns in the United States. Built just before the American Revolution, the tavern frequently served as a meeting place for the nation's founders. (Mira/Alamy Stock Photo)

space that measured the length and width of the building. The guests would have ascended stone steps to encounter a vast hall with a high ceiling (Sallinger 2002, 54; Thompson 1999, 149–51). Ellery describes the night's setup and entertainment as "elegant and well conducted," where they were entertained at four tables that formed a square that extended the length and width of the room. At one end of the room played an orchestra that consisted of "Clarinets, Haut-boys, French horns, Violins and Bass Viols." The centerpiece at the head table featured a "large baked Pudding, in the center of which was planted a Staff on which was displayed a crimson Flag." On the flag were symbols that would have reaffirmed each attendee's commitment to their revolutionary cause: "An eye, denoting Providence, a Label in which was inscribed an appeal to heaven; a man with a drawn sword in one hand, and in the other the Declaration of Independency, and at his feet a scroll inscribed 'The declaratory acts.'" These patriots must have become rather intoxicated over the course of their evening because Ellery records that the men engaged in a series of toasts with each being followed by the "discharge of Field-pieces." Of course, the "field pieces" were not in the tavern but were perhaps just outside the tavern and could be heard through the open windows (*Pennsylvania Magazine* 1887, 296–308).

While it is clear that the quality of City Tavern greatly impressed Ellery, for the sake of contrast, he also provides us an account of an establishment that he found distasteful. Fortunately for posterity, Ellery frequently recounted his tavern patronage in his diary. As with many men of his time, he assumed that while he was traveling, his meals, meetings, and lodgings would be accommodated at taverns, and he describes pleasant encounters in many of them. However, one particular tavern that he stayed at on November 12, 1777, he found to be unpleasant in the extreme. We have to assume that a gentleman such as Ellery would have sought out the best accommodations, so perhaps this tavern was the only one with space, or perhaps it was the only one in town (he does not indicate the name of the community). In comparison, he records that the night before he had a pleasant stay in a tavern in Bethlehem, Pennsylvania, where he had "fared exceedingly well, drank excellent Madeira, and fine Green Tea, and ate a variety of well-cooked Food of a good Quality and lodged well" (*Pennsylvania Magazine of History and Biography*, 296–308 and 326–27). Many of his daily entries simply recorded that he stopped at a tavern for lodging or meals without much commentary on the quality of the establishment. So, the Bethlehem tavern must have really left a good impression for him to have gone on at length about its fine fare. Also, while Ellery did sometimes lavish praise on a particular tavern, he almost never heaped scorn. Except for one: Levans Tavern. Ellery complained that his room was terrible and "admitted the cold air at a thousand chinks, and our narrow Bed had on it only a thin Rug and one Sheet" (*Pennsylvania Magazine of History and Biography*, 296–308 and 326–27). Ellery noted that even though he went to bed with his clothes on, it was still too cold for him to be able to sleep, and he reported that such was the case for the other lodgers as well. And it was not only the cold, poor bedding, and exposure to drafts that were problems. He described the other problems with the place this way:

> What added to the Infamousness of this tavern was the extreme Squalidy of the Rooms, Beds, and every Utensil. I will conclude my Story of this Sink of Filth & Abomination with a Circumstance which, while it shows that our dirty Landlady had some Idea of Neatness, must excite a contemptuous smile. The Table on which we were to breakfast was inexpressibly nasty, that we begged she would put a clean napkin on it, to which this simplex munditis objected that the Coffee might dirty the Cloth. (*Pennsylvania Magazine* 1887)

Such detailed written accounts provide us with fantastic time capsules with which to view colonial tavern spaces. We can also consider visions of tavern life in art. In 1762, the artist John S. C. Schaak produced an amazing painting of a tavern interior that provides a detailed glimpse of an 18th-century English tavern, one that would not have been much different from the typical American establishment that Ellery would have stopped at. In Schaak's artistic vision of tavern life, we can see a well-stocked establishment that not only served alcohol but also had ample victuals ready for hungry customers. Hanging in the kitchen and arrayed around a basket on the floor, one can see freshly killed fowls, a pig and a large slab of meat hanging from the ceiling, and fresh vegetables on the counter. A gentleman customer in the foreground is in pleasant conversation with a smiling young woman in a low-cut bodice who appears to be a serving girl. The customer wears a knowing look on his face, as if he enjoys having the attention of this pretty, young serving girl, if only for a while and for the price of a meal. In the background, we can see a seated gentleman in conversation with a British army officer with his arms folded smartly on his chest.

***The Tavern*, by John Schaak (1762), depicts an average tavern scene in what is probably England. In this painting we can see an inviting, well-stocked, and spacious community tavern. (ART Collection/Alamy Stock Photo)**

Perhaps he has just returned from service in the still-raging Seven Years War and is recounting his experiences there. Behind them we can see a welcoming fireplace with a large pot simmering on the fire. Schaak clearly meant to portray the tavern as a warm and welcoming community place. Perhaps this painting feels authentic because it is a reflection of a memory of a pleasant time the artist had spent in his own favorite haunt.

TAVERN SPACES IN THE EARLY REPUBLIC

In the early republic, as the nation went through a market revolution that increasingly relegated more people to lives of drudgery in factories and on farms, class lines hardened, and taverns increasingly followed suit, increasing in abundance and becoming more organized by socioeconomic status (see Sellers 1991). It was, as W. J. Rorabaugh calls it, "a period of unprecedented change," and in this milieu the tavern proliferated (Rorabaugh 1979, 145). Cities greatly expanded in size and so did their poorer neighborhoods, and as they grew in size and increased in squalor, more laborers, whose ranks were increasingly filled by immigrants, sought the refuge and entertainment of poor working-class taverns. Also fueling this trend was another by-product of the market revolution, cheap and abundant whiskey, which was replacing rum as the American drink of choice (Rorabaugh 1979, 87). As many became alarmed at the increase in taverns and whiskey consumption, a new popular name for working-class taverns took hold: "whiskey dens," which would come to denote a cheap and immoral tavern that catered to lower-class people. One concerned citizen in a letter to the editor in 1849 bemoaned that in his town such establishments had become more of a threat, "more fatal, and more dreadful" than cholera. He expounded further that "there is one blot, one plague spot, one cancer in our town, which mars the general beauty—one vile Dog-ge-ree—a whiskey den to pollute the atmosphere with its pestiferous fumes, its noisome stench, its baleful exhalations" (*Palmyra Weekly Whig* 1849). Gone were the days of the egalitarian community tavern.

During the first half of 1842, the famous British writer Charles Dickens conducted a tour of the United States that ultimately resulted in one of the greatest 19th-century travelogues ever produced regarding American society and culture, *American Notes for General Circulation* (1842). It is fortunate that during this travel adventure, Dickens toured one of the roughest quarters of the United States, the Five Points district in New York, immortalized in Herbert Asbury's 1927 work, *The Gangs of New York*, which is also the name of the great 2002 Martin Scorsese film starring Leonardo DiCaprio and Daniel Day-Lewis, who so aptly portray lower-class, rough-and-tumble denizens of what may have been the most notorious neighborhood in the 19th-century United States. In the book and the film, Bowery saloons play a prominent role and are aptly depicted for their rough and seedy atmospheres. The Bowery was notorious throughout the nation for its working-class violence and mayhem. For instance, in 1857, in faraway Richmond, Virginia, a local newspaper ran a long piece titled "The Bloody Riots in New York" about street battles in the Bowery between two notorious gangs, the Bowery Boys and the Dead Rabbits, noting that neither the police nor the military could stem the violence (*Richmond Enquirer* 1857). As Asbury notes, life in the Bowery was for its inhabitants one of violence and despair where one's "only escape from the misery of his surroundings lay in excitement," and a great deal of Bowery excitement could be found within its many taverns (Asbury 1927a, xix). Its streets contained a wide variety of taverns to choose from, and not just for drinking. They also offered newcomers information about jobs, lodging, and other opportunities. Some taverns there doubled as makeshift hotels. But one thing was certain: the Bowery was thick with taverns (see Devillo 2017; Ferrara 2011; Anbinder 2001). Dickens's sojourn into this underbelly of American society included a jaunt through these same taverns, providing us a firsthand account of their interiors by a master observer who takes us back in time to see these low-down establishments as they were experienced by their unwashed working-class patrons. Dickens would not have had trouble finding taverns to visit. As he exaggeratingly noted, "nearly every house is a low tavern." Dickens notes that he found that Bowery taverns "had a taste for decoration," citing that "among the pigeon-holes that hold the bottles, are pieces of plate-glass and coloured paper" to provide a sense of working-class style that may have in part been a mockery of upper-class style. Dickens found the walls covered with artwork that included such symbols of patriotism as "coloured prints of Washington, and Queen Victoria of England, and the American Eagle." He noted that perhaps the portraits of Queen Victoria were in honor of the many sailors he noticed who called on Bowery taverns at their ports of call. As a result, he noted "maritime pictures by the dozen" that included "portraits of William, of the ballad, and his Black-Eyed Susan; of Will Watch, the Bold Smuggler; of Paul Jones the Pirate, and the like," all observed by "the painted eyes of Queen Victoria, and of Washington to boot," implying that their eternally watching eyes were witness to the rowdy behavior of the wily patrons who haunted these taverns equally by day and by night (Dickens 1842, 212–13).

THE BARROOM IN THE SALOON AGE

Many lower-class individuals drank in Bowery taverns to find community and solace in welcoming places of refuge from the rawness of their working-class lives. In one of the greatest novels of the period, *The Jungle*, Upton Sinclair describes the struggles of his long-suffering main character Jurgis Rudkus, an immigrant trying to make his way in the harsh industrial jungle of Chicago. By the saloon era, not much had changed in regards to why people, largely working-class men, sought out taverns-cum-saloons. The only difference was that the intensity of the postbellum industrial revolution continued to increase the size of the army of the dispossessed, and simultaneously the phalanx of taverns multiplied throughout many communities in proportion. Working-class men in the Gilded Age were prolific saloon-goers, and they had plenty of reasons to be such. In this harsh age, the saloon could serve as a place of solace and comfort. In one of the greatest novels of the period, *The Jungle*, Upton Sinclair describes the struggles of his long-suffering main character Jurgis Rudkus: "He had faced difficulties before, but they had been child's play; now there was a death struggle, and all the furies were unchained within him" (Sinclair 1906, 135). Jurgis's losing struggle was one born by armies of Gilded Age industrial workers. In the saloon—and for some, only in the saloon—they could find shelter. Sinclair well describes the plight of working-class men who suffered from the precariousness of the availability of work that forced many to take to the streets to find shelter. For many, the interior of the saloon served therefore as the one place they could find succor and avoid the vengeful gaze of those who looked down on and sought to exploit such unfortunate men. Describing these circumstances, Sinclair relates Jurgis's experience with the one institution that took him in and made him feel that he had worth:

> At the saloon Jurgis could not only get more food and better food than he could buy in any restaurant for the same money, but a drink in the bargain to warm him up. Also, he could find a comfortable seat by the fire, and could chat with a companion until he was as warm as toast. At the saloon too, he felt at home. (Sinclair 1906, 274)

In this world, Sinclair paints a sympathetic picture of the saloon keeper who hosted desperate men such as Jurgis. While many accused saloon keepers of creating and profiting from misery, Sinclair explains that "part of the saloon-keeper's business was to offer a home and refreshments to beggars in exchange for the proceeds of their foragings; and was there any one else in the whole city who would do this—would the victim have done it himself?" (Sinclair 1906, 135).

As the once semiprofessional barfly and itinerant worker Jack London wrote of his early saloon-going days: "All ways led to the saloon, and thence led out and on over the world" (London 1913, 5). London wrote his amazing biopic *John Barleycorn* near the end of his relatively short time on this earth about his earlier saloon-frequenting and heavy-drinking life. He wrote as a man who looked back, just three years before his untimely death at the age of 40, with both regrets and affectionate memories. Both were found in the saloon, a place he describes both fondly and at the same time in disparaging terms reminiscent of the famous 19th-century tale of woe *Ten Nights in a Barroom* (Arthur 1854). The lure of the barroom had attracted London early in life, and he began frequenting various establishments as a youth. The barroom was his source of adventure and male camaraderie, but it was also his source of addiction and woe. But in the tavern, he, like so many others, found a social space that filled a void in his life:

> In the saloons life was different. Men talked with great voices, laughed great laughs, and there was an atmosphere of greatness. Here was something more than common every-day where nothing happened. Here life was always very live, and sometimes, even lurid, when blows were struck, and blood was shed, and big policemen came shouldering in. (London 1913, 35)

Even at the height of the anti-saloon movement, detractors of the establishment acknowledged that saloons offered something unique and inviting to customers, and they recognized that these things were lacking for working-class men outside of the saloon. Raymond Caulkins, a Gilded Age reformer, lamented that though the saloon was a "social evil," he understood that inside its swinging doors it provided something substantial to the workingman. As Caulkins wrote,

> This want is the demand for social expression, and how it is met becomes clear by noting what elements are needed to create what we may call a social centre. These elements are the absence of any time limit, some stimulus to self-expression, and a kind of personal feeling toward those into whose company one is thrown, which tempts one to put away reserve and enjoy their society. (Caulkins 1901, 2)

In 1897, a reformer associated with Chicago's Hull House, E. C. Moore, speculated about the lure of the institution, imagining that the typical customer would say the saloon "is a necessary feature of my life. It furnishes me with many things which I cannot get elsewhere. It does me no harm" (Moore 1897, 1). Moore's study was conducted in one of the most working-class and saloon-filled wards of Chicago, the 19th, which contained a population of 48,280 working-class souls, largely unskilled laborers, most of whom were recent European arrivals. The 19th had just four churches and little else, lacking other common forms of entertainment such as music halls and theaters. It did, however, contain a large number of miserable working-class jobs, crowded tenements, and filthy surroundings. Jane Adams of Hull House reported miserable conditions, including alleys that were impassable due to piles of manure and streets filled with garbage and the bodies of dogs and horses (*Chicago Evening Journal* 1895). One thing the 19th did have plenty of, however, was saloons. Addams described them as the only places in the ward "where social life may be free and untrammeled." And they seemed to be everywhere, "situated not only on every street corner . . . [but also] often in the blocks between" (Addams 1896, 54–58). Who could blame the workingman who sought refuge from such a world in his own world, the saloon? As Moore notes, this was where the men of the 19th spent much of their limited leisure time, and

> in it he finds more of the things which approximate to luxury than he finds at home, almost more than he finds in any other public place in the ward. In winter the saloon is warm, in summer it is cool, at night it is brightly lighted, and it is always clean. More than that there are chairs and tables and papers and cards and lunch. (Moore 1897, 4)

As Moore rightly observed, the saloon was a social space that provided a service for its vast army of patrons. Perhaps nothing illustrates this more than one of the mainstays of the saloon age, the "free lunch." This practice is a remnant of a bygone era that modern taverns generally do not replicate. The closest thing to this one could find today might be snack foods offered for free in taverns during a sporting event such as the Super Bowl or the now rare but iconic dish of complimentary peanuts or pretzels on the bar counter that customers are invited to put their fingers in so they may dish out a salty, but potentially contaminated, snack. When George Ade described the common nature of the tavern of his era, the free lunch certainly reinforced that idea, becoming a fixture that in many saloons was as much a part of the scenery as the mahogany bar or the brass footrail. For instance, in one study of the 163 saloons in Chicago's 17th ward, it was found that 111 of them offered the free lunch (Melendy 1900, 292–93). In 1894, in the midst of a terrible economic depression that rapidly inflated the ranks of the unemployed and desperate, one witty observer wrote an epic poem to honor the free lunch. One stanza in particular well captures the connection between the impoverished working-class customer and the oasis that was the saloon and its free lunch:

> When the specie, it once was our pleasure to share,
> Like friends in rejoicing, has wandered afar,
> When smote by the cyclone of want, and despair,
> How sweet to our vision the free lunching bar. (Corkscrew 1894, 11)

For the price of a beer, he could saunter up to this laid-out spread and, as Ade explained, turn to "the colored boy in the white apron [who] would slice off anything the customer seemed to crave and pile up a grand variety on a plate, especially if his palm had been crossed with silver" (Ade 1931, 34–35). Ade described the typical free lunch counter as he remembered it: "The long table across from the bar showed a tempting variety of good things to eat. There might be salted nuts, roast turkey, a spiced ham, a few ribs of beef, potato salad, potato chips, ripe olives, sandwiches, Herkhimer County cheese, summer sausage and napkins" (Ade 1931, 34). In 1908, Michael Kenna, who doubled as an alderman as well as one of the city's most famous saloon keepers, estimated that his Chicago colleagues spent an estimated $30,000 a day on laying out their free lunch spreads. Kenna claimed he arrived at his figure by estimating that the city's 7,000 saloons just about all offered some form or other of the free lunch, with costs for their spreads ranging from $1 per day in smaller, poorer saloons, to as much as $30 per day in fancier joints such as Kenna's Van Buren street saloon, the Workingman's Exchange. In that storied Chicago watering hole, it was claimed that at least 200 loaves of bread were consumed each day, accompanied by staples such as chili con carne, pigs' feet, cheese, radishes, and roast beef (*Chicago Inter Ocean* 1908). Ade claims that many saloon-goers took advantage of the free lunch. Typically, a beer in that period cost anywhere from a nickel to a dime, and for the price of a beer one could also expect a free ride at the free lunch table. Kenna claimed that he offered such a service as a sort of charity, arguing that due to recent layoffs a great many men were out of work, desperate for a meal, and he proffered that he was pleased to provide it to them, "We never ask them whether they have got any money to spend or not when they come into the place." Kenna claimed that he instructed his employees who worked the free lunch counter "to feed any one, no matter who he is. . . . Food is a necessity to men, so we give them what they want of it" (*Chicago Inter Ocean* 1908; Abbott 2008, 58).

Kenna's Workingman's Exchange could certainly afford such extravagance. After all, it was not an average saloon. It was estimated in 1903 that

Michael "Hinky Dink" Kenna (1858–1946) was one of the most famous saloon owners of his age. He was a notoriously corrupt Chicago alderman in the city's very working-class First Ward, where he was also the proprietor of the city's most famous saloon, the Workingman's Exchange. There, customers enjoyed social glasses of beer along with the famous "free lunch." (Chicago Sun-Times/Chicago Daily News collection/Chicago History Museum/Getty Images)

the establishment was taking in at least $100,000 per year. Kenna created a lavish workingman's resort, a place where a man could feel like a king for the cost of a beer. The *Chicago Tribune* described his "barrel house" as the largest in the world, with the barroom measuring at least 100 feet long by 50 feet wide, with the largest bar counter measuring 84 feet long and curving at the center. At the bar, thirsty working-class men lined up to drink out of giant schooners described as "large as an ordinary hat," filled with cold beer that cost the customer no more than a nickel (*Chicago Tribune* 1903). A publication called the *Lutheran Observer*, no fan of Kenna's business, claimed in 1903 that Kenna sold "thirty-one thousand barrels of beer in five years," which were consumed by working-class drinkers who entered the storied establishment by passing under a large sign that boasted "The largest and Coolest Glass in the City." The *Observer* estimated that with 300 glasses of beer in a barrel at five cents per glass, Kenna was clearing a profit of $10 per barrel, which after expenses would have left him with approximately $50,000 per year in profit, a tidy sum (*Lutheran Observer* 1903).

Kenna could offer such fare because he was of the rare breed of saloon keepers who maintained a large, financially stable operation (see Wendt and Kogan 2005). He was also interested in retaining the goodwill of potential voters, and feeding them well went a long way toward purchasing their electoral loyalty. However, this expensive practice begs the question as to why so many saloon keepers maintained the practice, typically for anyone who sauntered up to the buffet table. Such extravagance seems like it would have been a losing proposition for saloon keepers, and for many it was. However, the free lunch was clearly something that saloon-goers came to expect, and they sought out saloons that offered it.

Perry Duis argues that Chicago's saloon keepers chafed at this expectation but felt compelled to keep offering it in order to attract customers (Duis 1999 [1983], 296–97). After all, if, as Ade argued, most taverns were similar, why would the hungry and often poor workingman frequent an establishment that did not offer free food to go along with his nickel beer? In some cases saloon keepers turned to city government to help regulate the practice out of business. On April 30, 1917, with the United States just having entered the war in Europe, the city council passed a law that required every free lunch counter to have an attendant. This provided cover for smaller establishments to end the practice, while it continued on in more profitable saloons such as Kenna's (*Day Book* 1917).

WOMEN AND THE BARROOM

Barrooms have long served as spaces that promote masculine sociability, and throughout the tavern's long history there have been periods when women were sometimes excluded from the tavern's customer space. Early ordinaries usually catered to men and women; though late into the evening hours the common area served primarily as male centers of sociability. For instance, in Dr. Alexander Hamilton's account of his 1744 journey from Maryland to Maine, women are seldom mentioned in his daily stopovers in taverns along his journey. Instead, his many accounts of his evenings are filled with spirits, mirth, and conversation with male tavern-goers. Fortunately, he frequently described those he met, and most of these descriptions are about men. Typical of such entries was one concerning an evening about which he wrote, "I . . . went to the Ship Tavern, where we drank punch and smoaked [*sic*] tobacco with several colonels" (Gray and Kamensky 2012, 133). When Hamilton did mention women, they typically appeared as one of the tavern's hosts, usually the wife of the owner. By the saloon period, lines between male and female sociability hardened, with women mostly being excluded from the saloon's customer space. The historian Madelon Powers provides what is perhaps the best account of male culture in the saloon since Ade's *The Old Time Saloon* was published in 1931. Powers illustrates that inside the saloon there was an environment of "freewheeling masculinity" that was hostile to the presence of women.

Inside most saloons, one often heard foul language and saw various degrees of pornography on the walls, filthy sawdust on the floors, brass cuspidors filled with tobacco spit, and thick cigar smoke (Powers 1998, 30–31). Mary Ann Clawson asserts that a saloon environment that was hostile to women was a deliberate but inevitable part of the construction of masculine identity in the period. She writes, "The right to drink was a male privilege and the camaraderie fostered by men's public drinking was a significant part of masculine group identity" (Clawson 1989, 156). Men desired to create a place that reflected the ideals of male brotherhood, particularly in an era when men increasingly felt emasculated by their work; and in such a place, women were not welcome. The lack of women in the saloon gave reformers another explanation for why they were such immoral places (Duis 1999 [1983], 232). For these reformers, men left to their own devices apparently could only sink further into moral decay.

If the saloon atmosphere alone did not keep women away, both law and custom oftentimes provided barriers that prevented women from patronizing saloons. Women found in saloons risked being considered of low moral character and were sometimes labeled as prostitutes. The latter was sometimes a correct assumption, since some prostitutes did ply their trade in saloons (Noel 1982, 86–89). Many American cities went beyond mere custom and barred women from saloons or restricted their entry into certain parts of the saloon. In Aurora, Illinois, for instance, women were barred from "wine rooms" by statute (June 15, 1903, Section 4). These rooms, also called "sample rooms," oftentimes were places where men could find prostitutes (Duis 1999 [1983], 254). By the late 19th century, the use of the term "sample room" to describe an attached room in a saloon seems to have become a tongue-in-cheek reference to a room attached to a saloon where male customers could in fact meet prostitutes. The term "sample room" originated as a common reference to rooms where traveling salesmen might lay out their wares for public perusal, or in finer drinking establishments they were rooms where gentlemen might sample high-end liquors. However, it would seem that by the late 19th century, the term connoted an attached room where male customers might meet prostitutes. Sometimes these rooms were called wine rooms with the same sarcastic meaning, as many saloons did not, of course, specialize in wine (Blair 2010, 115–16).

Aurora went beyond merely passing laws against the presence of women in certain parts of its saloons. In 1917, the city hired a 51-year-old female police officer named Mary Phillips to both stop "flirts" from harassing women who passed by the doors of saloons and to remove women found on saloon premises. She describes her vision of her new job in the following way: "To find out the places in the city where young girls acquire bad habits and then take the necessary steps to have the places put out of business." She went on to warn the "idlers who stand on the downtown streets and giggle and stare when a girl or a woman passes," who largely would have been made up of working-class saloon patrons, that "every time a policewoman catches a man embarrassing a girl or a woman she is going to tap the man on the shoulder and invite him to accompany her to police headquarters" (*Aurora Daily Beacon News* 1917). It is easy to imagine the stir that Phillip's entry into Aurora's taverns would have provoked. It is possible that the intention of the city government, which was often at odds with its saloons, was in part to emasculate the working-class male customers and their keepers who would not have been happy with Phillip's intrusions into their carefully contrived masculine homosocial spaces.

FILTHY HABITS

The masculine nature of the saloon was reinforced by the many male accoutrements that were found in the typical barroom. One such item was the spittoon. At a time when tuberculosis ran rampant, the saloon was a place where masculine habits certainly helped its spread. First there was the habit that many men and probably most saloon-goers had of chewing tobacco and then spitting in the general direction of a spittoon. During the saloon era, spittoons were a fact of daily life, appearing everywhere from boarding houses to city halls, and of course they were a mainstay in saloons. Many photographs of barrooms from the period show their presence on the floor, often near the brass railing on the bar. An 1891 article in the *New Orleans Times-Picayune* points out that "probably no product of modern civilization is more familiar to the average citizen than the spittoon." After beer mugs, the article laments, the spittoon was frequently the weapon of choice in barroom brawls: "Hardly a day passes without a saloon scrap in which a spittoon plays a part in no wise inferior to that taken by the more pretentious billiard cue and the ever-popular beer mug." Even the receptacles of men's spit were divided by class, with workingmen's saloons containing spittoons and more fashionable men's clubs containing cuspidors, with the latter sometimes being made of porcelain and decorated with artistic designs. Really, they were both just receptacles for effluvium, and even in 1891 people understood that they were the breeders of disease, as this article's title attests: "The Fatal Spittoon: Germs of Deadly Disease Lurk in the Cuspidors." There, the writer stated, "Death lurks in the aristocratic cuspidor and the plebian spittoon alike." Inside these symbols of masculinity, one could find a stomach-churning mixture of "saliva, cigar and cigarette butts, discarded installments of fine cut and other debris," that when "mingled with beer drippings, water and other ingredients send forth a peculiar effluvia" (*New Orleans Times-Picayune* 1891).

If one did not get sick from proximity to the noxious contents in and around the spittoon, one could always try his luck with another ubiquitous object of the saloon era: the mustache towel. As with spittoons, pictures from saloon barrooms often show the presence of towels hanging from the bar. They seem to be white because they appear in old black-and-white photographs, and in truth they may have started their shifts as white towels, but they most certainly would have quickly turned all sorts of nauseating colors as their shifts wore on. So, imagine working a long day in a coal mine or factory. One's facial hair would likely pick up all sorts of terrible debris throughout the course of the day. No one would want this debris to make its way into a long-dreamed-about first beer or whiskey of the evening, so before taking that first drink, why not reach down and wipe one's face on the handy mustache towel hanging below the bar? In 1891, one curious observer decided to stand back and watch various men enter and use the offered towels over the course of an evening. He claimed that though one man out of 50 had a contagious disease, most men who visited saloons used communal towels to wipe their hands and faces. Of course, one might want to dry one's hands or face with a towel, but this writer warned his Gilded Age audience to remember, and hopefully not while eating, that beyond removing moisture, "the friction . . . forces off scales, pieces of head skin, lymph from cuts and abrasions, mucus from the nostrils, perspiration from the pores, pus from sores and ulcers, and anything liquid that may be excreted from the body or may have been thrown upon its surface." Of course, for the first man who uses such a towel, this is not a problem, but this observer noted that as many as 200 users were seen using saloon towels before they were washed (*Manhattan Mercury* 1887). So if this investigator understood these basic facts regarding hygiene, one has to wonder why so many men used the same towel.

Powers's most graphic example of the saloon's overwhelmingly male environment is a trough that was located at the base of the bar in some saloons. Such a contraption was primarily designed to allow customers to spit and perhaps clean manure from their boots, but many also used it as a urinal that allowed them to remain at their spot at the bar and not miss a beat in their conversation (Powers 1998, 30–31). As with the mustache-towel scenario, consider this: A workingman has just completed a 10-hour shift at a local factory, and the one thing on his mind is a cold beer at his favorite watering hole. Tired and thirsty, he ambles up to the bar and after

A saloon bar, ca. 1910, with "mustache towels" and spittoons. Taverns in the saloon period were primarily working-class male spaces that featured many male accruements, such as titillating artwork on the walls. Effluvia was also a common feature of saloon life, as men used common towels to wipe their hands and faces and spit haphazardly at spittoons. Many saloons also had troughs running along the bar that men spit in and also sometimes urinated in. (Kirn Vintage Stock/Corbis via Getty Images)

finishing that first satisfying draught he realizes that nature is calling, but he just got a good spot along the bar, and he certainly does not trust leaving his beer unattended. Fortunately, in the saloon age he sometimes did not have to. A recent *Baltimore Sun* article recommends that the next time one of its readers visits an old Baltimore watering hole, they should look down because they might see a remnant from that city's not-too-distant past during its "stag bar" era. The article's author had visited some of these establishments and describes what he saw there as "stainless steel troughs with a faucet at one end and a drain at the other" (Sessa 2010). This allowed customers to spit or dump other refuse right along the bar, and as Madelon Powers has noted, some customers also urinated in them (Powers, 31). Unfortunately, few of these troughs have survived to the present, but one tavern, the Brick, established in 1889 and located in Roslyn, Washington, boasts a 23-foot-long trough along its bar that customers today can still enjoy (Brick Saloon n.d.). However, they are surely no longer urinating in it. So popular is the trough at the Brick that each year the tavern holds a contest in which contestants float homemade boats down it, hoping to win nearly $200 in prize money (Forgotten Buffalo n.d.).

These examples point to conditions that might make modern observers squeamish about wishing that they could once again set foot in an actual Gilded Age saloon. In 1872, one writer at the *Chicago Post* defended the virtues and cleanliness of the saloon, arguing, "Women wonder why their husbands 'go into filthy saloons.'" This writer went on to claim, "The fact is that the saloon is not filthy. As far as neatness, taste, warmth, light, soft carpets, pictures, all can make it, it is attractive" (*Leavenworth Times* 1872). We cannot know what saloons this writer had visited, but the terms "filthy" and "saloon" often found their way next to one another in accounts regarding the institution, both from anti-saloon forces and from many others as well. In 1913, a temperance journal took glee in highlighting Cincinnati's Public Health Department's inspection of 773 saloons in the "Queen City." Their findings illustrate the many aspects of the saloon that promoted filthy and disease-spreading conditions. The journal noted that some of the many problems that inspectors reported included "common towels, unclean glasses, defective plumbing and drainage, filthy or obstructed toilets, common forks, dirty free lunch dishes, expectoration on the floor, etc." The article's author points out that sick and well men visit saloons equally, and yet they knowingly engage in practices that obviously spread disease. They noted 724 cases of commonly used towels. They inspected common drinking cups that several men used and discovered on them "tuberculosis, diphtheria and other bacterial germs of the throat and mouth." Another interesting and disgusting finding was the use of common forks. It seems that saloon patrons would grab forks from a common basket for use in enjoying their free lunch, and once finished they would simply return the fork to the same basket. They also found overflowing spittoons, so that men simply engaged in "frequent spitting on the floor—a filthy and dangerous habit." One would think that the men engaging in these behaviors had to know that what they were doing could result not only in spreading disease but also in catching disease, and it seems that a bit of policing of these conditions would have been customer-induced. However, this does not appear to have been the case. Perhaps sharing germy saloon amenities was a way of enhancing sociability. Fortunately, there were city governments such as that in Cincinnati that promised after this particular round of inspections to "force the saloonkeeper to do his part" (Graham 1914, 15). How well they actually did so as a result is unknown.

BARROOM ACTIVITIES

There are of course better ways than sharing nasty habits to enhance community. There are many competitive activities that reinforce conviviality and have long been associated with taverns, most more sanitary than the activities described above. Many of the most popular amusements that take place in today's taverns—such as pool, darts, bowling, and various card games—have been staple activities of taverns for centuries, and to better understand the timeless lure of the barroom a few of them are worth considering. While Puritan leaders frowned on such tavern recreations, punishments for engaging in them were generally light, and many partook in such activities in even the earliest ordinaries (Daniels 1995, 176–77). As the colonies grew and prospered, tavern gaming became an essential feature of tavern life. A French visitor to Virginia in 1765 noted that during his travels many of the American colonists he met spent their evenings in taverns gaming to excess as they engaged in "Carousing and Drinking In one Chamber and box and Dice in another, which continues till morning Commonly." He went on to note that gaming in taverns was one of the most common features of these colonial establishments, writing that "there is not a publick house in virginia but have their tables al baterd with boxes." He observed that the planters "have very great estates." But their gambling reduced them to a point where they "are mostely at loss for Cash" ("Journal of a French Traveler in the Colonies, 1765" 1921).

There are a wide number of activities that have enhanced community in barrooms, and there are of course too many to mention here. Some typical tavern activities such as darts and pool continue to thrive, while others have largely disappeared. For instance, quoits was an extremely popular activity that was played inside of large taverns or immediately adjacent to them, but today few even know of the sport's existence. In 1893, a Philadelphia newspaper praised the game and connected its origins in the Old World to its status as a mainstay activity in the New World, noting, "It dates back to the discus of the Greeks—The game Abraham Lincoln was playing when he received the news of his nomination" (*Philadelphia Inquirer* 1893). Its closest relative today might be lawn darts, horseshoes, or perhaps bags, a popular game played inside or outside of many Midwest taverns today. According to the *Sportsman's Year-Book for 1880*, quoits can trace its origins to ancient Greece, where it appeared as an Olympic event as far back as 1450 BCE, with some crediting it to Perseus himself (Angus 1880, 229–30). Quoits players toss a ring a set distance at a small pole on the ground that is sometimes referred to as a hob. Circling the hob results in two points, and getting one's ring closer to the hob than one's opponent also results in two points. It is hard to see how, but some argued that quoits was a rather physical sport. One 1866 account discussed two young men who took up the game because they had "heard that quoit pitching was a capital exercise for the development of muscles" (Gris 1866). Quoits contests were taken seriously, and serious money could be at stake in these matches. For instance, in 1868, a contest between a team from Chicago and another from Braidwood, Illinois, had a $1,000 prize at stake (*Daily State Register* 1868).

Some still play quoits, and tournaments can still be found, but not easily so. However, one of the most popular mainstays of the tavern continues to be billiards, today usually referred to as "pool." Pool tables are a common sight in most of today's taverns, and pool tournaments are a large draw at establishments with multiple tables. In 1850, a self-professed saloon keeper named Michael Phelan wrote a guide to billiards, claiming he had produced the "first American publication on the subject." Phelan asserts that the game originated from the French but had antecedents in ancient Rome and that, by the mid-19th century, out "of all the games now in vogue for the purpose of exercise and amusement . . . [billiards] stands preeminent, and is the most to be admired." Phelen argues strongly that his favorite pastime should not be maligned as a sport because it is associated with saloons, stating that billiards is "an innocent, harmless, and gentlemanly amusement," and though some wagering may go on, in general, Phelen asserts, "playing for money is prohibited in the Billiard Rooms and Saloons of this country" (Phelen 1850, 7). Of course, despite Phelen's protestations, many tavern patrons have played for money and continue to do so.

While card playing was more popular in Puritan society, billiards was also present, but because of the expense and needed space for billiards, it was primarily limited to larger, more well-off taverns (Daniels 1995, 181). By the late 19th century, billiards had indeed become a popular American pastime, with one Chicago newspaper noting in 1887 that "now there is scarcely a little country town or town-lot in America that does not boast of at least one billiard and pool table." The article went on to illustrate the mesmerizing nature of the game, relating the tale of two players who entered a pool hall at nine in the evening intending to play for a bit. However, "midnight came and they were still clicking the ivories; the night drew on toward morning, and morning gave way to afternoon, and they were still playing. At 4p.m. they decided that they had at last played billiards enough, and laid down their cues, having played for nineteen hours in a stretch without either eating or drinking" (*Chicago Inter Ocean* 1887).

There are many versions of billiards, ranging from pool to snooker, the former being the most common form of the game played in the United

States, while snooker is more popular in Great Britain. According to a world-renowned player and commentator of the game, Clive Everton, snooker originated among Britons in India, making its way to Great Britain in 1885. Everton claims that snooker is a more sociable game than traditional billiards because the latter allows a talented player to keep the other player out of the game for extended periods (Everton 1991, 2). Despite this, snooker did not become a mainstay of American tavern life, and this may be because American-style billiards had already become established by the time snooker was invented. This did not mean, however, that Americans were not innovative in regards to inventing new versions of the sport. In 1896, the *Pittsburgh Post* informed its readers about a new game called Little Cuba, which it claimed "is coming into popularity." Little Cuba featured a ball with an opening drilled into it that is fitted with a percussion cap. Shooters must try to hit the ball in such a way as to hit the cap, which then "explodes with a sharp little report, and the powder behind it makes enough smoke to be interesting" (*Pittsburgh Daily Post* 1896). Another billiards variation in the 1890s was "bottle billiards" in which a bottle is placed in the center of the table with just two balls on the table (Foster 1897, 598). In 2006, a writer for the *New York Times* commented that having only recently discovered the game when out one evening, he lamented that the game might be dying out. Perhaps his description of the game provides a clue as to why it is not more popular. He describes bottle pool as combining "elements of billiards, straight pool and chess under a set of rules that lavishly rewards strategic shot making and punishes mistakes with Sisyphean point reversals" (Hurt 2006). Perhaps in a tavern setting where patrons are seeking to relax while drinking alcoholic beverages it makes sense that complicated variations of billiards are not more popular than simple American-style pool.

Playing cards have been a staple of tavern life about as long as there have been taverns. Today's taverns see playing cards much less, unless one is in a casino. An 1890 history of card playing asserted that Puritans called playing cards the "Devil's Books," an assertion that is consistent with Puritan society (Van Rensselaer 1890, iii). One historian has noted that Puritans were actually avid card players and that indeed card playing took place in New England taverns. The most popular card game played in early American taverns was cribbage, an English invention that was thought to do an excellent job of improving mathematic skills. One restriction on card playing in New England taverns was that card players could not use them for gambling, and there were cases where tavern patrons were brought before magistrates for this infraction (Daniels 1995, 178–81).

While there are a multitude of card games with long and storied histories, by far the most famous of them to have been played in taverns is poker, a game referred to in an 1890 account as "the national game of the United States, and the one at present in fashion among many classes of society" (Van Rensselaer 1890, 117). While this assertion implies that poker was a game that bridged class divides, like so much else in American society in the Gilded Age, poker was also caught up in class distinctions. One 1906 newspaper article on the subject asked in its headline "Poker: Gambling, or a Gentleman's Game?" and implied that poorer working-class men could never be as good at the game as someone from the upper classes (*Chicago Inter Ocean* 1906). Of course, the well-off played poker in their private clubs, while the working class played in their saloons. Poker was one of the most popular games played in saloons and is certainly synonymous with Western saloons but it was also popular throughout the rest of the country (Powers 1998, 150). While gentlemen's clubs were largely unregulated, working-class saloons often caught the eye of reformers and authorities, and card playing was one aspect of tavern life that caught their attention. In 1913, the *Oakland Tribune* described the practice as a "public menace" and demanded that an "ordinance is needed." One young man, 18-year-old Harry Masters, was arrested in Oakland for "misdemeanor embezzlement" after having lost $300 to $400 playing poker. However, the reason that he was arrested was because, the paper lamented, he then stole that amount from his employer to make up the losses (*Oakland Tribune* 1913).

Stories of young men being led down paths similar to the one trod by young Masters have always been staple tropes for reformers and so have stories of mothers and wives who have descended on taverns to wreak havoc, Carrie Nation–style, because the men in their lives were believed to be ruining themselves and perhaps even their families inside. One such account concerned poker, a son, and his mother in Burlington, New Jersey, who learned in 1891 that her son, "a young man of a good family," had become "completely infatuated with the game, (poker) and played every night often losing heavily." Having learned of this, the intrepid mother entered the saloon where her son frequently played, "her face covered in a veil." On entering the room where her son was playing, she threw back her veil, upon which incredible drama ensued as "the players fled in all directions, one of them falling downstairs in his hurry to escape." It is hard to know if this scene played out exactly the way described, as this newspaper reporter's account demonstrates clear bias against the saloon and its patrons, with the writer stating that "the woman who brought this about is the heroine of the hour" (*Lebanon Daily News* 1891). Whether or not she was a heroine is up for debate, but she was obviously brave.

Saloon patrons could generally count on poker being present in saloons, and some banked on this as a way to earn a living. Big Bill Haywood of Industrial Workers of the World (IWW) fame noted in his autobiography how poker could become a source of income for a good player. He claims that for a time he earned a living exactly that way at a saloon in Winnemucca after the owner suggested to him that he could make good money by running a poker game in the establishment, which Haywood did, playing cards by night and laboring by day. He must have been good at the game because he claims to have made around $800 in a month, a tidy sum then (Haywood 1983; see also Carlson 1984). Perhaps the most famous poker game that ever took place was a result of the desire to make ends meet through poker winnings. Wild Bill Hickok, one of the most noted icons of the Old West, wandered into Deadwood in the Dakota territory in July 1876. Though famous, the then-39-year-old gunfighter was down on his luck when he strolled into one of the West's most famous cities. Legend has it that, based on his well-known prowess with firearms, he hoped to be named the town's marshal, a post that would have drawn an income, but in the meantime, while waiting to see how things would play out, Hickok spent time in the camp's very wild saloons. On August 1, 1876, Hickok was playing poker at Nutall and Mann's saloon (a.k.a. No. 10 Saloon) when he gave offense to another player, Jack McCall, who was losing heavily. The following day Hickok was back, hoping to maintain a winning streak, when the man he had slighted the day before, McCall, entered and shot Hickok at close range in the back of the head (Parker 1981, 197). This famous encounter led to the most famous poker hand in history, the "dead man's hand," which consists of two pair of black eights and black aces, the hand that Hickok was holding when he was gunned down in such a cowardly fashion.

VIOLENCE AND BARROOM CULTURE

As discussed in chapter 2, violence such as that which took place in Deadwood saloons has been a staple of barroom culture. On many an occasion, what has started as a fun night out has resulted in a violent altercation that in some cases has led to a night in jail or even a fatality. In an atmosphere of people who do not know each other well, where liquor flows freely and loosens the tongues of some while providing liquid courage to others, there is always the underlying threat of violence. A headline from a New Orleans newspaper in 1895, "A Duel to the Death," tells an all-too-familiar story of insulted honor being answered with horrific violence on the barroom floor. According to the account, two men were shot dead and a witness was wounded in a Big Easy barroom at 10:30 in the evening. And why did two men lose their lives on that fateful night? Because, according to the article, the murderer was "smarting under a fancied wrong to his family honor" (*New Orleans Times-Picayune* 1895). This familiar story was interesting enough to the editors of the *Times-Picayune* that they decided to spend nearly an entire news page telling every lurid detail of the event.

The public has always been fascinated by the barroom as a scene of mystery and violence, and the barroom as a place of violence has long served as a meme in fiction because it is so closely linked to reality. In her prodigious study of court transcripts from Gilded Age dramshop lawsuits, Elaine Parsons has found that one of the most oft-mentioned reasons for sudden and fierce barroom violence was the perception that someone failed to "mind one's own business" (Parsons 2003, 61). In the barroom people are expected to mingle, but they are also expected to respect boundaries. Alcohol can blur the lines of these boundaries and can also cause a patron to take offense at a perceived slight. Violence was also prevalent in many saloons as sport. Elliot Gorn has written about the prevalence of prize fights in barrooms in the Gilded Age when men would gather to watch other men pummel each other with their bare knuckles. As Gorn writes, such fights were part of "saloon-centered bloodsports" that thrived in working-class saloons as part of a culture that centered on "the old values of mutuality, reciprocity, loyalty to kin and community, bloodlust, prowess, and honor" (Gorn 2012, 181). There is certainly less violence in taverns today than there was in the saloon period, but the possibility that a violent encounter can ruin a fun night out remains a risk that tavern-goers take. Today's taverns are in general cleaner and less violent places. Perhaps the return of women to the barroom has been one reason.

WOMEN RETURN TO THE BARROOM

After the 13-year disaster of National Prohibition, many things changed about the tavern. In the years following the return of the legal tavern, few establishments called themselves saloons, and women began making a return to the barroom. Not all male customers were happy with this, and some complained about the appearance of women in the once male-only domain. An editorial writer in 1935 opined that women should "not sit on high stools with their feet on a rail and drink at the bar." Furthermore, he lamented that the problems the saloon had caused society were bad enough before National Prohibition, but after it the appearance of women was making the return of the tavern a much worse situation for society than before. Besides sometimes "NOT [all caps appear in the original] readjusting" their skirts after sitting on a high stool, women were making themselves a nuisance by "calling for foolish drinks to show how foolish they could be." Finally, in the writer's opinion, male-dominated spaces should be kept free of women: "Prizefights, cock-fights, regular saloon bars should put up the sign: 'Ladies not invited'" (*Lincoln Star* 1935). Of course, few feel that way today, and many male patrons are of course interested in finding establishments that have female patrons. Taverns understand this, and many promote "ladies' nights" to attract both women and men. Kool and the Gang, a popular music group, released the hit single "Ladies Night" in 1979, exemplifying the desire that male patrons have to find taverns with women present: "Oh, yes, it's ladies' night/And the feeling's right!" Many taverns offer specials on ladies' nights, ranging from no cover charge to free drinks. As the *Miami New Times* points out, the practice is one that women can take advantage of. Tavern-going in Miami Beach is expensive, but not for ladies who know where and when ladies' night is taking place. For instance, one establishment, Your Idol, gives ladies free drinks every Wednesday from 10:00 p.m. until 2:00 a.m. (Almeida 2017).

THE TIMELESS BARROOM

The barroom is timeless, and one of the most important aspects of the modern tavern is its desire to cater to the old, to create in the mind of the customer the atmosphere of a bygone era. After all, the tavern is a place of fantasy and escapism, and many customers enter them because they are seeking an escape from the workaday world. In 1921, the *Official Metropolitan Guide*, a publication designed for visitors to New York City to inform them about places and events they ought to visit, announced on May 29 that a new bar would be opening by the name of Old Town Tavern on West 42nd Street. A review of the tavern stated that Old Town Tavern would "revive something of the old-time spirit of New York that is oftentimes forgotten or overlooked in the rush and hurry of the present." Inside, patrons could hearken back to a seemingly familiar and yet abandoned past. This probably had special appeal in 1921, just a year after the Eighteenth Amendment and the Volstead Act had gone into effect. As discussed in chapter 1, much of New York City chose to violate National Prohibition with reckless abandon, so the announcement of an opening tavern could perhaps have been seen as an act of open defiance and reflected a longing for a return to both an experienced and an imagined past (Lerner 2007). Old Town Tavern promised to transport one there—and in style. It advertised walls "lined with buff Tracertine stone, the material of which the palaces of the Caesars were built and which was imported from Italy."

Forty years later, in 1961, a tavern boldly calling itself a saloon opened in Kalispell, Montana. By that year, the age of the saloon had passed over four decades earlier, but surely many old-timers still remembered their saloon-going days fondly, and younger people knew of the era from their elders and of course from films and books. The proprietor of Kalispell's new establishment, David "Moose" Miller, sought to capitalize on nostalgic memories of a bygone age when he opened his establishment, which he simply named The Saloon. Before opening, he accumulated items from the golden past, such as "an old player piano; old fashioned telephones you used to crank up to get the operator in order to get her off the party line. He found ancient cuspidors, historic photos, some swinging doors, and a general collection of paraphernalia that fit right into the saloon décor." As a result, the article claimed that The Saloon was one of the most important tourist attractions in the town, bringing in customers on the sawdust-strewn floor to marvel at the old as they reminisced about another age (*Daily Inter Lake* 1961). Miller's success stemmed from his understanding that the past lives in every barroom in every tavern. He sought to establish his saloon as a time machine that mixed nostalgia with alcohol, and he surrounded his patrons with the sights, sounds, and smells that have always characterized the barroom. But is it the mementos on the walls and the quintessential mahogany bar backed by a mirror that transports the tavern patron, or is the magical formula found in the mingling with old friends, new friends, and strangers that is enhanced through the enchanted elixir of alcohol? It is in this mixing, to quote William Faulkner, that we discover in the barroom that "the past is never dead. It's not even the past" (Faulkner 1951, 73).

Chapter 4

BEHIND THE BAR

> If I were hungry and friendless today, I would rather take my chances with a saloon-keeper than with the average preacher.
>
> —Eugene Debs (1908)

Bernard "Toots" Shor passed away in 1977 at the age of 73, and a nation noticed. At the time of his passing, he was running two successful taverns in Manhattan and was memorialized across the country in one of the best ways someone in his profession could be, as "a saloonkeeper who served strong drinks and good stories" (*San Antonio Light* 1969, 31). Lots of working-class New Yorkers visited Shor's, but so did many famous people, including the likes of celebrities and socialites such as Ernest Hemingway, Joe DiMaggio, and Frank Sinatra. Legend has it that FDR once stopped a presidential procession to pay Shor's a visit. His successor, President Truman, invited Shor and his wife to the White House (*San Antonio Light* 1969). As a result of Shor's fame, his passing was chronicled in newspapers around the country, and he was held up as a man who had been larger than life at the head of the pack in a tough business that he made look easy. Shor was known by all as a friendly and accommodating tavern man, but in the spirit of one of his famous patron's most famous songs, Shor could have said at the last, "I did it my way."

Shor had grown up tough. Born in 1903 as a Jew in a largely Italian and Irish neighborhood in Philadelphia, he lost his parents at a young age in separate tragedies. After being told by an uncle that he would not amount to anything, he went to New York and became one of the most celebrated tavern keepers in history. Prohibition proved to be good for many entrepreneurial and tough young men, and Shor was no exception. Starting out as a bouncer in a speakeasy, he soon worked for the likes of notorious mobster Owney "The Killer" Madden, where he earned respect for his intelligence

Benard "Toots" Shor (1903–1977) standing outside of one of his Manhattan establishments in 1959. Shor was one of the most well-known tavern keepers in history, serving the famous and the working class alike, always ready with an affectionate personalized insult. His passing in 1977 was noted in newspapers across the nation. (Library of Congress)

and toughness. Highlighting one incident that proved the latter, Shor once claimed in an interview that "one night I flattened a Revenue guy"(*Monroe News-Star* 1977, 11).

Capitalizing on what he had learned in the great age of organized crime, Shor opened his soon to be legendary tavern a few years after legal alcohol began to flow again. He had always proclaimed that his establishments were "for his pals," and not for people who rubbed him the wrong way, people he called "crumb bums," a term of endearment that he seems to have frequently also used for his friends. They were many, and they remembered Shor as "rambunctious, loud [and] sometimes even rude to people who didn't know him well" (*Panama City News Herald* 1977, 21). Highlighting the male bonding that went on in his tavern, Shor was known to greet those he liked with personalized insults. On entering Shor's, Frank Sinatra, for instance, could look forward to a warm greeting of "you skinny dago." Famous Yankees Whitey Ford and Yogi Berra were told, "You bums play lousy, but I feed you anyway." A friend of Shor's joked that he was exactly the kind of person Shor would kick out of his own saloon. But, as with most successful tavern keepers, it was said that "the real man was generous and warm." Despite some of his apparently more cantankerous traits, he was clearly a man with many friends and admirers and was affectionately proclaimed by many far and wide, Shor included, as the "world's greatest saloon keeper." He was proud of his lifelong profession, and it is clear that he was a successful businessman and socialite. But Shor eschewed such acclamations and embraced all the negative perceptions that his profession had had to carry since the first tavern keeper opened the first tavern, proclaiming, "I'm just a creepy saloonkeeper, and I ain't ashamed of it" (*Monroe News-Star* 1977, 11; *Panama City News Herald* 1977; Thomas 1991, 96–97; Barra 2007).

Shor might have made it look easy, but the tavern business has always been tough. But the tavern business has never been an easy one. During the Gilded Age, as discussed previously, when the number of saloons reached astronomical proportions in scores of American communities, many a working-class man was beguiled into trading in his tools for a chance at a better life behind the bar making a living dispensing a portion of the billions of gallons of alcohol that were being consumed each year (*Anti-Saloon League Yearbook* 1917, 252). George Ade observed that many a saloon keeper's customers stood at his bar and dreamed that they could do what he was doing, maybe even do it better. What laboring man who spent 10-plus hours a day working in a mine, meatpacking plant, or some other unpleasant industrial-age occupation would not have stood at the bar at the end of a long day, sipping a cold pint of lager and dreaming that he could leave his dark, dirty, and arduous job behind for a shot behind the bar as the master of the domain he so often frequented anyway? Many hard-working individuals have given up their workaday world for a try at life behind the bar, but the tavern business has always been a fickle mistress who can let down even the most persistent and serious of suitors.

The previous chapter considered the social space of the tavern as simultaneously created and enhanced by customers and tavern keepers in a kind of symbiosis. This chapter will examine what goes on behind the proverbial mahogany bar by considering the tavern owner and his staff and the environment in which they work. From the vantage point behind the bar, the barkeep surveys a world that he has contrived for the enjoyment of his customers and therefore for his ability to stay in business and thrive. Many may see him as the master of his domain, and after spending their days in the workaday world people look forward to an evening of fun in their favorite tavern where its keeper may seem like a friend and ringmaster of the tavern circus. His life may appear exotic and fun, and many a customer may envy his profession, but life for most tavern keepers is not easy. A tavern keeper's problems can be many. They include dealing with difficult city governments, problems with law enforcement officials and unruly customers who appear to be having a good time one minute but are creating a disturbance the next. They also have to worry about overserving customers and those who are underage. Some experience problems with their neighbors who complain about noise and the nuisance of having intoxicated individuals hanging out in front of their establishments. And then there is always the looming threat of dramshop lawsuits that can stem from a customer who is harmed or who harms another while intoxicated after having been served in his establishment. Finally, every tavern keeper knows that his business is a cutthroat one and that competition is fierce. There are only so many things that a tavern keeper can do to differentiate his establishment from the myriad of other establishments that serve essentially the same products he does.

Shor's customers formed a veritable list of who's who, ranging from mobsters to presidents to celebrities and athletes, but his patrons also included dock workers and cab drivers. In his tavern's heyday, these men would rub shoulders as members of the same club gathered around the communal cup of mirth. Shor was their ringleader, and he was their priest. Those who have made a life behind the bar have been portrayed by their detractors as pied pipers who lead their faithful followers to ruin. From the point of view of their patrons, however, those behind the bar can resemble shepherds who provide their flock with a place of refuge from the many cares of the world outside the tavern's doors. During early American history, tavern keepers provided a service that was valued and used by large swaths of society. That is largely true today as well, as some visit taverns frequently and others from time to time. Today, as was the case in early American history, there is little stigma attached to visiting a tavern to meet with friends or watch a sporting event, and owning a tavern or working in one is not a terribly controversial way to make a living. During the saloon age, detractors portrayed saloon keepers as an immoral and powerfully influential force who possessed an outsized amount of clout and influence. This perception is well illustrated in an 1889 observation about the undue influence that saloon keepers and others engaged in the alcohol trade supposedly had. In an article that appeared in newspapers throughout the country, titled "The Saloon Power: How It Runs Troy, N.Y., with the Aid of the Democratic Machine," it was claimed that the city of Troy was entirely in the hands of saloon keepers and brewers. This investigatory piece put forth that, ominously, all the city's aldermen were saloon keepers, while the mayor was a brewer. Nearly every other city officer from the city clerk to the charity commissioner were likewise listed as saloon keepers (*Osage County Chronicle* 1889).

Whether or not these claims were entirely true is not as important as the fact that such ideas about the power and pernicious influence of saloon keepers were a constant theme in the Gilded Age press and in many pulpits. Many middle-class reformers were bothered by the idea that immigrants who were flocking to U.S. cities were allegedly then being courted by city political machines, largely Democratic, that supposedly bought their votes. Saloons were portrayed as the center of these corrupt actions. As the great labor leader Terence Powderly explained in 1890, "Where a workingman for any cause was engaged in the sale of rum, it was imagined that he had an influence over his former associates, and his saloon was the resort of politicians of all parties before election" (Powderly 1890, 613). Of course, many immigrants spent a great deal of time in saloons, which were as easy to find as churches, often easier. Just as some politicians were seen as manipulators of the immigrant vote, so too were saloon keepers portrayed in the same light as overseers and manipulators of their customers. It was alleged that they influenced and bribed law enforcement, government officials, and politicians in order to maintain their pernicious practices, all the while building empires from the bones of working-class sorrows in the process.

"Toots" Shor was certainly a successful mid–20th-century tavern keeper, and many other legendary saloon men, such as Henry C. Ramos of New Orleans and Michael "Hinky Dink" Kenna of Chicago, will live forever as powerful and successful players in histories of the American tavern. They certainly wielded influence and wealth, but for most who have tried the business, this perception is nowhere near the reality. A large segment of those who sought to make a living behind the bar have ultimately experienced a fate similar to that of Martin Olson, who once kept a saloon in Centuria, Wisconsin. We do not know how he got into the saloon business or why, but like many of his brethren, Olson ultimately found himself in a courtroom facing bankruptcy. In the late spring of 1910, Olson stood facing a judge who informed him that he owed his creditors, the Twin City liquor, cigar, and mineral water dealers, $534.58 for merchandise. However, the only assets that the poor barkeep had left were valued at just $250 and included a "stove with appendages" and a "family Bible." Olson humbly asked for an exemption on the latter (*Star Tribune* 1910).

BLAME IT ON THE TAVERN KEEPER

Perhaps, with only the family Bible left, Olson could have gone into the ministry. He may have been suited for it, since the skills needed to be a saloon man were not much different from those needed to be a good pastor. In fact, many a saloon keeper may have been more adept at appealing to the masses. After all, he came straight from their ranks. And yet the tavern keeper has long endured the scorn of his fellow citizens, existing in the minds of many as an individual similar to the snake that tempted Adam and Eve in the garden. As one anti-saloon screed admonished in 1915, "There is evidence on every hand that young men have started drinking within the past three months who never thought of tasting liquor until the open saloon tempted them" (*Marysville Journal-Tribune* 1915). Reformers during the Gilded Age spent a great deal of energy lambasting saloon keepers as the source of all corruption in society and the fountain of poor morals among their working-class faithful. Even presidents used the bully pulpit to weigh in against the saloon man. Theodore Roosevelt warned about "lawbreaking among the saloonkeepers," while his successor, William McKinley, warned that by countenancing the legal liquor trade, "we agree to share with the liquor seller the responsibilities and evils of his business" (Pickett 1917, 365). Surprisingly, labor leaders whose members were typically avid saloon-goers also piled on the saloon keeper. Terence Powderly, who led one of the most successful labor unions of the 19th century, the Knights of Labor, reserved a great deal of vitriol for saloon keepers, blaming them for keeping the working class from rising in their station. Powderly's Knights was generally an inclusive organization, welcoming most workers and even women and minorities (see Weir 1996). However, Powderly banned some professions, including "lawyers, speculators, members of corporations, and . . . dealers in whiskey" (*Chicago Daily Tribune* 1882). In other words, saloon keepers. Powderly had once been a saloon-goer himself, but as the leader of the nation's largest labor organization, he decided that saloon keepers and their institutions were a blight on the working class. As he explained to his membership,

> His path [the saloon keeper], and that of the honest, industrious workingman, lie in opposite directions. The rum-seller who seeks admission into a labor society does so with the object that he may entice its members into his saloon after the meetings close. No question of interest to labor has ever been satisfactorily settled over a bar in a rum-hole. No labor society ever admitted a rum-seller that did not die a drunkard's death. (Powderly n.d.; Fernald 1890, 337)

Many opponents of the saloon described saloon keepers with terms similar to those used to describe slave owners in the antebellum South. In 1890, James Champlin Fernald, an advocate of Prohibition, accused saloon keepers of enslaving their working-class customers, who "work all day" and then come into the saloon and hand over their hard-earned pay "to the saloon-keeper, who very likely couldn't do their work if he would, and certainly wouldn't if he could." Fernald describes this relationship as a scheme in which the saloon keeper simply waits for his customers to obediently just hand over the money they earned for their hard labor. In this arrangement, he is their master, and they are his slaves. Fernald writes, "He has such mastery over them as no Legree ever had over his slaves. He needs no bloodhounds to keep them from running away." The use of Legree is in reference to Simon Legree, a cruel and mercurial slave owner made famous in Harriet Beecher Stowe's best-selling novel of the 19th century, *Uncle Tom's Cabin.* It is hard to imagine a worse person to compare one to. Of course, such descriptions deny agency to the tavern keeper's customers themselves, as if the tavern owner is the famed Pied Piper of Hamelin, and his customers are the village's children, led to their doom as they march along like automatons to his liquid-enhanced tune. His customers are willing dupes, and he is a thief, as Fernald argues, who steals from "the bronzed toiler [who] sits down in the den of his lily-handed, iron-hearted master, hands over to him his wife's dinner, and his children's shoes, and the very rent money" (Fernald 1890, 337).

Fernald was just one member of a vast army. There was no shortage of pastors of his variety who daily tore into saloon keepers from the pulpit and from the printing press, charging that they were leading their followers to their doom. None was better at serving up this sort of vitriol against that saloon keeper than the most famous itinerant minister of the Gilded Age, Billy Sunday. In his famous and well-attended sermons, the former baseball great turned minister relentlessly stalked his audience from the stage, sometimes beating his fists into the air and at other times suddenly falling on the ground in fits of hysteria. In one such sermon, he charged with fire that "the saloonkeeper is worse than a thief and a murderer. The ordinary thief steals only your money, but the saloonkeeper steals your honor and your character. The ordinary murderer takes your life, but the saloonkeeper murders your soul" (Sunday 1908; Mole 2012, 89). In 1895, a Methodist minister, Louis Albert Banks, likewise castigated the saloon keeper from the pulpit in a similar vein. In a sermon titled "The Saloon Debtor to Pauperized Labor," Banks told his rapt audiences the tale of a "laboring man" who on walking out of a saloon "saw a costly carriage . . . occupied by two ladies elegantly attired." On witnessing this spectacle, the saloon customer turned to the saloon keeper and inquired as to whom the carriage belonged. The saloon keeper replied that it was his own carriage, "It cost thirty-five hundred dollars. My wife and daughter cannot do without it." On hearing this and pondering the implications, the saloon patron suddenly had an amazing epiphany. After years of drinking and wasting his time and money in this saloon, he exclaimed, "I see it! I see it!" to which the saloon keeper inquired, "See what?" At this point the newly enlightened saloon customer launched into an eloquent soliloquy in which he laid the blame for his own economic woes at the feet of the saloon keeper: "[I] see where, for years my wages have gone, I helped pay for that carriage, for those horses and gold-mounted harnesses, and for the silks and laces for your family." Meanwhile, this fictional workingman lamented that his own family had had to do without. He castigated the saloon keeper: "My wages, and the wages of others like me, have gone to support you and your family in luxury." From that day forward, proclaimed this new and improved man, the wily saloon keeper would no longer enrich himself at his expense. Instead, he proclaimed, "Hereafter my wife and children shall have the benefit of my wages; and, by the help of God, I will never spend another dime for drink"(Banks 1895, 76).

Not all saloon keepers took these assaults on their character by the clergy lying down. The Reverend E. B. Sutton discovered this the hard way after castigating saloon keepers from the pulpit in June 1890. Sutton, an agent with the Washington Temperance Alliance, was on a speaking tour in Eastern Washington. In the city of Almira, he received a letter from local saloon keepers warning him to leave town. Perhaps believing that God would protect him in his holy mission, Sutton chose not to heed the warning. After a sermon in which he had poured invectives upon hard-working saloon keepers, invectives that were probably similar to those poured on by the likes of the pastors described above, a saloon keeper named George Clark knocked upon his hotel door. When Sutton answered, Clark chose not to explain himself or his purpose. Instead, he chose to begin beating on Sutton, just as had been promised in the letter. It must have been quite the scene. According to an account, Clark "trampled on his victim, stamping and kicking him until outside interference was made." After Sutton was rescued, he was taken to a nearby hospital where it was discovered that his skull was fractured, and it was proclaimed doubtful that he would recover. He was delirious but was said to have periods of lucidity in which he must have wondered where the Lord was when he was being beaten. It probably never crossed his mind that the Lord might have been on the side of Clark, more than likely a hard-working family man, like most saloon keepers, who was tired of getting verbally kicked. Perhaps, he had just decided it was time to kick back. (*Seattle Post-Intelligencer* 1890, 6).

This event did not, of course, end there. At first, when it was believed that Sutton would die, Clark beat town on a fast horse, hearing that "the sheriff was in hot pursuit." However, after four days, and upon learning that Sutton would survive, Clark returned to face the music. He did after all have a business to run. After recovering, Sutton took Clark to court, and six jurors were empaneled to hear the case. The pugilistic saloon keeper, in what seems to have been a further act of defiance, did not participate in his defense. Instead, he "refused to plead either way, or to bring out any witnesses, and he refrained from cross-examining any witnesses." This bold strategy appears to have paid off. After a short recess, this jury of his peers found him guilty for having savagely beaten Sutton, but the punishment was quite light. Clark would have to pay a fine of $25. A newspaper article speculated that this was because in Almira—"a little railroad town, recently built in the woods"—the "saloon element rules everything by a sort of tyranny." It is not hard to imagine that as the article describes it, "Clark was greatly pleased at the verdict." Such an occasion of course required a celebration, and the recently declared guilty man had people to celebrate with. In fact, three of the jurors accompanied Clark from the courtroom in order to tip back some social glasses together. It may be true that the "saloon element" held great sway in Almira. But this may have been because this was a working-class lumber and railroad town where workers liked to drink and where they liked their saloon keepers. Consequently, they may have seen Sutton as the abuser and Clark as the victim. In this light, they may have thought that they had indeed served justice (*Seattle Post-Intelligencer* 1890, 8). In addition to being portrayed as moral reprobates, others described saloon keepers as lazy and oafish. Even George Ade in his nostalgic look back at the institution described a sizable number of them as lazy, and at times in his writing he showed open contempt for the profession. He wrote that many who went into the business did so because "keeping a saloon seemed an easy way of making a living, while surrounded by jovial acquaintances." In this effort to make an easy living, Ade laments that the prospect of saloon keeping drew in "a great number of citizens, who were too lazy or too fat to lay bricks or nail on shingles," implying that while the customers were hard-working individuals their keepers sometimes were anything but (Ade 1931, 101). Such descriptions abounded, and the term "lazy saloon keeper" often made it into print and into the sermons of the many pastors who decried the tavern. As described above, it was often reasoned that because so many workingmen were spending their money at saloons that saloon keepers were running some sort of racket that deprived the workingman's family of his earnings while enriching the saloon keeper. In 1883, a Chicago Catholic priest explained that since there was a saloon for every 120 persons in the Windy City, and excluding women and children, this put the customer base at 25 customers per saloon, then it stood to reason that "each family on an average contributed one twenty-fifth part to the support of some lazy saloonkeeper and his family" (*Waterloo Press* 1883). Lazy, immoral, corrupt—throughout the saloon age the invectives piled higher and higher.

Eugene Debs, a labor leader and the most prominent socialist politician in American history, took a different tack. Debs did not blame the saloon nor the saloon keeper for the problems that the working class endured. Instead Debs rightly put the blame on the nature of American industrial capitalism in the Gilded Age. He chafed at the idea that so many reformers would get worked up "over a man taking a drink at 11:30 or playing a game of cards, but they are not concerned about wage-slavery, or child-sweating, which have a thousand victims where the saloon has one." It is easy, Debs noted, "to pounce upon the saloonkeeper and hold him up as a monster of iniquity." However, Debs argued, the saloon is a legal *business* "as lawful as any other business in the profit-mongering system." In such a system Debs declared that the "saloonkeeper is no more responsible for the saloon than the preacher is for the church, and the saloonkeeper is not necessarily a bad man, nor the preacher necessarily a good one" (Debs 1908, 1). The equating of the preacher with the saloon keeper, the church with the saloon, has long been a common theme, and in many communities today the number of each institution is fairly similar, and many visit the tavern to minister to the soul in ways similar to those who go to religious gathering places to do so. As George Ade wrote, regarding the great age of the saloon, "The saloons did one hundred times as much business as the prayer-meetings and the genial bar-keep was more of a public character and more highly esteemed by the crowd than the pale and pious preacher" (Ade 1931, 98). Of course, ministering to the customer's soul through drink and community may be one aspect of the business, but as is also true with any church, bringing in enough revenue to pay the bills is the first order of business if the tavern ministry is to continue.

THE BAR

Just as a preacher conducts his business from behind a pulpit, a tavern keeper conducts his from behind the fabled tavern bar. The term "bar" dates to the 16th century and describes the barrier that separates the bartender from those being served. Today, when we enter a new tavern, we expect to see a long bar that typically dominates the barroom, and for an initiate to a never-before-visited tavern, the bar can seem like home base, the center of the tavern universe. The very routine of sitting down at the bar and ordering a drink is a comforting universal ritual. The bar is the tavern and the tavern is the bar. In 1826, a New York City newspaper columnist decried that drinking excessively was no longer confined to the "low and vulgar" but was becoming a habit for "the educated youth of the metropolis to a fearful extent," who could now be seen "crowding around a tavern bar, in the broad day" (*Long-Island Star* 1826). As this suggests, the bar itself has become synonymous with the act of tavern-going, so that when we plan on going to a tavern we often say we are "going to the bar." We call the individual who makes our drinks a "bartender." The space in which we drink and socialize is the "barroom." Female servers have long been called "bar maids," though this term has largely fallen out of the lexicon. In some taverns the bar is coarse and utilitarian, while in others it is elegant and stylish, but its form and function are largely universal.

In many early American taverns, the bar was often a small affair, located off in the corner of the room. It frequently had a cage around it made of wooden slats. The bartender could enter the bar through a back door and lift the slats, indicating that he was ready to serve customers. When he was not serving alcohol to customers, he could close the cage doors, allowing the owner to lock up his alcohol stock and perhaps other valuable items (Carlin 2012, 40–41; Craig 2012, 125). When new communities formed hastily, bars could be very rudimentary affairs. The American West attracted large numbers of men seeking employment, land, and the fulfillment of dreams of getting rich, and taverns followed them, and in some cases preceded them. Elliot West describes a journalist's account of a hastily constructed tavern that used a sack of flour to serve as a bar. Other makeshift bars consisted of pine boards laid across barrels. Once a community was up and running, its taverns became more established and sought to provide better amenities to their customers. Most barkeeps constructed bars that rarely exceeded 10 feet in length, using local carpenters. Others imported their bars by train or wagon, with some having come all the way from Europe (West 1979, 31).

For many saloon keepers the bar was often their biggest expense. In the saloon age, bars were frequently elegant affairs, even in poorer establishments. This may have something to do with the etymology of the word "saloon" itself, its origin deriving from the French word *salon*, denoting a fancy gathering place for elite citizens (Hammell 1908, xx). In the saloon common, working-class men gathered to feel special in their own clubs, clubs that in some ways mirrored higher society in their décor and affectations. Bar fixtures were frequently advertised in newspapers by the companies that manufactured them and by tavern keepers who were leaving the business, and we can gain a better understanding of the fixtures an aspiring saloon man would have sought to acquire by considering a 1908 advertisement placed by the Valentine Auction Company in a Richmond, Virginia, newspaper offering an entire bar setup that consisted of "a Solid Genuine Mahogany Bar Counter, with a panel mirror front." The cost of these fixtures was advertised at $2,600, a considerable sum in 1908, translating to roughly $70,000 in 2018 dollars. But these fixtures came with many extras, some being essential for conducting business and others acting as decorative devices. The following detailed accounting from this advertisement provides a picture of the many essentials the saloon keeper would have been looking for:

> Large double Ice Box in centre, with beer coils, spigots, etc. (will hold four half barrels beer at one time), and has fine copper work boxes, magnificent back bar Fixture of rich Mahogany finish on solid Cherry, with a large plate mirror in centre and a number of smaller mirrors; has two glass inclosed [*sic*] wine cabinets on ends and inclosed [*sic*] cupboard base, handsome Wall Case to match back box fixture, with carvings and mirrors, glass doors, etc.: Solid Brass Foot Rail, handsome leaded Glass Mahogany Bar Door, Partitions, etc. (*Times Dispatch* 1908)

This advertisement describes an expensive setup, and many saloon keepers were intent on creating a stylish atmosphere for their customers. A write-up for a bar opening in Saint Albans, Vermont, in 1903 provides a wonderful description of a new saloon-era tavern and the lavish style that some saloon keepers aspired to. The proprietor, J. J. Thompson, seems to have spared no expense, laying out $3,500 for his new barroom. The room was wainscoted with "elaborately carved" oak that reached a height of over five feet. The floor was a mosaic of elaborate squares, and the ceiling was made of steel and was "elaborately decorated in red and gold." But the most important feature of the new saloon was an extravagant bar and backbar arrangement, both crafted from antique oak, with the back of the bar crafted from copper, brass, and silver. The backbar stood 26 feet long and 11 feet high and sported three large plateglass mirrors. As the customer sat at the bar getting deeper into his cups, he could contemplate the many "handsome engravings" that hung on the walls. But perhaps the most interesting feature of all was a painting that sums up well the nature of the all-male camaraderie and misogyny of the Gilded Age saloon. Centered above the mirror behind the bar, imbibers could contemplate a large painting of "a woman's head in the jaws of tiger" centered above the bar (*St. Albans Daily Messenger* 1903).

Behind the wooden bar, one could typically see the ubiquitous backbar mirror, which served several practical purposes. The modern mirror is a relatively new invention, making its debut in Germany in 1835 when German chemist Justus von Liebig coated one side of clear glass with silver, but the process was not perfected until a few decades later (Pendergrast 2003, 182–84). So modern mirrors and the saloon age grew up together with the mirror becoming an iconic feature of the space behind the bar, and it served several purposes. First, a large mirror can create a sense of a larger space, which can be a plus in a smaller establishment. Second,

Customers enjoying a social drink at the bar of the famous Palace Saloon in Virginia City, Nevada. The back bar mirror was a ubiquitous feature in many saloon-era taverns. They can still be found in many taverns today. (Ron Yue/Alamy Stock Photo)

a mirror allows a bartender to see what is going on behind him if he has his back to his customers while conducting chores such as cleaning glasses or mixing drinks. Third, a mirror allows customers at the bar to have a better sense of their own surroundings, a feature especially helpful in the Old West saloon where a patron might fear being sneaked up on. Wild Bill Hickok, for instance, might have enjoyed life as a retired former gunman had he been facing a mirror while playing poker for the last time in a Deadwood saloon. He might have seen Jack McCall coming, or McCall may have decided to not make his play had he seen the eyes of Hickok fixed on him. Some have conjectured that saloon mirrors serve another purpose, helping customers stay calmer. According to this reasoning, as patrons imbibe, they can view themselves in the reflection, and perhaps this has the effect of calming them as they see their own face becoming angry and distorted during a confrontation. One Missouri newspaperman, named Arthur Aull, suggested another purpose of the mirrors when in 1910 he argued that they exist in saloons for the vanity of the male customer who likes to watch "himself across the bar." And, Aull contends, there were many opportunities to do so as "there are mirrors in front, behind, at the sides and everywhere." The workingman, Aull argues, loves to watch himself drink, and if the mirrors were not there, he proclaims "fifty per cent less liquor will be sold over the bar" (*Jasper News* 1910).

SMASHING MIRRORS

Mirrors have always been a fascination. Of course, everyone knows that breaking a mirror is a sure way to bring on bad luck. Early societies wondered if the mirror captures the soul, while others have believed that mirrors contain magical powers (Oliver 2009, 200). Perhaps saloon mirrors are the soul of the saloon. Anti-saloon women seem to have thought so, and from time to time they entered saloons and proceeded to shatter them. By far the most famous of the saloon mirror smashers was Carrie Nation of Kansas, who, after hearing the voice of God in 1900, decided that the Lord wanted her to begin a career smashing saloon fixtures, and mirrors became particularly susceptible to her wrath. On June 6 of that year, Nation entered Dobson's saloon in Kiowa, Kansas, proclaiming to poor Dobson and his bewildered customers, "Men, I have come to save you from a drunkard's grave," before unleashing a barrage of rocks, leaving the establishment's unsuspecting mirror a pile of shards of glass (Taylor 1966, 114–15). Her wrath against Kansas saloon keepers and their precious and fragile fixtures continued from there as Nation believed she could act with impunity. She had reason to believe so. First, God had told her to do it, and second, saloon keepers were operating in Kansas illegally since the state had become dry in 1881 (see Smith Bader 1986). Therefore, she believed that they could hardly appeal to authorities after she had wrecked their establishments.

It was reported in one incident in Wichita, just six months after her first smashing spree, that she smashed up that city's Carey Hotel, destroying "a mirror valued at $100" and a titillating painting titled *Cleopatra at Her Bath* valued at $300 (*Wheeling Daily Intelligencer* 1900). Carrie Nation would continue her campaign against saloons and their fixtures until her death in 1911. But until then her wrath knew no bounds, and she followed up her first attack on saloon fixtures with many more. For instance, some of her highlights include a return to Kiowa in November, where she busted up four saloons, breaking three mirrors, 211 glasses and bottles, and 13 gallons of beer and whiskey. In Enterprise, Kansas, in January, she attacked a saloon, breaking its mirror and 45 glasses and bottles and 11 gallons of beer and whiskey (*Omaha Daily*

Bee 1901). Her antics were reported far and wide, and she would inspire other women to carry on what she called "hatchetations" against saloon fixtures.

Kansas native Carrie Nation (1846–1911) posing with her trademark hatchet and Bible in 1900. Nation became the scourge of Kansas saloon keepers, as she took antisaloon rhetoric to a violent conclusion. Nation entered many a saloon with her hatchet and commenced to smashing it to pieces. Inspired by Nation, some other women took up her cause. (Bettmann/Getty Images)

Stories of women smashing saloon mirrors abounded, and many attributed these actions to Nation's inspiration. For instance, one 1904 incident that involved an angry saloon-mirror-smashing wife included in the headline that she "Carrie Nationizes Things at Pelican Saloon." The wife, one "Mrs. Burke," was angry when she discovered her husband inside the Pelican Saloon in Fort Scott, Kansas, "preparing to take a drink of whiskey." With this discovery, Burke was said to have flown "into a rage," which prompted her to grab a glass and throw it at the unsuspecting mirror, shattering it (*Fort Scott Weekly* 1904). Nearly a decade later, on January 17, 1913, Mrs. Annie Quinn entered Peter Balmes's Chicago saloon looking for her husband "with a brick in each hand." Her wrath resulted from what she claimed was the scorn of "the saloon men" who before this incident she had asked not to sell her husband alcohol. However, she realized that despite her request he had been drinking in Balmes's establishment since that morning, so as she remembered it, on entering the saloon, "I seemed to have the strength of a dozen men come to me." She screamed at Balmes, "You have shattered my home, now I'll shatter your mirror." She then hurled a brick at the $100-mirror behind the bar followed by a second as "glass shivered, split, and flew" (*Rock Island Argus* 1913). Perhaps at that moment a thousand pent-up frustrations were released as the crescendo of breaking glass must have sounded to her like the ringing of a thousand church bells. But for Balmes, who made a living selling alcohol to men like her husband, her rage was a costly thing, just another hazard of life behind the bar.

KEEPING ORDER FROM BEHIND THE BAR

It is easy to imagine a stunned Balmes as he witnessed Mrs. Quinn enter his establishment, threaten to damage it, and then begin hurling bricks at his precious mirror. During such a confrontation, his natural reaction would have been to take cover behind his bar, ducking down as the brickbats shattered the glass behind him. The bar may be the main social hotspot in the tavern, but its imposing bulk also provides a barrier between those who work behind it and their customers. When there is a problem, the bar can become a place of refuge, a foxhole in a sense, giving the term "behind the bar" a whole new meaning. As such, this term has appeared frequently in stories about saloon violence in which those seeking shelter in a bar fight or bar shootout have sought the space behind the bar as a place of protection. It is also common knowledge that many tavern keepers keep some sort of weapon behind the bar for use in a confrontation with an unruly customer or even a robber. There are a variety of weapons that can be found behind the bar, ranging from guns to blunt objects. One of the most famous and perhaps notorious of the latter is the "blackjack" or "sap." These are typically small, leather-covered clubs that are weighted in one end and take some skill to use properly. However, one of the most popular blunt objects for use behind the bar is the trusty baseball bat. In a recent *Daily News* interview with New York bartenders, one long-time bartender relayed that the bat is her barroom weapon of choice because one look at it and most would-be troublemakers think twice. As she explains, "It's like the lowest of the low-tech weapons. It's the handgun of the Stone Age. And it really works." A Brooklyn bartender relayed a story that emphasizes this point: "The one time I grabbed it, the guy just looked at me and realized: This is what's going on." On this quick reflection, the would-be troublemaker "decided it'd be better for him to turn around and walk out the door" (*New York Daily News* 2013). For most people working behind the bar, this is the most desired outcome.

Knowing that a bartender has access to a weapon behind the bar may, in some instances, defuse a situation, but this knowledge can also escalate a problem. For instance, in 1906, Max Miller shot J. F. Turley dead in an El Paso saloon called the Legal Tender. In a trope as old as time, Miller had walked into the saloon in a temper because he knew his wife was in there, and he believed she was being a bit too chummy with the other customers. In a fit of hurt and rage, Miller accused her in front of the other customers of "buying beer for every bum in the house." It is interesting to note that Miller was himself a saloon keeper who like most of his brethren had already had many run-ins with the law for violations ranging from staying open on Sundays to allowing gambling and minors in his establishment. So perhaps life as a barkeep had made Miller a bit more quick-tempered than he otherwise would have been. When Miller confronted the crowd about his wife's behavior, it seems that one customer, J. F. Turley, grew agitated and denied having engaged in any wrongdoing with Miller's wife, stating, "She didn't buy any drinks for me," followed by some choice adjectives directed at Miller. At this point Miller drew his gun and killed Turley. This would appear to be a fairly simple case of murder. But when Miller later laid out his defense, he argued that he shot Turley because he saw him trying to get behind the bar. Miller's argument was that he assumed that Turley was going for a weapon because, as everyone knew, "it was customary to keep a revolver on the work bench of a saloon under the bar" (*El Paso Herald* 1906).

Likewise, in a saloon in Anaconda, Montana, in the spring of 1898, bartender Robert Works killed a customer named Edward Daly when the latter went behind the bar during a dispute with Works, who had cut him off and refused to serve him any more drinks. Enraged by this, Daly went behind the bar to confront Works and to serve himself, at which point Works shot him at point-blank range. As was the case with Miller and Turley, one of the main defenses in the subsequent trial to justify the shooting was that Daly "went behind the bar." And just as Miller had known, pistols were often as common a tool of the saloon trade as shot glasses. Works argued that Daly knew the saloon kept a pistol lying behind the bar, and that if he did not get to it first then Daly might, and that would be the end of the bartender. So, Works's defense was that he feared for his life and shot Daly because he had no choice. Someone was going to get to the pistol first, and Works counted himself lucky that it was him. This defense was bolstered by testimony from others that put forth that Daly had threatened Works, promising to "throw him out from the bar." One witness for the defense stated that "all the defendant was guilty of was the exercise of a God-given right to defend himself against a violent and vicious attack from a young Hercules" (*Anaconda Standard* 1898). We can assume that on the night of this unfortunate incident Works had gone to his job just like any other night in hopes of earning a paycheck by serving drinks and perhaps some conversation. He could not have known that the evening would end with him behind bars facing a murder charge. In the end, despite Daly's reputation and Works's explanation for his actions, the latter was found by a jury to be guilty of manslaughter. He was sentenced to 10 years in prison (*Butte Daily Post* 1898; *Anaconda Standard* 1899).

Of course, unruly and even violent customers are an occupational hazard for those working behind the bar. While one moment all might be convivial, in the next a simple misperceived slight can lead to an outbreak of violence. As Ade puts it, the bartender "had to deal with assorted humanity and attune himself to all of the moods which overcame customers who went out of gear after the third round had been served." What may seem one moment to be a good time for all can suddenly turn violent, and even the calmest of customers can suddenly change. As a tavern keeper well knows, and as Ade put it, "drink had a way of transforming the timid shoe salesman into a noisy debater and bringing to him the delusion that he could overcome, in physical combat, either a brakeman or a blacksmith" (Ade 1931, 93). And, of course, dealing with an out-of-control customer typically falls on whoever is behind the bar. Tavern keepers have all sorts of strategies to deal with the problem, and as the above cases demonstrate, it is always best to deescalate a situation. One tavern keeper, Pete Frisch from Bloomington, Illinois, who retired in 1953, looked back on his career behind the bar, which began in 1900 and spanned the next 53 years, reminiscing about how he successfully dealt with difficult customers. Vilified by many, the typical saloon keeper was just another working-class individual struggling to get by. Frisch was a German immigrant who arrived in Bloomington at the age of 17 in 1890. He got by as a dishwasher but dreamed of bigger things, eventually becoming a bartender and later the owner of his own saloon, where he took pride in running a clean and orderly establishment where troublemakers were not tolerated. Frisch claimed that "nobody ever got too drunk in my place, and if a drunk came in I showed him the door." But from time to time someone would get out of control, and on such occasions he claims that he did not resort to calling the police. Instead, he relied primarily on his knowledge of the ways of working-class men. But he also maintained a physical means of keeping the peace in his establishment: his trusted friend that he referred to as "a persuader," which was the thick end of a pool cue that he kept behind the bar. However, the "persuader" seems to have never cracked a troublemaker's skull. Perhaps potential troublemakers just knew that the persuader was there, and they chose not to see what would happen if Frisch were to get it out. Others may have taken one look at it and decided to behave. After all, the intrepid barkeep claimed that he never had to use it, that he was "never forced to tap an unruly customer in the head." Apparently, the existence of the persuader and the belief that Frisch would use it was all it took because according to him "one look at the heavy bill . . . was enough to make a gentleman of the hardest-headed trouble maker" (*Pantagraph* 1953).

TAVERN KEEPING AND THE TROUBLE WITH LAW ENFORCEMENT

Frisch's pride in never having had to call the police would make sense to many tavern keepers. Since the first tavern opened, many in the business have had a complicated relationship with law enforcement. Undoubtedly, it is important for a bartender to know that the police are a phone call away should troubles arise that they are unable to deal with. However, there can be many downsides to calling in law enforcement. News that the police are on their way will undoubtedly lead to many customers choosing to leave post haste, and the sight of a police car in front of a tavern is a sure way to keep potential customers from entering. And of course no tavern wants a reputation for having frequent visits by cops. Essentially, people in various states of intoxication generally do not want to interact with law enforcement officials and will avoid places where they are known to be. A tavern keeper may need to call the police in some circumstances, but when officers enter taverns, having been called or not, what happens next is not always predictable. For instance, in 1967, a tavern keeper and one of his customers testified that police entered their San Antonio tavern and without warning hit another customer in the back of the head with a blackjack. We cannot know definitively why a police officer struck this man. Witnesses stated that the blow was unwarranted and that the victim was entering the establishment when he was struck from behind unaware (*Lubbock Avalanche-Journal* 1967). One thing that is certain, however, is that such incidents highlight the possible consequences when police enter a tavern. One such case, *Ybarra v. Illinois* (444 U.S. 85 1979), went all the way to the United States Supreme Court. At issue was an incident that occurred in 1976, when seven to eight police officers entered the Tap Tavern in Aurora, Illinois, in order to search the tavern and the bartender because they suspected that heroin was being sold on the premises. At the time there were 13 surprised customers in the tavern who suddenly found themselves up against the wall being patted down by officers. Police later argued that they were within their rights to conduct these pat-downs. However, the customers certainly did not expect that their patronage of the Tap Tavern would result in having their persons searched and their Fourth Amendment rights potentially violated.

We can consider two other incidents that further highlight the risks of having police officers enter a tavern. While in most states and many locales police are allowed to arrest those who display public intoxication, it seems that law enforcement has at times taken this practice to a new level. At 1:30 a.m. one morning in June 2009, for instance, Fort Worth police arrived in force at the Rainbow Lounge, a recently opened gay nightclub. Several police entered the establishment seeking intoxicated patrons, or so they claimed. Ultimately, they arrested six patrons on the charge of public intoxication. To be clear, these patrons were inside the establishment. One of those who suffered at the hands of overzealous law enforcement that evening was an army veteran who claimed that police "bulldozed" him through the crowd out to an awaiting paddy wagon. Another individual claimed that he was "slammed against a wall, elbowed, and fell on the ground." Because of the injuries he received, he spent a week in intensive care. After the fact, he was charged with public intoxication and assault (*Mother Jones* 2010). And it is not just Texas where such overzealous law enforcement actions take place. An American Broadcasting Corporation (ABC) news report noted in 2012 that Alaska law enforcement was beginning to step up its efforts to identify and arrest tavern patrons who display signs of intoxication, going so far as to send plainclothes officers into taverns to look for patrons who appear intoxicated. One Anchorage police officer justified the practice by arguing that alcohol is a huge factor in crimes committed in his state: "Alaska has a huge, huge alcohol problem. Most people in jail, whatever they did, their decision-making process was affected by alcohol" (*ABC News* 2012). Of course, most believe that a tavern should be a space where some level of intoxication is allowed. So, the idea that the police would arrest a person for being intoxicated in a tavern seems like a bad public relations choice if the police would like to maintain a good relationship with tavern keepers and their customers. As one bar owner quipped in regards to police looking for intoxicated patrons, he is fine with "police coming through" his establishment, but he does not believe that they are a better judge of who has been overserved and who has not, stating, "You can't tell me the cops know better who's drunk on premises [than we do]" (*ABC News* 2012). Certainly a customer would prefer to be cut off by his or her bartender rather than face an unknown outcome at the hands of police officers.

Stories of actions by law enforcement such as these do not tend to endear officers to some tavern owners, who on the one hand should be able to rely on law enforcement to assist them with unruly patrons, but on the other, fear what can happen if police appear in their establishment. Therefore, for many bartenders, it remains preferable to deal with difficult situations themselves. Those tending bar who deal with bad situations themselves run the risk of running afoul of the law if they lose control of the situation or their own tempers. Take the case of Charles Arnold, who kept a saloon in New York City and was charged with "felonious assault" in September 1874 after getting into an altercation with a customer. The customer, a butcher by the name of James Reilly, entered Arnold's establishment at 3:00 a.m. with "a friend named Edwards." We cannot know what state of intoxication Reilly and Edwards were in, but we do know that they were two working-class men looking for a place to drink at three o'clock in the morning, so it is a fairly safe bet that they may have already been in their cups before entering Reilly's establishment. After two glasses of beer, a confrontation ensued between Edwards and the proprietor. Of course, there was not a phone to pick up in 1874, so bartenders in that age had to rely on their own wit and moxie to deal with a situation. It seems that in the case of Edwards and Arnold, the latter lost his cool in this pursuit. Witnesses claimed that Reilly tried to intervene in order to cool things down between his friend and the saloon keeper. However, Arnold had a glass in his hand during the confrontation and chose to use it as a weapon on the alleged peacemaker, dealing "him three terrible blows on the head with the glass, inflicting very dangerous wounds." Arnold was arrested and, realizing that the future of his business was at stake, appears to have obfuscated and told the officers at the station house that he had assaulted Reilly in self-defense, but he later changed his story, explaining that he had not dealt vicious blows to Reilly at all but instead insisting that "Reilly had fallen against the end of the counter and so wounded himself" (*New York Times* 1874). Changing his story in this manner may seem comical, but we can imagine that as Arnold sat in the police station he began to realize just how high the stakes could be for him if the charge of felonious assault were to stick. His business and his livelihood, not to mention his freedom, were at stake after all.

Another aspect of dealing with the police has sometimes involved police corruption in the form of graft and even extortion. In 1962, Louis Lindinger, a Gary, Indiana, tavern owner, accused at least 12 local police officers of having taken bribes from him so that he could conduct gambling and after-hours alcohol sales. It is interesting to note that Lindinger kept detailed records of his weekly payments, which included cigars and liquor, so when he decided to out the officers he had been paying off he was certainly ready to prove his case. In what may have been revenge for having outed them, Lindinger's attorney charged that afterward the police raided the establishment and smashed merchandise. The police denied this (*Daily Reporter* 1962). For other examples of police shakedowns of tavern owners, one need look no further than Chicago, where stories regarding police corruption have been part of Chicago lore since 1855 when the department was founded (see Lindberg 1991 and Mitrani 2013). Stories of police officers shaking down tavern owners in the Windy City was commonplace knowledge, and in the early 1970s several high-profile scandals hit the news. In 1973, a Chicago police commander and several officers were accused of having shaken down several of that city's tavern owners. In all, the investigation into this incident returned a total of 39 indictments (*News Journal* 1973). Two years later, several Chicago tavern owners testified that they had to make routine monthly payoffs to the police for years in order to stay in operation. One tavern owner, a former police officer himself, testified that he had to make payments of $50 per month over the course of a year. Another testified that he had been making payments of $140 per month for five years, and he had recently been told that the payments would be raised to $200 (*Waxachacie Daily Light* 1975). Apparently, these incidents did not solve the problem of police shakedowns in Chicago. On December 17, 1984, a 52-year-old veteran police officer and his partner entered Carey's Lounge and Liquors in Chicago's Rogers Park neighborhood and discovered an underage drinker. Rather than make arrests, the officer decided to make some money, offering to look the other way if the tavern owner paid him $400. However, in what could be a scene from a sitcom, the brave tavern keeper told the officer that the amount he was proposing was a "ripoff" and counteroffered to pay $50. For him to have a sense of what amount constituted a "ripoff" tells us that he probably had experience dealing with this sort of scenario. He probably also knew of colleagues and similar situations that they had faced. After some haggling, they agreed to a payoff of $100. But, at some point after the exchange, apparently feeling uneasy or maybe even angry, the intrepid tavern owner reported the incident (*Chicago Tribune* 1986). This was bold on his part, considering the potential for a backlash from this officer or others.

THE LAW AS A WEAPON AGAINST THE TAVERN

A tavern keeper's relationship with local law enforcement is just one aspect of the many legal considerations he or she faces. The potential for lawsuits by customers or those harmed by customers is another constant threat. In recent decades, organizations such as Mothers Against Drunk Driving (MADD), founded in 1980 by a mother who had lost her child to a drunk driver, have been supporting tough dramshop liability laws that make it easier to sue alcohol servers for the actions of their customers, arguing that "this liability makes it in the economic interest of establishments to have responsible serving practices" (Mothers Against Drunk Driving, 1). However, such suits are not new. They have been the bane of tavern keepers since the 19th century when the temperance and anti-saloon movements sought to hold saloon keepers accountable for their customers' actions and perhaps drive saloons out of business in the process (see Blocker 1985).

The Bar of Destruction political cartoon by Thomas Nast (1874). This protemperance illustration shows Death as a bartender serving rum to a patron while two small children beckon from the doorway. This cartoon originally appeared in the March 21, 1874, edition of *Harper's Weekly*. (Library of Congress)

In the years before the Civil War, the war against intemperance and tavern keepers had begun its relentless forward march. Maine, for instance, banned saloons in the early 1850s, and if the expansion of slavery and the Civil War had not happened, it is possible that temperance and Prohibition would have gained an even stronger foothold in that decade (Furnas 1965, 209–10). With the end of the Civil War and the nation's expansion to the west, reformers once again turned their attention to the issue of alcohol, and the movement against it spread rapidly, taking off in the early 1870s. In 1873, the Woman's Christian Temperance Union spread like wildfire across the land. While temperance implied that adherents to the movement were relying on moral suasion to convince drinkers to willingly pledge to give up drinking, there was another side to the movement, which sought to use the law to assault the saloon. The promotion of dramshop laws was seen as one way to go after saloon keepers even if reformers could not force drinkers to stop drinking nor force saloon keepers to close their doors. By enabling lawsuits against saloon keepers, reformers hoped to bankrupt them, and they sometimes did. As a trade journal for saloon keepers in Chicago called *Fair Play* noted at the turn of the century, "The laws of this state governing the liquor trade are so severe that there is not a licensed saloon-keeper in Illinois that does not lay himself liable to prosecution under the law a dozen times each day" (Barker 1905, 61).

In Illinois, for instance, the state legislature and Governor John Palmer approved legislation in 1872 that placed a target squarely on saloon keepers. Many states passed similar legislation at this time as well. The Illinois law revised dramshop statutes to make it fairly easy to bring suit against a saloon keeper for damages. Many of the statutes also opened the door for saloon keepers to be arrested for infractions. Local communities also placed strict requirements on saloons that put saloon keepers in jeopardy every time they opened their doors and served customers. Consider for instance the saloon license issued in 1884 to John Weibel, a Bloomington, Illinois, saloon keeper. His license stipulated that he could keep his license as long as he did not "keep a disorderly house, or shall permit any Gaming therein, for money, liquors or any other valuable thing, or shall permit therein and playing at cards, dice, bagatelle, dominoes, or any other game whatsoever, for amusement or otherwise; then . . . this License shall become absolutely null and void" ("Saloon License Issued" 1884). Of course, what constituted a "disorderly house" was up to local government consideration. Weibel had to realize that his livelihood hung each day upon the whims of local officials whose strict stipulations laid traps that could be sprung at any time. Consider licenses issued to Aurora, Illinois, saloon keepers that required them to be closed on Sundays, election days, and other days stipulated by the mayor. They were also required to close at eleven o'clock at night, an early hour for many imbibers. Reminiscent of the strict laws placed on the keepers of taverns in Puritan New England, the behavior of Aurora's tavern customers was also tightly regulated. They were forbidden from permitting singing or dancing or any playing of musical instruments. They also faced the threat of losing their licenses if on their premises were found "any person . . . who is in the habit of getting intoxicated" (Aurora City Ordinances, June 16, 1902, Section 2 and June 15, 1903, Section 4). This last stipulation was a fairly common one and well demonstrates the potential pitfalls faced by saloon keepers who wanted to follow the law. It was, of course, difficult for saloon keepers and their bartenders to keep up with who in their communities was in the habit of getting intoxicated. But running afoul of this provision, and many others, could lead to jail time, fines, and the loss of a license. A Kentucky newspaper ran a piece in 1876 that sought to have a little fun with the concept of saloon keepers and their relationship to "known inebriates" by imagining a courtroom exchange between a lawyer and a saloon keeper on the witness stand charged with "selling drink to a known inebriate." First, asks the lawyer, "Is he a known inebriate?" "Don't know what you mean," answers the saloon keeper. "Does he drink whiskey?" asks the lawyer. "Yes, and every thing else," answers the saloon keeper. Well, "Is he a hard drinker?" asks the exasperated lawyer. "No," exclaims the saloon man, "he is the easiest drinker you ever seed. He could drink three times to any other man's one" (*Owensboro Examiner* 1876).

But, of course, such legal pitfalls were no laughing matter and frequently landed saloon keepers in serious trouble. Consider, for instance, a cold January morning in 1877 when several Joliet, Illinois, saloon keepers found themselves together in front of a judge facing a variety of charges with 15 of them having been charged with "selling intoxicating liquor on the first day of the week" (Sunday); for "dispensing intoxicating liquors on election day"; one for "selling intoxicating drink to an intoxicated person"; one for "selling intoxicating drink to a habitual drunkard"; five for "selling intoxicating liquors without a license"; and seven for "selling intoxicating drinks to a minor" (*Joliet Signal* 1877). Selling to minors either knowingly or unknowingly laid a trap for many saloon keepers. For instance, in the First Judicial District in the State of Oklahoma in the courthouse in Sallisaw in the first few days of May 1911 witnessed 27 saloon keepers being tried for making the mistake of serving minors (*Star-Gazette* 1911). Selling to a minor is considered a grave offense today, and today's tavern keepers and bartenders endeavor to avoid falling into this trap, but as many of the stories told above attest to, the best of strategies can still find one in the hot seat as will be further discussed below. Nowadays persistent and resourceful minors find ways to trick alcohol servers into serving them. But imagine trying to avoid serving minors in the days before modern, state-issued identification cards and when many young men worked in the same professions as other saloon customers. In Illinois and in many other states, the legal drinking age in the saloon period was 21, just as it is today.

To make matters worse, many an anti-saloon activist laid in wait for saloon keepers in order to catch them violating this law. For instance, in 1911, in Lincoln, Nebraska, one activist took a complaint to that city's police chief, stating that saloon keeper Frank Hollingworth, owner of a saloon called Bright Spot, had been seen selling alcohol to several minors, including 18 pints of Pabst Blue Ribbon beer on three different occasions to one minor under the age of 21 and three glasses of beer to another, but just one to 19-year-old Martin Flanagan (*Nebraska State Journal* 1911a). Later Hollingworth would have to sit in a courtroom as the three boys were called as witnesses against him. The question of how youthful the boys looked was addressed. Supposedly the first boy, who was 20, appeared "seemingly that old." While the other two, aged 17 and 19, were respectively described as "appearing fully that young" and "rather more youthful in appearance." All three boys testified that they had never actually bought alcohol from the saloon owner, Hollingsworth, but had made their purchases from his employees, his bartenders. On the stand, Hollingsworth, whose business was at stake, stated that had it been him behind the bar he never would have sold to the boys, while his three bartenders stated under oath that they had never served the youths, though one of them stated that the boys had indeed been seen in the saloon. Finally, one of the bartenders argued that the oldest of them looked like a man over the age of 21 and that he had stated that he was 23 (*Nebraska State Journal* 1911b). This detail hints that this bartender probably had served him. If, after all, the youth looked older and claimed to be 23, why would he have not served him? Ultimately, this incident put Hollingsworth's license on the line, and it was canceled for a time. The beleaguered saloon keeper would have to petition to get it back (*Lincoln Journal Star* 1911). For Hollingsworth, such an incident highlighted the precariousness of his ability to earn a living and support his family in a society that was increasingly at war with his profession. On the day that he walked out of the courtroom with his license suspended, he probably anticipated getting it back in time after a period of contrition and lost income. He could not know then, however, that in less than 10 years, the struggle against him and his brethren would put them out of business for good.

THE RAINES LAW

Perhaps the most notorious and certainly some of the strangest of the saloon-era dramshop laws were passed in New York state in 1896. In December of that year, as a direct result of this legislation, eight saloon keepers faced justice in criminal court in Buffalo, New York, for having violated the Raines Law. All pleaded not guilty, but all had to post a bail of $500, a hefty sum in 1896. They were caught in a sting operation by an undercover excise agent. Some were indicted for selling on Sunday, some for selling after hours, and one for selling to a minor (*Buffalo Evening News* 1896). They were the first of many who would fall prey to the Raines Law. This law was named after an anti-saloon New York legislator named John Raines who authored the legislation and celebrated its passage on March 3, 1896. This notorious set of regulations contained many provisions. The law raised the cost of saloon licenses, already one of many expensive burdens faced by saloon keepers. The law also prohibited the sale of alcohol on Sundays in saloons. Of course, this was the one day that workingmen had off, and this provision was clearly aimed at keeping them out of the saloons and perhaps sober on the Sabbath. An anti-saloon publication noted this, stating that for saloon keepers, "the week-day trade [was] merely sufficing to pay expenses." It was the Sunday trade especially that brought in the profits (Committee of Fifteen 1905, 2). It is clear that the law was not simply aimed at better regulating saloons but rather at putting saloon keepers out of business. Raines himself admitted that one purpose of the law was to reduce the number of establishments through high taxes and regulations (Raines 1896, 483). In 1908, an anti-saloon commission, the Committee of Fourteen, could report that as a result of the law's enforcement, 450 establishments had been put out of business, and they were in the process of targeting 600 more (*New York Tribune* 1908).

However, the New York saloon endured, and saloon keepers thwarted the law as much as possible. Much to the chagrin of reformers, a 1908 report noted that a majority of saloons, in fact most of them, were violating the Raines Law and serving alcohol on Sundays (Lerner 2007, 25). The law may have been an attempt to more strictly regulate saloons and curb working-class drinking, but it is also a great example of the law of unintended consequences. The statute did allow for hotels to continue to serve alcohol on Sundays as long as the establishment had at least 10 beds and as long as the alcoholic drinks were served along with food (Lerner 2007, 25). The goal in allowing this was to avoid targeting already existing hotels that served alcohol when the law went into effect. These exceptions provided a large loophole that many saloon keepers drove right through. The famous muckraker Jacob Riis wrote in 1902 that saloon keepers openly mocked the law, noting for instance that some saloon keepers set out "brick sandwiches," which consisted of "two pieces of bread with a brick between." Saloon keepers did this, states Riis, "in derision of the state law which forbids the serving of drinks [without food present]" (Riis 1902, 224).

Further, the requirement that establishments serving drinks have at least 10 beds simply led saloon keepers to put 10 beds or bedlike structures in some part of their saloon. As Riis notes, some of these new beds served as places for impoverished men to find a place to sleep, but in some cases they simply furthered opportunities for prostitution, or as Riis puts it, such setups were "chiefly used for purposes of assignation" (Riis 1902, 224). An anti-saloon tract noted this in 1902, arguing that there was a clear connection between "the 'Raines Law hotel' and professional vice." In fact, this tract argues that the Raines Law made prostitution a much worse problem since the marriage of beds and saloons gave women plying the trade an easy and logical place to do so. This reform-minded tract writer laid out a scenario to help readers understand how this arrangement, made possible by the saloon keeper, could entrap the unsuspecting saloon customer who, he argues, generally enters a saloon "to drink his glass of beer and to listen to the bad music and worse jokes." Once in the saloon, this unwary workingman might then become unwittingly "subject to solicitation which has the appearance of a mere flirtation." Then, perhaps weakened by drink, this individual may succumb to temptation: he may "feel he did not seek vice, but was overcome by circumstances." This is, after all, a fellow that typically "would hesitate to enter a brothel, but now finds himself 'easily 'victimized' in the Raines Law hotel." It is interesting to note that this middle-class moralist went after the saloon and its keepers because he cared so much about the fate of the seemingly naïve workingman, who, after all, he claimed is just one of many "such moral imbeciles" (Committee of Fifteen 1905, 3). So, a law that was meant to curb immoral behavior became, just a few years after its passage, a law that encouraged immoral behavior. Of course, it was claimed, this was only made possible by the trickery of the wily saloon keeper.

THE DIFFICULTIES REMAIN

Things have changed a great deal since the great saloon age, but running a tavern today is still a difficult business. Startup costs can range from nearly $200 to over $800,000, and then there can be recurring high licensing fees and insurance, the cost of staff, and many other routine expenses (Tarver 2018). As with the saloon age, there are many pitfalls in the tavern trade that can turn just another night of business into a tavern-closing event. Some of the biggest issues faced by tavern keepers still include the risk of serving underage drinkers, being held accountable for "overserving" a customer, and accidents or acts of violence that occur on the tavern's property. The potential for such events places a burden on tavern owners to carry expensive insurance, and many tavern owners carry multiple policies ranging from general liability insurance to liquor liability insurance, also known as dramshop insurance. Such policies cost thousands of dollars a year, and needing them illustrates the risks that come with operating a business that serves alcohol (King 2016).

Being held accountable for overserving customers is a serious issue for tavern owners and their servers. The Texas Alcoholic Beverage Code, for instance, "requires sellers and servers to refuse alcoholic beverage service to intoxicated persons and minors." Texas law stipulates that a server may be held accountable if at the time he or she serves "the individual being sold, served, or provided with an alcoholic beverage was obviously intoxicated to the extent that he presented a clear danger to himself and others" (Texas Alcoholic Beverage Commission 2017). For a tavern owner, such an arrest or fine is a major issue, but the burden of following this law can also fall heavily on his or her staff. Serving alcohol in a restaurant or tavern tends to be a low-paying profession. However, servers have a great deal of responsibility placed on them to pay close attention to the behavior of their customers and notice when a customer is displaying signs of intoxication and then tell that individual that he or she can have no more to drink. Such a decision is potentially awkward for a server who is employed at the whim of the tavern's owner, and the ensuing encounter is a fairly certain way to offend a customer and therefore end up without a tip. And since in many states employers of servers who receive tips are allowed to pay well below minimum wage, such a threat is a real problem for one's livelihood. There is also the conundrum of trying to figure out who has indeed been overserved. If overserved means showing public signs of intoxication, many tavern patrons display such signs. It is interesting to note that when law enforcement accuses an individual of being intoxicated, there is an expectation that they must demonstrate that the accused individual is indeed intoxicated by giving him or her a field sobriety test and a breathalyzer test. However, a server is expected to make this decision based solely on his or her instincts and observations.

The cost for not noticing or not acting on these instincts and observations can be devastating for those who serve. For instance, in the fall of 2013, a 48-year-old man, Sammy Ford, was walking home from a bar in Tulsa, Oklahoma, at one o'clock in the morning when he was struck and killed by two different drivers, neither of whom were charged. However, two servers from the tavern in which he had been drinking were charged with felonies for having overserved Ford. They claimed that the deceased did not appear intoxicated when he left their place of work. Maybe he appeared obviously intoxicated, and maybe he did not. Maybe the establishment he was drinking in was really packed that evening, and the two servers were too busy with multiple customers to notice how intoxicated he was. It is interesting to note that servers are responsible for keeping tabs on their customers' levels of intoxication, but tavern keepers are generally not responsible for keeping the ratio of servers to customers low enough so that the former can keep better tabs on the latter. What we do know is that two poorly paid women, who had no previous criminal record, were slapped with felony charges (Fullbright 2014). In a similar case, a 22-year-old server, Anthony Helsley, himself barely old enough to drink legally, was arrested in Greenfield, Indiana, in the summer of 2017 for "sales to intoxicated persons and violation of alcohol server criteria" (Steele 2017). What turned out to be a terrible incident in a young person's life occurred because one of the bar's customers died in a vehicle crash along with one of his passengers. Another passenger sustained injuries. A subsequent investigation revealed that just before the crash they had been drinking at Ro's Bar and Grill, where it was determined that Helsley had served them (Steele 2017). Ultimately, after being arrested, having his mugshot taken, and forever having this incident recorded on the World Wide Web, Helsley was sentenced to probation after pleading guilty to a Class B misdemeanor (VanOverberghe 2018).

Besides worrying about overserving customers, servers have to be concerned about the ages of those they serve. Across the United States, with some exceptions, the legal drinking age is 21 years old. It is ironic that 18-year-olds are adults in nearly every way: they have the right to marry, vote, join the military, and so forth; however, they cannot enter a tavern and consume alcohol. It was not always this way. During much of the 20th century, several states and locales allowed people under the age of 21 to drink. However, in 1984, Congress passed the National Minimum Drinking Age Act, which required all states to raise the minimum drinking age to 21. Many argued that such decisions should be left up to the states, and it is interesting that President Ronald Reagan, who claimed to be a strong supporter of states' rights, very much approved of and pressured states to comply with the law. Prior to the law's passage, the General Accounting Office claimed that there were 19 states that did not have a minimum drinking age of 21. The method of forcing compliance was to threaten to withdraw a portion of federal highway funds from states that did not comply (Alcohol Problems and Solutions n.d.). Many, however, did resist such pressure. For instance, two years after the law was passed, the Washington, DC, city council reluctantly decided to comply. Council chairman David A. Clarke noted, "We are doing it because we have to do it." Even at that point, however, there were still seven states that were holdouts (Evans 1986).

For those serving alcohol, knowing who is of legal age and who is not can be a tricky endeavor, and those who get caught serving underage patrons face legal ramifications that can range from fines to arrest. In Illinois, for instance, it is a Class A misdemeanor to "sell, serve, deliver or give alcoholic beverages to a person under 21 years of age or to any intoxicated person" (Spielman 2017). Fines for doing so range between $500 and $2,500 and can lead to a jail sentence of up to a year. It is interesting to note that in many states, such as Illinois, persons between the ages of 18 and 20 can serve alcohol, meaning that they are responsible for checking the identifications of potential patrons and turning away those who might be their same age (Spielman 2017). Of course, the tavern owner faces the prospect that a violation in his or her establishment can result in a fine or his or her liquor license being suspended or revoked. Such was the case for

Pappy's Grill and Sports Bar in Berkeley, California, which lost its liquor license in early 2018 for selling alcohol to minors. Following this incident, one walking past what appears to be a popular college bar in a town known for its prestigious university would have seen the following notice posted on the door: "Notice of Suspension: Alcoholic Beverage Licenses Issued for These Premises Have Been Suspended By Order of the State Department of Alcoholic Beverage Control Act." From this notice and the consequences faced by the owner, one might assume that Pappy's was a flagrant violator of laws regarding the serving of minors. However, Pappy's license was suspended because the establishment's staff "sold alcohol to minors on three separate occasions within a three-year period." A quick glance at Pappy's website tells a story of a college bar where young college students and other young twentysomethings go to have a fantastic time. So a busy college bar that must have seen thousands of young people come in and out of its proverbial swinging doors lost its license for having made the mistake of serving an average of one underage customer per year.

Another Berkeley establishment that advertises itself as a "taqueria and bar" had a similar problem in 2017 when agents with the California Alcoholic Beverage Control witnessed underage patrons who used fake identifications being served. As a result of this infraction, the business paid a $3,000 fine. Later in the year, a similar incident resulted in the establishment's license being suspended for 25 days, an eternity for a business that relies on revenue from liquor sales. As Shuchi Rana, the co-owner of another Berkeley establishment, the Café Durant, laments, "We're doing everything in our power (to adhere to ABC guidelines)" (Mayes 2018). And it only makes sense that this statement is true. Profits from knowingly serving minors could hardly outweigh the risks involved with knowingly serving them. As Rana further states, "As a small business, everything impacts us in a big way" (Mayes 2018). Café Durant claims they have taken several precautions to avoid such problems in the future, including purchasing flashlights that help determine the validity of an identification and more regular table checks. But in reality, even if servers follow all possible precautions, a good fake identification or a server that is too busy to catch an underage patron can lead to disaster (Mayes 2018).

While tavern owners can experience fines, the loss of their liquor license, and even closure, serving underage drinkers is hazardous for their employees who serve alcohol. Consider the story above of Anthony Helsley, who was arrested and convicted for having overserved patrons at his place of employment. It is important to note that at the time he was the only server on duty. It is unknown how many other customers he had on that fateful night, but what we do know is that at the young age of 22 a possibly overworked and probably poorly paid Helsley likely had a lot on his plate. Another of his responsibilities, besides monitoring who should be cut off, would have been to check identifications and make sure that no one who was underage was being served. Those who are underage and attempting to be served are trying, in many cases very hard, to fool their potential server. Of course, the consequences for being fooled or for missing an underage customer that is being served can be severe. In the summer of 2011, six bartenders were arrested from three different establishments in Southampton, New York, after a police investigation into the serving of minors. The way the investigation was conducted was that an "agent" showed fake identification for the purpose of being served. It seems that this agent was served because at one establishment, called 75 Main, two servers, one aged 22 and the other 20, were arrested and charged with "unlawfully dealing with a child in the first degree." At another establishment a little later, called Dream Nightclub, three more bartenders, aged 19, 22, and 34 were arrested for the same offense (Reynolds 2011). It is easy to imagine that being splashed on the internet, potentially for the rest of one's life, for the stated offense of "unlawfully dealing with a child in the first degree" could cause future problems. It is hard to imagine that most of these individuals were planning to make a career of serving alcohol in a bar, but one thing for certain is that their future career prospects will forever be tainted by this charge. It is easy to simply dismiss this by arguing that they should have been more careful, but anyone who has ever been in a crowded drinking establishment with harried servers should be able to understand the challenges they face.

DRAMSHOP LAWSUITS

Legal trouble that involves a threat to one's license, arrest, or fines is just one aspect of the tavern business. Another facet that can be just as destructive to one's business is the threat of dramshop lawsuits. These lawsuits, which stem from statutes found in most states, entitle those who have been harmed by an intoxicated person to seek monetary damages against those parties who supplied alcohol to the intoxicated person. According to Carl Bogus, a professor at Roger Williams University School of Law, these lawsuits have grown "exponentially" in number since the 1970s (Bogus 2001, 144). This rise coincides with the rise of MADD and its pursuit of reducing drunk driving. Typical of these laws is Vermont's statute, which reads as follows:

> Action for damages. A spouse, child, guardian, employer or other person who is injured in person, property or means of support by an intoxicated

> person, or in consequence of the intoxication of any person, shall have a right of action in his or her own name, jointly or severally, against any person or persons who have caused in whole or in part such intoxication by selling or furnishing intoxicating liquor. ("Vermont Dram Shop and Social Host Liability Laws" Statute 7 V.S.A. 501)

Of course, the intoxicated individual who harms another is usually held accountable for his or her actions, but such broad language in these statutes opens the tavern keeper up to potential lawsuits, and it is easy to understand why some might develop a dislike of the legal profession. In 1875, a trade book for the saloon-keeping profession remarked that it is the very nature of tavern keepers that makes them susceptible to the wiles of errant attorneys. According to this guide, it is "because the saloon keeper is a jolly, easy-going fellow, free with his money" that attorneys "always consider him a legitimate source of prey" (Newton 1875, iii). A tavern keeper knows that on any given day he enters his tavern he has to wonder if that will be the night that a patron engages in behavior that will lead to a ruinous lawsuit. Take the tragic case, for instance, of the untimely death of 18-year-old Jane Emily Clymer, a junior at the University of Vermont, when on September 14, 1985, she was struck and killed by a drunk driver in Burlington, Vermont, while walking her bike by the side of the road. The driver of the vehicle was intoxicated at the time and had been drinking at the Rotisserie and Wesson's Family Diner. This case set a legal precedent in Vermont by allowing for the collection of punitive damages under the state's dramshop statutes. Ultimately, the establishment's owners had to pay $250,000 in damages. Of course, the driver was held accountable as well, serving 30 months in prison (*New York Times* 1992). But this fact would have done little to assuage the monetary damage done to the owner's business. As with checking identifications, the responsibility to keep tabs on those being served alcohol typically falls on the tavern owner's employees. They may be dependent on their employer for their livelihoods, but the owner is entirely dependent on them to make sure his livelihood is not threatened in a court of law.

Even when servers take what seem like sensible precautions to avoid disaster, things can still take a tragic turn and cost their employer dearly. Take the 2010 case of Matt and Meredith Eastridge, whose paths crossed with 25-year-old David Huffman, who was traveling at 100 miles per hour when he struck the Eastridges, causing Meredith to lose a pregnancy that was in the sixth month. Huffman had become intoxicated after a visit to Eddie's Place, a tavern in Charlotte, North Carolina. Granted, Huffman was intoxicated, and the attorney that represented the owners of Eddie's Place admits that he had been served 10 drinks in just over two hours.

However, according to the attorney, the staff took precautions to make sure that Huffman would not drive. One of the employees organized a ride for Huffman with another patron. However, according to the attorney, "He accepted it and then went and drove his own car anyway." As a result of the tragedy, the Eastridges received a very large settlement against Eddie's Place totaling $1.7 million. This amount was awarded despite the fact that the tavern, according to the attorney representing its owners, had never in the establishment's 15-year history been cited for an alcohol-related violation. Also, the attorney further pointed out, the Mecklenburg County Alcoholic Beverage Control Board had concluded that Huffman had no longer been served alcohol after he showed signs of being visibly intoxicated (Copeland 2012).

One of the problems with using observational cues to decide when to cut someone off is that everyone reacts differently to the effects of intoxication. It is possible that Huffman was intoxicated but not showing blatant outward signs of being intoxicated. For instance, the Oregon Liquor Control Commission (OLCC) has put out an exhaustive list called "50 Signs of Visible Intoxication" to help servers. The OLCC breaks these signs into five categories: appearance, speech, attitude, behavior, and other, which includes "excessive perspiration." The list has some rather commonsense cues, such as bloodshot eyes, slurred speech, being obnoxious, and swaying. How someone reacts to alcohol is in part based on one's tolerance level. Everyone is born with a certain tolerance level, and this level can increase if one routinely drinks more than two or three drinks at a time (Alleyne 2008). Increased tolerance means that an individual might be intoxicated but not show the kind of outward signs of intoxication that a server learns about when being trained to spot an intoxicated person. Tolerance is not how much a person can drink but how he or she reacts and behaves at different levels of intoxication. For instance, two customers might be sitting together having a good time, while each consumes a six-pack of beer. However, afterward, one of them is showing the kind of signs described above, while the other one might still look like a sober individual who is in control of his behavior. The bartender where they are drinking might feel obligated to cut off and call a taxi for the visibly intoxicated of the two while continuing to serve the other. But it might be the person not exhibiting outward signs of intoxication that gets into an accident that results in a lawsuit against the establishment that he had been drinking in. Busy bartenders are expected to know and pay attention to such things.

Such a reality calls into question the efficacy of relying on visible signs of intoxication to know when to cut someone off. However, taverns are in the business of selling drinks to customers. The more drinks sold on any given evening, the more profits in the till. Also, most people do not want to frequent a tavern where they can expect to be cut off when they want to order more drinks and are not showing blatant outward signs of intoxication. Many who criticize dramshop laws that allow tavern keepers to be sued based on the behavior of their customers argue that such lawsuits diminish the idea of personal responsibility for one's actions. Under such laws, tavern keepers are at risk of losing their businesses by serving a legal product to adult customers, some of whom might behave irresponsibly after having consumed that product. As the attorney for Eddie's Place, Rick Pinto, argues, such laws are too vague and confusing and place an onerous burden on tavern owners. Referring to North Carolina's dramshop statutes, Pinto argues, "The Law is, you can't serve someone who is visibly intoxicated when you have cause to believe they are going to drive." However, he further argues, such a requirement places too much of a burden on taverns: "It's not our duty to make sure no one ever leaves a restaurant with more than .08 alcohol in their system. That's not what the law is. But that may be what the jury decided." And a decision along these lines by a North Carolina jury resulted in a ruinous verdict for Pinto's client (*USA Today* 2012). Professor Bogus argues that dramshop lawsuits have been effective in reducing the overall number of drunk driving deaths, and that is, of course, a good thing. However, it has been low-paid, often overworked employees and struggling businesspeople who have often paid a high price for this common good (Bogus 2001, 144).

WOMEN BEHIND THE BAR

Much has changed in the business during the several decades following the rollback of National Prohibition and the return of the legal tavern. Throughout this book, the vast majority of examples have featured male tavern keepers and patrons. This is because for much of the tavern's history men have dominated the business and the barroom. As was discussed in the last chapter, women customers have become a common presence in the barroom in recent decades. This has also been the case for those working behind the bar. The mustachioed, slightly potbellied, and aproned male bartender of the saloon age has been replaced in many instances with a much younger female bartender, a sight that most patrons now take for granted. During the colonial period, women could often be found behind the bar as many establishments were family affairs and the entire family pitched in as staff. Many also ran their own taverns. As an expert on colonial Williamsburg notes, widows were a common feature of colonial life, and many could be found running taverns (Woodward 1994). However, during the 19th century, bartending became more of a man's world. In the Gilded Age, women were barred, sometimes by force of law, from working behind the bar, but in most cases they were simply excluded by custom. This explains, for instance, why the good citizens of Omaha, Nebraska, were shocked to learn in 1898 that a local establishment had violated this unwritten rule and "had hired a female bartender as a drawing card." This revelation resulted in a new rule, passed by the city's excise board, which banned female bartenders (*Omaha Daily Bee* 1898). It was rare to find a female bartender in the great saloon age, but there were some. It was reported, for instance, in one press account that in 1904 in the entire state of Indiana, there were 27 female saloon owners and 44 female bartenders (*Oakland Tribune* 1904).

It has been estimated that between 1900 and 1940, just 2 percent of bartenders were women, and after National Prohibition ended, many locales banned women from serving as bartenders (Hurt 2017). Some argued that women's reputations should be protected. Others argued that women were simply being used in taverns to entice men to spend more of their hard-earned money. Labor leaders expressed another concern, echoed in 1936 by Edward Fiore, president of the Bartenders' International Union in Salt Lake City, who stated simply that "female sudslushers are a menace to our profession" (*Ogden Standard-Examiner* 1936). In the fall of 1941, on the eve of the United States' entry into World War II, the city council of Freeport, Illinois, banned female bartenders by a vote of 11 to 2 (*Freeport Journal-Standard* 1941). World War II opened many doors to women to work in new professions. Some of them found working opportunities behind the bar as many men put down the apron and took up arms to fight for their country. Nonetheless, even during the war, many men continued to oppose women as bartenders. In 1943, the Springfield Federation of Labor took an official stand against female bartenders "and urged that all union members shun taverns employing lady drink-mixers" (*Decatur Daily Review* 1943). Following the war, the millions of men who had served in uniform began the process of returning to civilian life. When the veterans sought to return to their old professions, they often pushed women out of the way, and this included female bartenders. Hugo Ernst, president of the Hotel and Restaurant Employees and Bartenders International, reflected this sentiment in 1946 when he proclaimed, "Tending bar is a man's job" (*Freeport Journal Standard* 1946, 1). Unions were looking out for their members, but since they had actively sought to keep women from bartending, their membership was male, so when they sought to protect union bartending jobs, they were protecting male jobs. Typical of this effort was Local 588 of the Bartenders International League of America, which lobbied Champaign, Illinois, city council to ban female bartenders in 1946, arguing on moral grounds that "actions between male and female bartenders and customers of the bar are deleterious to the reputation of the tavern and reflect on the standards the union makes an effort to maintain" (*Freeport Journal-Standard* 1946). In fact, many localities continued to ban women from working as bartenders for several decades after the war. For instance, in 1971, Waukesha, Wisconsin, still banned women and those under the age of 21 from being bartenders, despite passage of the landmark 1965 Civil Rights Act that banned gender discrimination in employment. In that city it took the head of the Waukesha County Tavern League to bring a suit against the city in order to have the ordinance overturned (*Waukesha Daily Freeman* 1971). Such laws were eventually rolled back throughout the country, and today it is likely that a tavern customer will have a female bartender as it is estimated that around 60 percent of today's bartenders are women (Hurt 2017).

"I'M HERE FOREVER"

As the prevalence of women behind the bar demonstrates, much about tending bar has changed, but much has also stayed the same. For the most part, the role of the person behind the bar has remained eternal. Sure, the number of drinks has grown exponentially, particularly types of shots. But still, in many establishments, typical customers order fairly simple drinks such as beer or maybe a rum and Coke. Some mix it up with their customers, and some just mix drinks. For some, life behind the bar is a temporary job, perhaps just a gig during youth to help pay for college or until something better comes along. For others, however, life behind the bar is a lifetime profession. We began this chapter considering the remarkable life and career of legendary tavern owner Bernard "Toots" Shor. We will end by considering the amazing career of Patty Ford, who was interviewed in 2015 by Corey Kilgannon and featured in a *New York Times* article. At the age of 61, Ford reminisced that his long working life behind the bar had been more adventurous than arduous. In describing his career to Kilgannon, he mused, "I've never worked a day in my life." By 2015, the 61-year-old had been laboring as a bartender for over 40 years, working at the same establishment, Smith and Wollensky, in Manhattan for the previous 30 of those years. Ford notes that he began in the profession at the age of 17 and has never looked back with regret since taking his current union bar job with benefits three decades prior. Now, so many years later, he notes, "I'm the last of an era of career bartenders who chose it as a lifelong vocation." Ford is beloved by his customers, who have supported him as he has battled cancer while continuing to carry on as their bartender. Now, he wants them and the world to know that in life and as their bartender, "[he has] swung with both fists." And, "I tell my customers, 'I'm here forever' " (*New York Times* 2015).

EPILOGUE

> Taverns are the places where madness is sold by the bottle.
>
> —Jonathan Swift (Day 1884, 926)

The human penchant for seeking intoxication and sociability are timeless desires, and the nexus of these desires is found in the tavern. As George Ade noted near the end of Prohibition, the attempt to wipe out these two mainstays through force of law had proven to be a Sisyphean effort, so that by 1931 when *Old-Time Saloon* was published, he could confidently write: "EVEN the most ardent Dry will admit that it is almost impossible to eradicate the daily habits, the social customs and the time-honored practices which have been in evidence and tolerated for centuries—merely by taking a couple of roll-calls in Congress and saying, 'Presto, change!'" The tavern has always been there, in most societies, and in most periods of time, or as Ade puts it: "History does not go back far enough to uncover any period during which the wine-imbiber could not find a 'Welcome' sign in front of some cool retreat within which he could bib as long as his bronze coins held out" (Ade 1931, 62).

This book has explored the role of the tavern in society by focusing on the institution as one of the primary spaces where people have always socialized and interacted with others: close friends, casual acquaintances, and strangers. A prominent focus of this effort has centered on some of the physical features of the tavern. As an eternal institution, the basic features

A cage bar in the tap room of the John Atkinson Tavern, originally located in Prescott, Massachusetts, ca. 1933. Early taverns often featured a cage bar, typically constructed with wooden slats, in which a bartender could enter the cage through a door and raise the front of the cage in order to serve drinks. (Library of Congress)

of the tavern have remained consistent. From the earliest taverns in which bartenders served alcohol from behind cage bars to the taverns we recognize today where bartenders still hand customers drinks from behind bars, the tavern is still essentially an open space where people mingle and drink. In a sense, everything else that a tavern offers is just extra. Ade quipped that if someone had seen one saloon, he had seen them all, and for the most part he was right (Ade 1931, 28). Throughout time, the exterior has undergone changes. Signs have gone from a simple wooden board affixed to a post to flashier neon signs. Storefronts have evolved from those that resembled residences and later the archetypal false-front architecture of the Old West to today's taverns, which come in a variety of different physical appearances. But no matter the architecture or the quality of the signage, a tavern almost always has an obvious presence. The nature of life behind the bar has fluctuated. Early tavern keepers were respected community members who provided important services. Saloon-age tavern keepers were vilified by large swaths of society as men responsible for the ruin of their fellow man. Today, fewer people disapprove of the profession. Tavern owners have once again become just like most other small business owners. The tools of the trade have changed minimally. The biggest change, refrigeration, came to the industry in the late 19th century, and over time tavern keepers adapted. But if we consider the items found behind the bar in that age and those used by a modern bartender, such as Patty Ford, we would not see many differences.

The reasons people have sought out taverns has not changed much either. However, in the modern age, some factors related to tavern patronage have changed. For instance, there are risks related to driving while intoxicated. Patrons choose to leave the comfort of their homes to pay perhaps three times more for a beer or other alcoholic beverage at a tavern than they would pay at a store. While enjoying that beverage in a tavern, a patron must be mindful of not having too many if he or she intends to drive home. According to the Foundation for Advancing Alcohol Responsibility, 29 percent of vehicle-related fatalities in 2017 were a result of alcohol-impaired driving (Foundation for Advancing Alcohol Responsibility n.d.). According to the Centers for Disease Control and Prevention, more than a million drivers were arrested for being under the influence. But that represented just 1 percent of the 111 million Americans that self-reported that they had driven under the influence (Centers for Disease Control and Prevention 2017). A great many of those incidents would have involved drivers leaving taverns. Despite such costs, inconveniences, and risks, the tavern business has continued to thrive. As in the age of National Prohibition, people still seek the social glass where they can find it.

As discussed in the introduction, the tavern continues to thrive while so many other institutions where Americans socialize are diminishing in number and influence. This reflects Robert Putnam's thesis that fewer Americans are joining voluntary associations that result in face-to-face interactions with people they may not already know well. Certainly, the advent of the internet and social media has led more people to feel they are having these types of interactions online. As Jacob Silverman notes in his 2015 study of social media, socializing is the main activity that happens on the Web, and as he writes, "few aspects of contemporary life have gone unaffected by this shift." Silverman describes one aspect of this shift as "the lure of constant connection" (Silverman 2015, ix). I certainly see this phenomenon as a college professor. I frequently walk into my classroom a few moments before class begins to find that students are in no way interacting with one another. Instead, most are intently interacting with their smartphones. I then struggle to keep them off these devices during class. And many of them tend to immediately get back on them the moment I tell them class is over. While face-to-face social interactions may increasingly be a casualty of societal shifts, it is true that there are still public spaces where such social interactions continue to take place. Maybe one day I will walk into my classroom and say, "Put down the phones. Go have an authentic experience. Go to a tavern." In fact, I know the perfect song to play for them in order to explain why. Perhaps no piece of literature or music has ever captured the essence and allure of the tavern as well as Billy Joel did in his timeless 1973 ballad, "The Piano Man." Joel reminds us that if we are feeling nostalgic, if we are seeking human interaction, if we would like to "forget about life for a while," there is a place for that. Whenever these desires arise, the tavern will be there.

BIBLIOGRAPHY

Abbott, Karen. 2008. *Sin in the Second City: Madams, Ministers, Playboys and the Battle for America's Soul*. New York: Random House.

Ackerley, C. J. 2010. *Demented Particulars: The Annotated Murphy*. Edinburgh: Edinburgh University Press.

Adamson, Melitta Weiss, and Francine Segan, eds. 2008. *Entertaining from Ancient Rome to the Super Bowl: An Encyclopedia*. Westport, CT: Greenwood.

Addams, Jane. 1896. "The Settlement." In *Proceedings* 1:54–58. Illinois State Conference of Charities and Correction. Jane Addams Memorial Collection, University Library, University of Illinois at Chicago, Jane Addams Papers, Microfilm Reel 46-0738-0742.

Ade, George. 1931. *The Old Time Saloon*. New York: Ray Long and Richard R. Smith.

Alcohol Problems and Solutions. n.d. "National Minimum Drinking Age Act of 1984." Accessed April 8, 2017. https://www.alcoholproblemsandsolutions.org/YouthIssues/1092767630.html.

Aldrete, Gregory S. 2008. *Daily Life in the Roman City*. Norman: University of Oklahoma Press.

Allen, Eric. 1960. "Oldtimer Recalls Wild Days of Corner Saloon." *Ada Weekly News*, November 10, 1960.

Alleyne, Richard. 2008. "Scientists Identify Alcohol Tolerance Gene." *Telegraph* (UK), December 8, 2008.

Almeida, Celia. 2017. "The Ten Best Ladies' Nights in Miami." *Miami New Times*, July 26, 2017. https://www.miaminewtimes.com/music/the-ten-best-ladies-nights-in-miami-9518828.

Anaconda Standard. 1898. "The Jury Is Still Out." Anaconda, MT, April 22, 1898, 7.

Anaconda Standard. 1899. "What Happened in Montana in 1898." Anaconda, MT, January 1, 1899, 24.

Anbinder, Tyler. 2001. *Five Points: The Nineteenth Century New York City Neighborhood*. New York: Simon and Schuster.

Angus, Keith, ed. 1880. *The Sportsman's Year-Book for 1880*. London: Cassell, Petter, Galpin.

Arthur, T. S. 1854. *Ten Nights in a Barroom*. Philadelphia: J. W. Bradley.

Asbury, Herbert. 1927a. *The Gangs of New York: An Informal History of the Underworld*. New York: Vintage Books.

Asbury, Herbert. 1927b. "The Old Time Gangs of New York." *American Mercury*, August, 478–86.

Associated Press. 2017. "Man Wounded in Shooting during Fight in Tombstone Saloon." October 14, 2017. https://www.businessinsider.com/ap-man-wounded-in-shooting-during-fight-in-tombstone-saloon-2017-10.

Aurora Daily Beacon News. 1917. Aurora, IL, July 1, 1917, 3.

Aurora Daily Beacon News. 1932. "Now and Then." Aurora, IL, November 27, 1932.

Bacon, Edwin W. 1893. *Boston Illustrated*. Boston: Houghton, Mifflin.

Banks, Louis Albert. 1895. *The Saloonkeepers Ledger: A Series of Temperance Revival Discourses*. New York: Funk and Wagnalls.

Barker, John Marshall. 1905. *The Saloon Problem and Social Reform*. Boston: Everett.

Baron, Stanley. 1962. *Brewed in America: A History of Beer and Ale in the United States*. Boston: Little, Brown.

Barra, Allen. 2007. "Where Everybody Knows Your Name." *New York Sun*, September 14, 2007.

Berry, Melissa D. 2015. "The Wolfe Tavern: The Place Where Our Ancestors Tarried." *Daily News of Newburyport*, February 28, 2015.

Billings, John S., et al., eds. 1905. *The Liquor Problem: A Summary of Investigations Conducted by the Committee of Fifty, 1893–1903*. Boston and New York: Houghton, Mifflin.

Blair, Cynthia M. 2010. *I've Got to Make My Livin'*. Chicago: University of Chicago Press.

Blocker, Jack S., Jr. 1985. *Give to the Wind Thy Fears: The Women's Temperance Crusade, 1873–1874*. Westport, CT: Greenwood.

Blocker, Jack S., Jr. 1989. *American Temperance Movements: Cycles of Reform*. Boston: Twayne.

Blocker, Jack S., Jr. 2006. "Did Prohibition Really Work?" *American Journal of Public Health* 96, no. 2 (February): 233–43.

Blum, Peter H. 1999. *Brewed in Detroit: Breweries and Beers since 1830*. Detroit: Wayne State University Press.

Bogus, Carl T. 2001. *Why Lawsuits Are Good for America*. New York: New York University Press.

Borthwick, J. D. 1857. *Three Years in California*. London: William Blackwood and Sons.

Boswell, James. 1830. *The Life of Samuel Johnson, LLD*. London: John Sharpe, Piccadilly.

Boyer, Paul. 1978. *Urban Masses and Moral Order in America, 1820–1920*. Cambridge, MA: Harvard University Press.

Bradford, William. 1856. *History of Plymouth Plantation*. Boston: Little, Brown.

Bradford, William. 2002. *Of Plymouth Plantation: 1620–1647*. Edited by Samuel Eliot Morrison. New York: Alfred A. Knopf.

Brewers Association. n.d. "Number of Breweries." Accessed August 21, 2018. https://www.brewersassociation.org/statistics/number-of-breweries/.

Brick Saloon. n.d. "The World Famous Brick Saloon." Accessed September 3, 2018. http://www.bricksaloon.com/events-calendar.html.

Brooks, Charles. 1886. *History of the Town of Medford, Middlesex County, Massachusetts*. Boston: Rand, Avery.

Bryan, Wilhelmus B. 1904. "Hotels of Washington Prior to 1814." *Records of the Columbia Historical Society* 7. Washington, DC.

Buffalo Evening News. 1890. "Saloon Fixtures." Buffalo, NY. April 29, 1890, 4.

Buffalo Evening News. 1896. "Indicted Saloonkeepers." Buffalo, NY, December 4, 1896, 4.

Butte Daily Post. 1898. "A Verdict Arrived At." Butte, MT, April 22, 1898, 3.

Cabras, Ignazio, and David Higgins, ed. 2017. *The History of the Beer and Brewing Industry*. New York: Routledge.

Canton Daily News. 1928. "Night Club Traps Enmesh Young Girls." Canton, OH. December 9, 1.

Capital Times. 2013. "Data: Only Two States Have More Bars Than Wisconsin." Madison, WI, May 8, 2013. http://host.madison.com/ct/news/local/data-only-states-have-more-bars-than-wisconsin/html_1a7a0e58-b732-11e2-99a0-001a4bcf887a.html.

Carlin, Joseph M. 2012. *Cocktails: A Global History*. London: Reaktion Books.

Carlson, Peter. 1984. *Roughneck: The Life and Times of Big Bill Haywood*. New York: W. W. Norton.

Caulkins, Raymond. 1901. *Substitutes for the Saloon*. Boston: Houghton, Mifflin.

Centers for Disease Control and Prevention. 2017. "Impaired Driving: Get the Facts." https://www.cdc.gov/motorvehiclesafety/impaired_driving/impaired-drv_factsheet.html.

Centralia Evening Sentinel. 1908. "Liquor Loses Everywhere." Centralia, IL, April 8, 1908, 1.

Charnwood, Lord. 2009. *Abraham Lincoln*. New York: Cosimo Classics.

Cherrington, Ernest Hurst, ed. 1917. *The Anti-Saloon League Year Book, 1917*. Westerville, OH: Anti-Saloon League of America.

Chicago Daily Tribune. 1882. April 16, 1882, 4.

Chicago Evening Journal. 1895. "Alleys Are Cleaner: Vast Improvement in Nineteenth Ward Byways." July 29, 1895, 2.

Chicago Inter Ocean. 1887. "Knights of the Cue." November 20, 1887, 15.

Chicago Inter Ocean. 1906. "Poker: Gambling, or a Gentleman's Game?" January 28, 1906, 37.

Chicago Inter Ocean. 1908. "$30,000 a Day for Free Lunch in Chicago." January 26, 1908, 35.

Chicago Tribune. 1903. "Home of the Big Beer." May 20, 1903.

Chicago Tribune. 1986. "Former Cop Guilty in Tavern Shakedown." July 17, 1986.

China Daily. 2015. "Palace Hotel Endures as One of San Francisco's Most Alluring Havens." November 21–22, 2015, 10.

City of Chicago Landmark Designation Report. 2011. Commission on Chicago Landmarks, April 7, 2011.

Clawson, Mary Ann. 1989. *Constructing Brotherhood*. Princeton, NJ: Princeton University Press.

Cleveland Plain Dealer. 1923. "Dry Forces Labor Day and Night but Rum Still Flows." February 17, 1923, 1.

Cohen, Patricia Cline. 1998. *The Murder of Helen Jewett*. New York: Alfred A. Knopf.

Cole, Peter. 2007. *Wobblies on the Waterfront: Interracial Unionism in Progressive-Era Philadelphia*. Urbana: University of Illinois Press.

Committee of Fifteen. 1905. *The Raines Law Hotel and the Social Evil*. New York: G. P. Putnam's Sons.

Copeland, Larry. 2012. "Horrific N.C. Crash Puts Spotlight on Dram Shop Laws." *USA Today*, November 24, 2012.

Corbett and Ballenger's Third Annual Leadville City Directory for 1882. 1882. Leadville, CO: Corbett and Ballenger.

Corkscrew, Christopher. 1894. *Hardscrabble; or, Ballad of the Free Lunch Bar*. New York: W. I. Whiting.

Courtwright, David T. 2001. *Forces of Habit: Drugs and the Making of the Modern World*. Cambridge, MA: Harvard University Press.

Cowell, Andrew. 2001. *At Play in the Tavern*. Ann Arbor: University of Michigan Press.

Craig, Bruce, ed. 2012. *The Oxford Encyclopedia of Food and Drink in America*. Vol. 1. Oxford: Oxford University Press.

Daily Arkansas Gazette. 1894. "Sparks from the Wires." Little Rock, AR, December 21, 18942.

Daily Inter Lake. 1961. "All Around Town." Kalispell, MT, July 27, 1961, 13.

Daily Mail. 1976. "County's Old Saloon Era Largely Unchronicled." Hagerstown, MD, October 1, 1976, 4.

Daily Reporter. 1962. "Probe Charges Gary Police Took Bribes." Greenfield, IN, October 18, 1962, 1.

Daily Republican. 1883. "License in Illinois Cities." Decatur, IL, March 23, 1883, 2.

Daily State Register. 1868. Des Moines, IA, August 5, 3.

Damrosch, Leo. 2010. *Tocqueville's Discovery of America*. New York: Farrar, Straus, and Giroux.

Daniels, Bruce C. 1995. *Puritans at Play: Leisure and Recreation in Colonial New England.* New York: St. Martin's.

Day, Edward Parsons. 1884. *Day's Collacon.* New York: International Printing and Publishing Office.

Day Book. 1917. Chicago, IL, April 30, 1917, Noon Edition, Image 5. https://chroniclingamerica.loc.gov/lccn/sn83045487/1917-04-30/ed-1/seq-5/De Bow, J. D. B. 1858. *De Bow's Review and Industrial Resources, Statistics, etc.*, Vol. 24 and 4. New Orleans and Washington, DC: Forgotten Books.

Debs, Eugene V. 1908. "Progress by Prohibition." *Terre Haute Tribune*, March 1, 1908.

Decatur Daily Review. 1943. "No Female Bartenders." Decatur, IL, September 15, 1943, 15.

DeLyser, Dydia. 1999. "Authenticity on the Ground: Engaging the Past in a California Ghost Town." *Annals of the Association of American Geographers* 89, no. 4 (December): 602–32.

DeLyser, Dydia. 2006. *Western Places American Myths: How We Think about the West.* Edited by Gary J. Hausladen. Reno and Las Vegas: University of Nevada Press.

Denver Public Library. [1870–1880?]. "Palace Variety Theater." *Denver Public Library Digital Collections*, call number X-24703. http://cdm15330.contentdm.oclc.org/cdm/ref/collection/p15330coll22/id/36023.

Department of the Navy. 1946. "Old Tun Tavern, Philadelphia." *National Archives*, 532355. https://catalog.archives.gov/id/532355.

Devillo, Stephen Paul. 2017. *The Bowery: The Strange History of New York's Oldest Street.* New York: Skyhorse.

Dickens, Charles. 1842. *American Notes for General Circulation.* London: Chapman and Hall.

Dow, Neal. 1898. *Reminiscences of Neal Dow.* Portland: Evening Express.

Drake, Samuel Adams. 1917. *Old Boston Taverns and Tavern Clubs.* Boston: W. A. Butterfield.

Drowne, Henry Russell. 1919. *A Sketch of Fraunces Tavern.* New York: Publisher Unknown.

Dubuque City Directory. 1939. Dubuque, IA: R. L. Polk.

Duis, Perry. 1998. *Challenging Chicago: Coping with Everyday Life, 1837–1920.* Urbana: University of Illinois Press.

Duis, Perry. 1999 (1983). *The Saloon: Public Drinking in Chicago and Boston, 1880–1920.* Urbana: University of Illinois Press.

Earle, Alice M. 1900. *Stage Coach and Tavern Days.* New York: Macmillan.

Economist. 2018. "Why America Still Has Dry Counties." June 5, 2018. https://www.economist.com/the-economist-explains/2018/06/05/why-america-still-has-dry-counties.

Egerton, Douglas R. 1993. *Gabriel's Rebellion: The Virginia Slave Conspiracies of 1800 and 1802.* Chapel Hill: University of North Carolina Press.

Eighth Census of the United States: 1860. 1864. Washington: Government Printing Office.

Ellis, David. 2012. *The Truth about William Shakespeare: Fact, Fiction and Modern Biographies*. Edinburgh: Edinburgh University Press.

El Paso Herald. 1906. "Max Miller Swears That All the Witnesses Against Him Lied on Oath." El Paso, TX, December 13, 1906, 5.

Emerson, Lewis L. 1921. *Blue Book State of Illinois, 1921–1922*. Springfield: Illinois State Journal.

Erdoes, Richard. 1979. *Saloons of the Old West*. New York: Alfred A. Knopf.

Eshleman, George Ross. 1904. *The Lancaster Law Review*. Vol. 21. Lancaster: Wickersham.

Evans, Sandra. 1986. "D.C. Raises Drinking Age to 21." *Washington Post*, September 24, 1986.

Everton, Clive. 1991. *Snooker and Billiards*. Ramsbury, UK: Crowood.

Faulkner, William. 1951. *Requiem for a Nun*. New York: Random House.

Fernald, James C. 1890. *The Economics of Prohibition*. New York: Funk and Wagnalls.

Ferrara, Eric. 2011. *The Bowery: A History of Grit, Graft, and Grandeur*. Charleston, SC: History Press.

Forbes, Allan, and Eastman, Ralph M. 1954. *Taverns and Stagecoaches of New England*. Vol. 2. Boston: State Street Trust.

Forgotten Buffalo. n.d. "Rare Tavern Relics." Accessed September 2, 2018. http://forgottenbuffalo.com/forgottenrochester/spittoonwatertroughs.html.

Fort Scott Weekly. 1904. "She Smashes the Mirror." Fort Scott, KS, January 16, 1904, 6.

Foster, R. F. 1897. *Foster's Complete Hoyle: An Encyclopedia of All Indoor Games Played at the Present Day*. London and New York: Frederick A. Stokes.

Foundation for Advancing Alcohol Responsibility. n.d. "Drunk Driving Fatalities." Accessed September 15, 2018. https://www.responsibility.org/get-the-facts/research/statistics/drunk-driving-fatalities/.

Francaviglia, Richard V. 1991. *Hard Places: Reading the Landscape of America's Historic Mining Districts*. Iowa City: University of Iowa Press.

Freeport Journal-Standard. 1941. "Women Banned as Bartenders in Taverns Here." Freeport, IL, October 21, 1941, 1.

Freeport Journal-Standard. 1946. "Seek Ordinance That Would Outlaw Women Bartenders in Illinois." Freeport, IL, February 27, 1946, 1.

Fullbright, Lori. 2014. "Tulsa Man Hit and Killed by Two Cars, Bartenders Charged with Over Serving." *NewsOn6*, January 29, 2014. http://www.newson6.com/story/24584500/tulsa-man-hit-by-two-cars-bartenders-charged-with-over-serving.

Furnas, J. C. 1965. *The Late Demon Rum*. New York: Capricorn Books.

Gately, Iain. 2008. *Drink: A Cultural History of Alcohol*. New York: Gotham Books.

Gill, Harold B., Jr., and George M. Curtis III, eds. 2009. *A Man Apart: The Journal of Nicholas Cresswell, 1774–1781*. Lanham, MD: Lexington Books.

Gleen, Thomas Allen. 1896. "The Blue Anchor Tavern." *Pennsylvania Magazine of History and Biography* 20 (4): 427–34.

Gorn, Elliot. 2012. *The Manly Art*. Ithaca: Cornell University Press.

Goyens, Tom. 2014. *Beer and Revolution: The German Anarchist Movement in New York City, 1880–1914*. Urbana: University of Illinois.

Graham, H. K., ed. 1914. "Saloon Sanitation." *Temperance: A Monthly Journal of the Church Temperance Society* 4–6 (August).

Gray, Edward G., and Jane Kamensky, eds. 2012. *Gentleman's Progress: The Itinerarium of Dr. Alexander Hamilton, 1744*. Chapel Hill: University of North Carolina Press.

"Gris." 1866. "A Match Game of 'Quoits.'" *Fremont Weekly Journal*, December 21, 1866, 1.

Gulick, Charles Burton. 1902. *The Life of the Ancient Greeks: With Special Reference to Athens*. New York: D. Appleton.

Hammell, George M. 1908. *The Passing of the Saloon: An Authentic and Official Presentation of the Anti-Liquor Crusade in America*. Cincinnati: Tower.

Harned, Richard. 2009. *The Palace Hotel*. Charleston, SC: Arcadia.

Harper, R. 1904. *The Code of Hammurabi, King of Babylon, about 2250 B.C.* Chicago, IL: University of Chicago Press.

Hatch, Nathan O. 1989. *The Democratization of American Christianity*. New Haven, CT: Yale University Press.

Hawkins, Sir John. 1787. *The Life of Samuel Johnson*. London: J. Buckland.

Haywood, Bill. 1983. *Bill Haywood's Book: The Autobiography of William D. Haywood*. Westport, CT: Greenwood.

Hess, Corrinne. 2018. "Historic Schlitz Tied-House in Riverwest Could Become Condominiums." *BizTimes: Milwaukee Business News*, July 16, 2018.

Hirschfeld, Al. 2003. *The Speakeasies of 1932*. New York: Glen Young Books.

Holt, Michael F. 1999. *The Rise and Fall of the American Whig Party: Jacksonian Politics and the Onset of the Civil War*. Oxford: Oxford University Press.

Hunt, William C. 1910. *Thirteenth Census of the United States. 1910: Number and Distribution of Inhabitants*. Washington, DC: Government Printing Office.

Hunt, William C. 1912. *Thirteenth Census of the United States 1910. Addendum, Illinois*. Washington, DC: Government Printing Office.

Hurt, Harry, III. 2006. "Billiards with a Bottle. And This Game Is Dying?" *New York Times*, August 26, 2006.

Hurt, Jeanette. 2017. "A Short History of Women Working behind the Bar." *Supercall*, February 14, 2017. https://www.supercall.com/culture/women-bartender-history.

Imbarrato, Susan Claire. 1998. *Declarations of Independency in Eighteenth Century American Biography*. Knoxville: University of Tennessee Press.

Jacoby, Jack. 2012. *The Biggest Joke Book Ever*. Bloomington, IN: Trafford.

James, Ronald M. 2012. *Virginia City: Secrets of a Western Past*. Lincoln: University of Nebraska Press.

Jameson, Franklin, ed. 1908. *Original Narratives of Early American History: Winthrop's Journal: 1630–1649.* Vol. 1. New York: Charles Scribner's Sons.

Janesville Daily Gazette. 1920. "Eighteenth Amendment Puts 19 Saloons Out of Business in City." Janesville, WI, July 9, 1920, 14.

Jasper News. 1910. "Saloon Mirrors Responsible." Jasper, MO, March 10, 1910, 5.

Johnson, Marylin S. 2009. *Violence in the West: The Johnson County Range War and the Ludlow Massacre*. Longrove, IL: Waveland.

Joliet Signal. 1877. Joliet, IL, January 16, 1877, 1.

"Journal of a French Traveler in the Colonies, 1765." 1921. *American Historical Review* 26 and 27, no. 4 and no. 1 (July and October): 742–43.

Keats, John. 1909. *Poems Published in 1820*. Oxford: Clarendon.

Keire, Mara L. 1997. "The Committee of Fourteen and Saloon Reform in New York City, 1905–1920." *Business and Economic History* 26, no. 2 (Winter).

Kelley-Blazeby, Clare. 2001. "Tavernas in Ancient Greece c. 475–146BC: An Archaeological Perspective." *Assemblage: The Sheffield Graduate Journal of Archaeology*, no. 6 (August).

Kilgannon, Corey. 2015. "An Old-Fashioned Bartender Known for His Pour and His Personality." *New York Times*, June 26, 2015.

King, Kenneth. 2016. "5 Liability Issues Restaurant, Bar and Tavern Owners Need to Watch Out For." *Property Casualty 360*, February 18, 2016. https://www.propertycasualty360.com/2016/02/18/5-liability-issues-restaurant-bar-and-tavern-owner/?slreturn=20181024190053.

Kyriakodis, Harry. 2011. *Philadelphia's Lost Waterfront*. Charleston, SC: History Press.

Kyvig, David. 2000. *Repealing National Prohibition*. Kent, OH: Kent State University Press.

Larson, Cedric. 1937. "The Drinkers Dictionary." *American Speech* 12, no. 2 (April): 87–92.

Laubach, Frank Charles. 1911. "The Social Value of the New York Saloon." Electronic reproduction. New York: Columbia University Libraries. http://www.columbia.edu/cu/lweb/digital/collections/cul/texts/ldpd_7083211_000/index.html.

Leavenworth Times. 1872. "Domestic Virtues." Leavenworth, KS, March 31, 1872, 2.

Lebanon Daily News. 1891. "One Nervy Woman." Lebanon, PE, April 2, 1891, 1.

Le Baron, William, Jr., and Company. 1879. *History of McLean County, Illinois: Portraits of Early Settlers and Prominent Men*. Chicago: Wm. Lebaron, Jr.

Lee, Sydney. 1904. *A Life of William Shakespeare*. London: Smith, Elder.

Lender, Martin Edward. 1982. *Drinking in America: A History*. New York: Free Press.

Lepore, Jill. 2005. *New York Burning: Liberty, Slavery, and Conspiracy in Eighteenth-Century Manhattan*. New York: Vintage Books.

Lerner, Michael A. 2007. *Dry Manhattan: Prohibition in New York City*. Cambridge, MA: Harvard University Press.

Liebenson, Bess. 2001. "For Tavern Signs, a Fitting Tribute." *New York Times*, January 20, 2001. http://www.nytimes.com/2001/01/21/nyregion/for-tavern-signs-a-fitting-tribute.html.

Lincoln Journal Star. 1911. "The City in Brief." Lincoln, NE, July 28, 1911, 10.

Lincoln Journal Star. 1935. Lincoln, NE, July 9, 1935, 9.

Lindberg, Richard C. 1991. *To Serve and Collect*. Santa Barbara, CA: Praeger.

London, Jack. 1913. *John Barleycorn or Alcoholic Memoirs*. London: Mills and Boon.

Longfellow, Henry Wadsworth. 1863. *Tales of a Wayside Inn*. Boston: Ticknor and Fields.

Long-Island Star. 1826. "From Noah's Enquirer." Long-Island, NY, October 12, 1826, 1.

Lord, Elliot. 1883. *Comstock: Mining and Miners*. Washington: United States Government Printing Office.

Lossing, Benson J. 1884. *History of New York City*. New York: A. S. Barnes.

Lubbock Avalanche-Journal. 1967. "Police Inquiry into Third Day." Lubbock, TX, June 29, 1967, 37.

Luley, Benjamin P., and Gael Piques. 2016. "Communal Eating and Drinking in Early Roman Mediterranean France." *Antiquity* 90 (349).

Lutheran Observer. 1903. "Statesman Making Money." Vol. 71. Lancaster and Philadelphia, PA, February 20, 1903.

Lyons, Clare A. 2006. *Sex among the Rabble: An Intimate History of Gender and Power in the Age of Revolution, Philadelphia, 1730–1830*. Chapel Hill: North Carolina Press.

Macveach, Lincoln, ed. 1924. *The Journal of Nicholas Cresswell*. New York: Dial.

Malley, Richard C. 2000. "From the Hand of the Master: The Signs of William Rice." WNPR News. http://wnpr.org/post/hand-master-signs-william-rice.

Manhattan Mercury. 1887. "Hotel Soap and Towels." Manhattan, KS, November 30, 1887, 3.

Martin, A. Lynn. 2008. "The Role of Drinking." In *Medieval Sexuality: A Casebook*, edited by April Harper and Caroline Proctor. New York: Routledge.

Martin, A. Lynn. 2009. *Alcohol, Violence, and Disorder in Traditional Europe*. Kirksville, MO: Truman State University.

Marysville Journal-Tribune. 1915. "Advertisement." Marysville, OH, June 24, 1915, 3.

Mather, Cotton. 1726. *A Serious Address to Those Who Unnecessarily Frequent the Tavern and Often Spend Time in Publick Houses*. Boston: S. Gerrish.

Mather, Cotton. 1911. *Diary of Cotton Mather, 1681–1724*. Boston: Massachusetts Historical Society.

Mayes, Shelby. 2018. "Pappy's Grill and Bar Loses Liquor License after Selling Alcohol to Minors." *Daily Californian*, March 1, 2018.

Mazrim, Robert. 2007. *The Sangamon Frontier: History and Archeology in the Shadow of Lincoln*. Chicago: University of Chicago Press.

McGirr, Lisa. 2015. *The War on Alcohol: Prohibition and the Rise of the American State*. New York: W.W. Norton & Company, Inc.

Melendy, Roy. 1900. "The Saloon in Chicago." *American Journal of Sociology* 6, no. 3 (November).

Mendelson, Richard. 2009. *From Demon to Darling: A Legal History of Wine in America*. Berkeley: University of California Press.

Middlesex County Government. n.d. "Indian Queen Tavern." Accessed January 12, 2017. www.middlesexcountynj.gov/Government/Departments/BDE/Pages/Indian-Queen-Tavern.aspx.

Mitrani, Sam. 2014. *The Rise of the Chicago Police Department: Class and Conflict, 1850–1894*. Urbana: University of Illinois Press.

Mokarry, Adrienne. 2009. "Glimpse of History: Old Indian Queen Tavern in New Brunswick." *NJ.com*, April 7, 2009. www.nj.com/news/local/index.ssf/2009/04/glimpse_of_history_old_indian.html.

Mole, Rich. 2012. *Whiskey Wars of the Canadian West: Fifty Years of Battles against the Bottle*. Victoria, BC: Heritage.

Monahan, Sherry. 2017. *The Golden Elixir of the West: Whiskey and the Shaping of America*. New York: Two Dot.

Monroe News-Star. 1977. "Famous Saloonkeeper 'Toots' Shor Is Dead." Monroe, LA, January 24, 1977, 11.

Moore, E. C. 1897. "The Social Value of the Saloon." *American Journal of Sociology* 3, no. 1 (July): 1–12.

Morton, Joseph C. 2006. *Shapers of the Great Debate at the Constitutional Convention of 1787*. Westport, CT: Greenwood.

Mothers Against Drunk Driving. 2012. "Dram Shop and Social Host Liability." Washington, DC (June 2012). https://www.madd.org/wp-content/uploads/2017/08/Dram_Shop_Overview.pdf.

Mt. Carroll Mirror-Democrat. Mount Carroll, IL, December 13, 1973. https://carroll.illinoisgenweb.org/history/poffys.htm

Nathan, Gavin R. 2006. *Historic Taverns of Boston*. New York: Universe.

National Register of Historic Places. 1971. "White Horse Tavern." July 25, 1971. United States Department of the Interior National Park Service.

Nebraska State Journal. 1911a. "Chief Hunger's Complaints." July 15, 1911, 3.

Nebraska State Journal. 1911b. "Testimony of the Boys." July 20, 1911, 5.*New Dictionary of Quotations from the Greek, Latin, and Modern Languages*. 1874. London: John F. Shaw.

New Orleans Times-Picayune. 1891. "The Fatal Spittoon: Germs of Deadly Disease Lurk in the Cuspidors." New Orleans, LA, July 26, 1891, 10.

New Orleans Times-Picayune. 1895. "A Duel to the Death." New Orleans, LA, January 6, 1895, 2.

News Journal. 1973. "Police Probe Levels Former Austin Chief." Chicago, IL, January 17, 1973, 1.

Newton, Adison V. 1875. *The Saloon Keeper's Companion and Book of Reference*. Worcester, MA: West and Lee Game.

New York Times. 1874. "A Saloon-Keeper's Dangerous Weapon." September 21, 1874.

New York Times. 1992. "Drunken Driving Lawsuit Settled." May 22, 1992, 21.

New York Tribune. 1908. "Says It Has Killed 450 Hotels." New York, February 14, 1908, 2.

Ng, Christina. 2012. "Alaska Cops Arresting Drunks in Bars." *ABC News*, January 10, 2012. http://abcnews.go.com/US/illegal-drunk-alaska-bars-law/story?id=15330748.

Nietzsche, Friedrich Wilhelm. 1964. *Complete Works: The First and Authorized English Translation*. Vol. 10. New York: Russell and Russell.

Noel, Thomas J. 1982. *The City and the Saloon: Denver, 1858–1916*. Lincoln: University of Nebraska Press.

Nolte, Carl. 2013. "Restored Pied Piper Returns to Namesake Bar." *San Francisco Chronicle*, August 23, 2013. https://www.sfgate.com/bayarea/article/Restored-Pied-Piper-returns-to-namesake-bar-4754251.php.

Oakland Daily Evening Tribune. 1875. "Advertisements." Oakland, CA, November 27, 1875, 1.

Oakland Tribune. 1904. "Chips from Other Blocks." Oakland, CA, April 11, 1904, 6.

Oakland Tribune. 1913. "Ordinance Is Needed on Saloon Gambling." Oakland, CA, July 29, 1913, 6.

Official Metropolitan Guide. 1920. Hotel Association of New York City. March 7, 1920.

Official Metropolitan Guide. 1921. Hotel Association of New York City. May 29, 1921.

Ogden Standard-Examiner. 1936. "So They Said." Ogden, UT, May 24, 1936, 22.

Ogle, Maureen. 2006. *Ambitious Brew: The Story of American Beer*. Orlando, FL: Harcourt.

Old Style Saloon No. 10. 2015. "Saloon #10." https://www.saloon10.com.

Oliver, Harry. 2009. *Black Cats and April Fools*. London: John Blake Books.

Omaha Daily Bee. 1898. "Excise Board Matters." Omaha, NE, October 16, 1898, 3.

Omaha Daily Bee. 1901. "Mrs. Carrie Nation—The 'Joint Smasher.'" Omaha, NE, February 10, 1901, 17.

Osage County Chronicle. 1889. "The Saloon Power: How It Runs Troy, N.Y., with the Aid of the Democratic Machine." Burlingame, KS, December 5, 1889, 3.

Osborn, Matthew Warner. 2014. *Rum Maniacs: Alcoholic Insanity in the Early American Republic*. Chicago: University of Chicago Press.

Owens, Christopher. 1973. "National Register of Historic Places Inventory—Nomination Form." Application to National Park Service, March 2, 1973.

Owensboro Examiner. 1876. Owensboro, KY, May 12, 1876, 6.

Palmyra Weekly Whig. 1849. "Editor Whig." Palmyra, MO, November 15, 1849, 2.

Panama City News Herald. 1977. "World's Greatest Saloonkeeper Shor Buried." Panama City, FL, January 27, 1977, 21.

Pantagraph. 1898. From a file on Mayor Franklin Price, McLean County Historical Society. Bloomington, IL, December 24, 1898.

Pantagraph. 1953. "City's Oldest Saloon Goes Dry." Bloomington, IL, November 8, 1953, 11.

Parker, Watson. 1981. *Deadwood: The Golden Years*. Lincoln: University of Nebraska Press.

Parsons, Elaine. 2003. *Manhood Lost*. Baltimore: Johns Hopkins University Press.

Past and Present of LaSalle County, Illinois. 1877. Chicago: H. F. Kett.

Peck, Gunther. 1993. "Manly Gambles: The Politics of Risk on the Comstock Lode, 1860–1880." *Journal of Social History* 26, no. 4 (Summer): 701–23.

Pegram, Thomas R. 1998. *Battling Demon Rum: The Struggle for a Dry America, 1800–1933*. Chicago: Ivan R. Dee.

Pendergrast, Mark. 2003. *Mirror Mirror: A History of the Human Love Affair with Reflection*. New York: Basic Books.

Pennsylvania Magazine of History and Biography. 1887. No. 1 of Vol. 11, April. Philadelphia: Publication Fund of Historical Society of Pennsylvania, 296–308, 477.

Pew Research Center. 2015. "Attendance at Religious Services." Religious Landscape Study. May 12, 2015. http://www.pewforum.org/religious-landscape-study/attendance-at-religious-services.

Phelen, Michael. 1850. *Billiards without a Master*. New York: D. D. Winant.

Philadelphia Inquirer. 1889. "War on Speakeasies." November 26, 1889, 8.

Philadelphia Inquirer. 1893. "Quoits." August 20, 1893, 24.

Pickett, Deets, ed. 1917. *The Cyclopedia of Temperance, Prohibition, and Public Morals (1917 Edition)*. New York: Methodist Book Concern.

Pierson, Francis J. 2006. *Getting to Know Denver*. Denver: Charlotte Square.

Pittsburgh Daily Post. 1896. "Little Cuba, the New Game of Billiards That Is Coming into Popularity." December 6, 1896, 15.

Plumb, Brian E. 2011. *A History of Longfellow's Wayside Inn*. Charleston: History Press.

Porterhouse Brewing Company. n.d. "Fraunces Tavern." Accessed December 18, 2016. http://www.frauncestavern.com/.

Powderly, Terence Vincent. 1890. *Thirty Years of Labor, 1859–1889*. Columbus: Excelsior.

Powderly, Terence Vincent. n.d. *Workingmen and Drink: Extracts from Circular of T.V. Powderly to the Knights of Labor*. New York: National Temperance and Publication House.

Powers, Madelon. 1998. *Faces Along the Bar: Lore and Order in the Workingman's Saloon, 1870–1920*. Chicago: University of Chicago Press.

Public Opinion: Comprehensive Summary of the Press Throughout the World on All Important Current Topics. Vol. 31, *July, 1901–December, 1901*. 1901. New York: Waverly Place.

Putnam, Robert D. 2000. *Bowling Alone: The Collapse and Revival of American Community*. New York: Simon and Schuster.

Raines, John. 1896. "The Raines Liquor-Tax Law." *North American Review*, April 1, 1896.

Reynolds, Colleen. 2011. "Six Bartenders Arrested for Serving Alcohol to Minor." *27east.com*, June 29, 2011. http://www.27east.com/news/article.cfm/General-Interest/389041/Six-Bartenders-Arrested-For-Serving-Alcohol-To-Minor.

Richmond Enquirer. 1857. "The Bloody Riots in New York." Richmond, VA, July 10, 1857, 4.

Riedel, Charles. 1860. "A Defender of Lager Beer." *Scientific American: A Journal of Practical Information in Art, Science, Mechanics, Agriculture, Chemistry, and Manufactures* 3, no. 6 (August).

Riis, Jacob. 1902. *The Battle with the Slum*. New York: Macmillan.

Ripley, George, and Charles A. Dana, eds. 1858. *The New American Cyclopedia: A Popular Dictionary of General Knowledge*. Vol. 3. New York: D. Appleton.

Rock Island Argus. 1913. "Woman Smashes a Saloon Mirror." Rock Island, IL, January 17, 1913, 20.

Rockwell, Norman. 1936. "The New Tavern Sign." *Saturday Evening Post* 208, no. 34 (February): 18–19.

Roediger, David R., and Philip S. Foner. 1989. *Our Own Time: A History of American Labor and the Working Day*. London: Verso.

Rorabaugh, W. J. 1979. *The Alcoholic Republic: An American Tradition*. Oxford: Oxford University Press.

Rose, Kenneth D. 1996. *American Women and the Repeal of Prohibition*. New York: New York University Press.

Rosenzweig, Roy. 1983. *Eight Hours for What We Will: Workers and Leisure in an Industrial City, 1870–1920*. Cambridge: Cambridge University Press.

Ross, Steven J. 1998. *Working Class Hollywood*. Princeton, NJ: Princeton University Press.

Sallinger, Sharon V. 2002. *Taverns and Drinking in Early America*. Baltimore: Johns Hopkins University Press.

"Saloon License Issued by the City of Bloomington to John Weibel." 1884. *City Council Proceedings, 1871–1965*. Accession Number 44/01. Illinois Regional Archives Depository, Illinois State University.

Saloon Survey, New York City: Changes in Saloon Property after the First Three Years and after Five Years of Prohibition. 1924. Westerville, OH: World League Against Alcoholism.

San Antonio Light. 1969. "Considine Puts Toots Shor 'On the Line.'" San Antonio, TX, November 23, 1969, 31.

San Francisco Call. 1904. "Business Chances." September 12, 1904, 8.

Sandburg, Carl. 1954. *Abraham Lincoln: The Prairie Years and the War Years*. New York: Harcourt.

Schneider, Joseph W. 2003. "Deviant Drinking as Disease: Alcoholism as a Social Accomplishment." In *Drugs, Alcohol, and Social Problems*, edited by James D. Orcutt and David R. Rudy. Lanham, MD: Rowan and Littlefield.

Schoelwer, Susan P. n.d. "Tavern Signs Mark Changes in Travel, Innkeeping, and Artistic Practice." Connecticut History. Accessed March 3, 2018. https://connecticuthistory.org/tavern-signs-mark-changes-in-travel-innkeeping-and-artistic-practice/.

Schoelwer, Susan P. 2001. "For Tavern Signs, A Fitting Tribute." Interview by Bess Liebenson, *New York Times*, January 21. https://www.nytimes.com/2001/01/21/nyregion/for-tavern-signs-a-fitting-tribute.html.

Schubas Tavern. 2019. Accessed February 4, 2019. https://www.schubastavern.com/.

Seattle Post-Intelligencer. 1890a. "A Martyr to Faith." June 29, 1890, 6.

Seattle Post-Intelligencer. 1890b. "Rev. Sutton is Avenged." August 25, 1890, 8.

Sellers, Charles. 1991. *The Market Revolution: Jacksonian America, 1815–1846*. New York: Oxford University Press.

Sessa, Sam. 2010. "That's Not Just Any Foot Rest. It's a Trough." *Baltimore Sun*, April 6, 2010.

Seventh Census of the United States: 1850. 1853. Washington: Robert Armstrong, Public Printer.

Shurtleff, Nathaniel B. 1871. *A Topographical and Historical Description of Boston*. Boston: Printer Unknown.

Sidbury, James. 1973. *Ploughshares into Swords: Race, Rebellion, and Identity in Gabriel's Virginia, 1730–1810*. New York: Cambridge University Press.

Silverman, Jacob. 2015. *Terms of Service: Social Media and the Price of Constant Connection*. New York: HarperCollins.

Sinclair, Upton. 1906. *The Jungle*. New York: Doubleday.

Smith, Jack. 1990. "Thomas Jefferson Declared under the Influence." *Los Angeles Times*, July 10, 1990.

Smith Bader, Robert. 1986. *Prohibition in Kansas*. Lawrence: University Press of Kansas.Snyder, W. P. 1892. "Working the Growler on a Saturday Night." *Harper's Weekly* 4 (9): 356.

Solomon, Deborah. 2013. *American Mirror: The Life and Art of Norman Rockwell*. New York: Farrar, Straus and Giroux.

Spielman, Fran. 2017. "Minors Cleared to Serve Alcohol at Restaurants and Grocery Stores." *Chicago Sun Times*, March 22, 2017.

St. Albans Daily Messenger. 1903. "Thompson Opens Bar." St. Albans, VT, May 14, 1903, 7.

Star-Gazette. 1911. "Criminal Docket District Court." Sallisaw, OK, April 28, 1911, 1.

Star Tribune. 1910. "Holy Book a Saloon Asset." Minneapolis, MN, June 10, 1910, 5.

Statista. 2017. "Food and Drink Sales of Bars and Taverns in the United States from 2009 to 2017." https://www.statista.com/statistics/218851/us-bars-and-taverns-food-and-drink-sales/.

Statista. 2018. "Market Value of Alcoholic Drinks in the United States from 2013 to 2018." https://www.statista.com/statistics/491248/alcoholic-drinks-united-states-market-value/.

Steele, Noelle. 2017. "Greenfield Bar Cited, Server Charged with Crime Following Fatal Drunken-Driving Crash." *Daily Reporter* (Greenfield, IN), July 20, 2017.

Stott, Richard B. 1990. *Workers in the Metropolis: Class, Ethnicity, and Youth in Antebellum New York City*. Ithaca, NY: Cornell University Press.

Street Number Directory and Classified Business Directory, Bloomington and Normal, 1909. 1909. Bloomington, IL: Pantagraph.

Stutz, Howard. 2011. "Rough Road for Taverns." *Las Vegas Business Press* 28 (34): 6–9.

Summit Daily. 2016. "The Mint." August 15, 2016. https://www.summitdaily.com/restaurants/silverthorne-restaurants/the-mint/.

Sunday, William Ashley. 1908. *Get on the Water Wagon*. N.p.: E. A. K. Hackett.

Swenson, Jim. 2017. "Poopy's Continues to Expand as Illinois' 'Largest Biker Bar.'" *Telegraph Herald* (Dubuque, IO), June 4, 2017.

Szasz, Thomas. 1993. *A Lexicon of Lunacy: Metaphoric Malady, Moral Responsibility, and Psychiatry*. New Brunswick, NJ: Transaction.

Talamo, Rachel, and Jonathan Forani. 2013. "New York City Bartenders Keep a Baseball Bat Handy Should Danger Arise." *Daily News* (New York), July 14, 2013.

Taliaferro, John. 1996. *Charles M. Russell: The Life and Legend of America's Cowboy Artist*. Norman: University of Oklahoma Press.

Tarbell, Ida M. 1896. "Lincoln's Life at New Salem from 1832–1836." *McClure's Magazine* 6 (3): 213–40.

Tarver, Evan. 2018. "The Economics of Owning a Bar." *Investopedia*, October 25, 2018. https://www.investopedia.com/articles/personal-finance/011216/economics-owning-bar.asp.

Taylor, Robert Lewis. 1966. *Vessel of Wrath: The Life and Times of Carrie Nation*. New York: New American Library.

Telegraph Herald. 1933. "Urges Public to Forget about Bootleggers." Dubuque, IA, December 6, 1933, 1.

Telegraph's Dubuque City Directory. 1899–1900. Dubuque, IA: Telegraph.

Telegraph's Dubuque City Directory. 1934. Dubuque, IA: Telegraph A.

Texas Alcoholic Beverage Commission. 2017. "Sell and Serve Responsibly."

Thomas, Evan. 1991. *The Man to See*. New York: Simon and Schuster.

Thompson, Patrick. 2017. "Tied Houses: A Lesson in Omaha's Saloon History." Accessed February 4, 2019. https://www.restorationexchange.org/2017/07/27/pabst-schlitz-omahas-saloon-history/#comment-10177.

Thompson, Peter. 1999. *Rum Punch and Revolution*. Philadelphia: University of Pennsylvania Press.

Times Dispatch. 1908. "Solid Mahogany Bar Fixtures at Auction." Richmond, VA, May 21, 1908, 11.

Tivoli Brewing Company. 2018. "The Tivoli Story." Accessed September 1, 2018. https://tivolibrewingco.com/story/.

Tracy, Sarah W. 2005. *Alcoholism in America: From Reconstruction to Prohibition*. Baltimore: Johns Hopkins University Press.

Trenton Evening Times. 1923. "Judge Aware of Liquor Violations." Trenton, NJ, August 10, 1923, 5.

Treu, Martin. 2012. *Signs, Streets, and Storefronts*. Baltimore: Johns Hopkins University Press.

Turner, George Kibbe. 1907. "The City of Chicago: A Study of the Great Immoralities." *McClure's Magazine* 28 (April): 576–79.

Twain, Mark. 1872. *Roughing It*. Hartford: American.

United States Census. n.d. "Resident Population and Apportionment of the U.S. House of Representatives." Accessed April 15, 2017. https://www.census.gov/dmd/www/resapport/states/oregon.pdf.

U.S. House of Representatives. 1894. "Gathered around the Kegs at Kelley's Saloon 'The Bijou.' Round Pond, Okla. Terr. by Kennett, January 1894." National Archives. 540092. https://catalog.archives.gov/id/540092.

VanOverberghe, Caitlin. 2018. "Bar Waiter Sentenced to Time on Probation." *Daily Reporter* (Greenfield, IN), February 16, 2018.

Van Rensselaer, Mrs. John King. 1890. *The Devil's Picture-Books: A History of Playing Cards*. New York: Dodd, Mead.

Washington, George. 1887. "Extracts from Washington's Diary, Kept While Attending the Constitutional Convention of 1787." *Pennsylvania Magazine of History and Biography* 11, no. 3 (October): 286–308.

Waterloo Press. 1883. "The New Slavery." Waterloo, IN, May 31, 1883, 3.

Watson, John Fanning. 1857. *Annals of Philadelphia and Pennsylvania in Olden Time*. Philadelphia: Elijah Thomas.

Waukesha Daily Freeman. 1971. "Stubbornness on Lady Bartenders Could Be Costly." Waukesha, WI, December 23, 1971, 7.

Waxachacie Daily Light. 1975. "Five Tavern Owners Tell of Payoff." Waxachacie, TX, July 2, 1975, 8.

Weekly Gazette. 1872. "Out West." Colorado Springs, CO, October 10, 1872, 8.

Weekly Oregon Statesmen. 1851. "Silver House." November 25, 1851, 3.

Weinstein, Adam. 2010. "Cop Walks into a Bar and . . . Arrests You. For Having a Drink." *Mother Jones*, March–April 2010. https://www.motherjones.com/politics/2010/02/texas-racist-laws-drinking-while-brown/.

Weir, Robert. 1996. *Beyond Labor's Veil: The Culture of the Knights of Labor*. University Park: Pennsylvania State University Press.

Wendt, Lloyd, and Herman Kogan. 2005. *Lords of the Levee: The Story of Bathhouse John and Hinky Dink*. Evanston, IL: Northwestern University Press.

Wert, J. Howard. 1907. "Old Time Notes of Harrisburg." *Harrisburg* (PA) *Star-Independent*, March 1, 1907, 10.

West, Elliot. 1979. *Saloons on the Rocky Mountain Mining Frontier.* Lincoln: University of Nebraska Press.

Wheeling Daily Intelligencer. 1900. "She Broke Saloon Mirrors." Wheeling, WV, December 28, 1900, 1.

Whitehorse Tavern. n.d. Accessed June 6, 2017. http://whitehorsenewport.com/.

Wiebe, Robert. 1967. *The Search for Order, 1877–1920.* New York: Hill and Wang.

Winsor, Justin. 2001. *A History of the Town of Duxbury, Massachusetts, with Genealogical Registers [1849].* Bowie, MA: Heritage Books.

Winthrop, John. 1996. *The Journal of John Winthrop, 1630–1649.* Abridged ed. Edited by Richard S. Dunn and Laetitia Yeandle. Cambridge, MA: Harvard University Press.

Woodward, Donna Dene. 1994. "With All the Grace of the Sex." *Colonial Williamsburg Journal* (Spring).

Worth, Richard. 2009. *Teetotalers and Saloon Smashers: The Temperance Movement and Prohibition.* Berkeley Heights, NJ: Enslow.

Ybarra v. Illinois. United States Supreme Court 444 U.S. 85. 1979.

BIBLIOGRAPHY

INDEX

About the Author

Steven D. Barleen earned a PhD in history from Northern Illinois University. His primary historical focus is labor history. He has previously published articles related to drinking, the tavern, and Prohibition, and in 2014 he was awarded the Harry E. Pratt Memorial Award for Outstanding Scholarly Publications in Illinois History. He currently teaches at Clinton Community College in Clinton, Iowa. He has worked as a bartender, and he has been known to frequent taverns.

www.ingramcontent.com/pod-product-compliance
Lightning Source LLC
Chambersburg PA
CBHW070411100426
42812CB00005B/1711
9781440852725